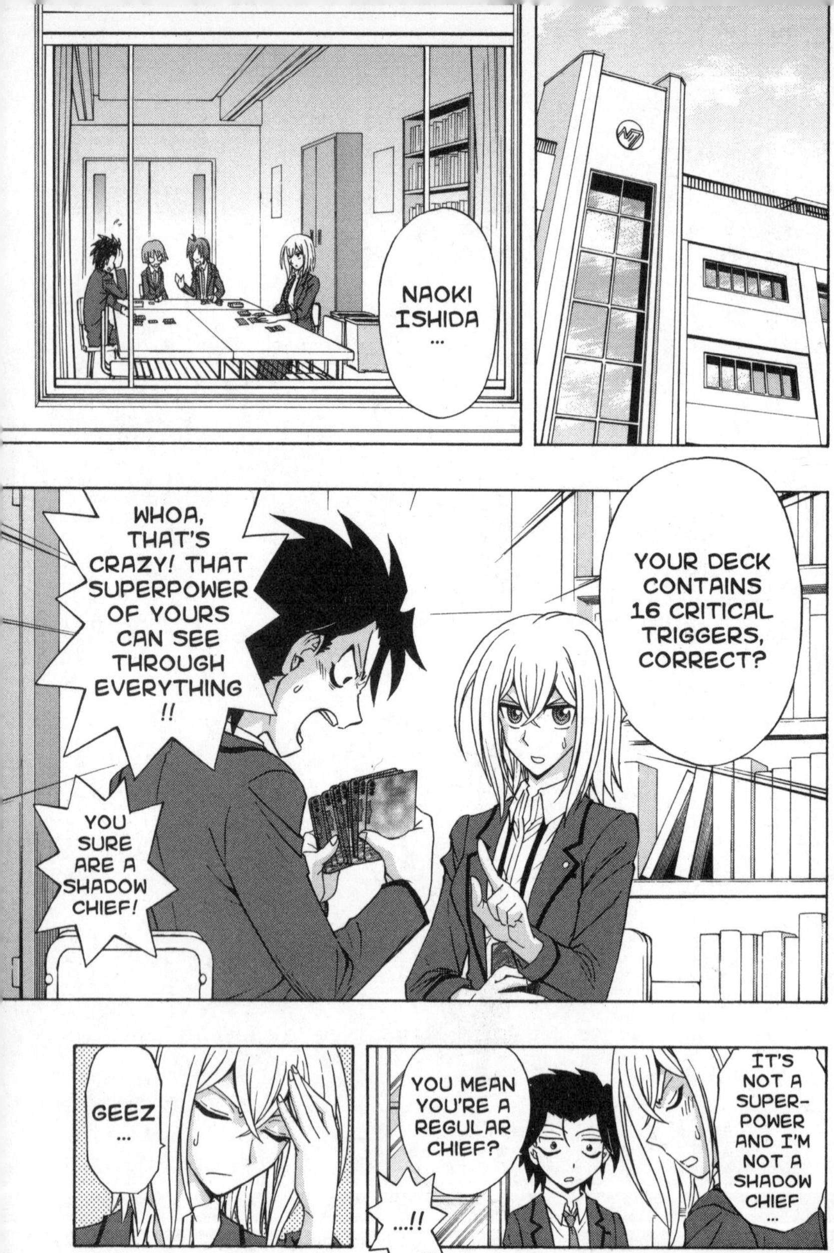
NAOKI ISHIDA ...
YOUR DECK CONTAINS 16 CRITICAL TRIGGERS, CORRECT?
WHOA, THAT'S CRAZY! THAT SUPERPOWER OF YOURS CAN SEE THROUGH EVERYTHING !!
YOU SURE ARE A SHADOW CHIEF!
IT'S NOT A SUPER-POWER AND I'M NOT A SHADOW CHIEF ...
YOU MEAN YOU'RE A REGULAR CHIEF?
...!!
GEEZ ...

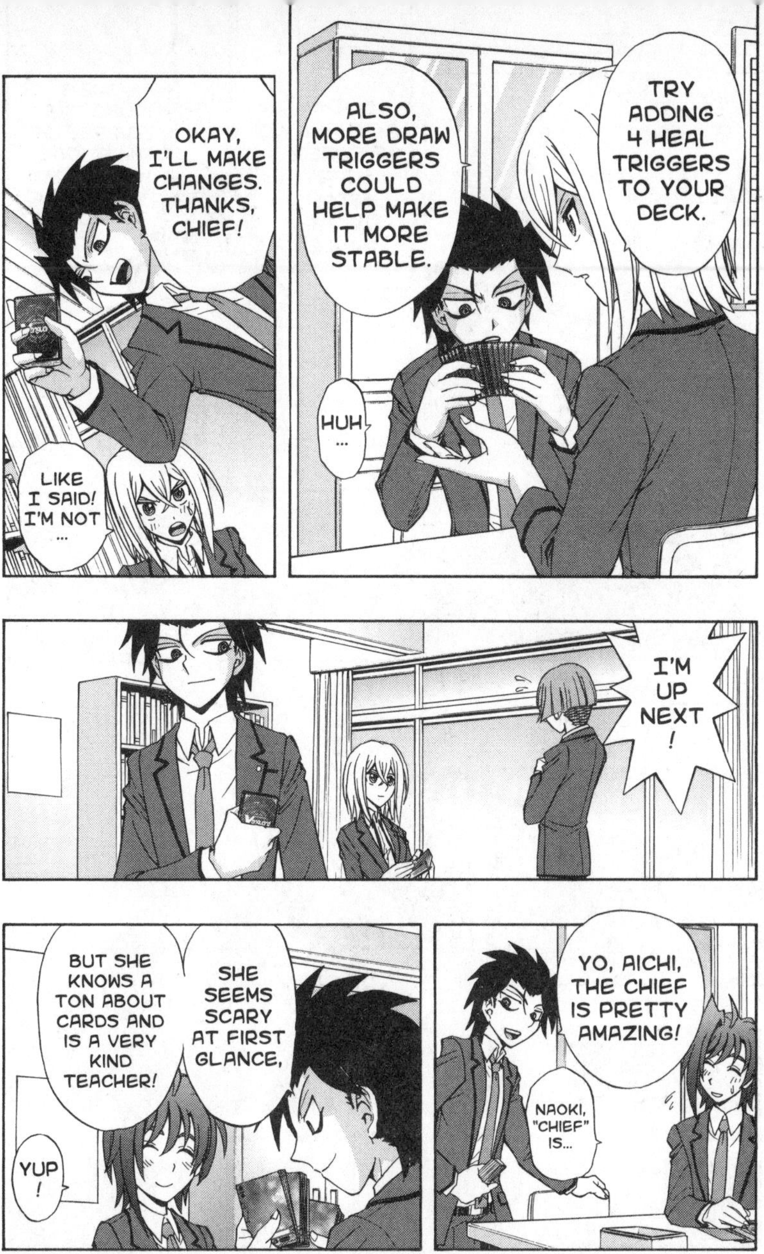
TRY ADDING 4 HEAL TRIGGERS TO YOUR DECK.
ALSO, MORE DRAW TRIGGERS COULD HELP MAKE IT MORE STABLE.
HUH ...
OKAY, I'LL MAKE CHANGES. THANKS, CHIEF!
LIKE I SAID! I'M NOT ...
I'M UP NEXT!
YO, AICHI, THE CHIEF IS PRETTY AMAZING!
NAOKI, "CHIEF" IS...
SHE SEEMS SCARY AT FIRST GLANCE,
BUT SHE KNOWS A TON ABOUT CARDS AND IS A VERY KIND TEACHER!
YUP!

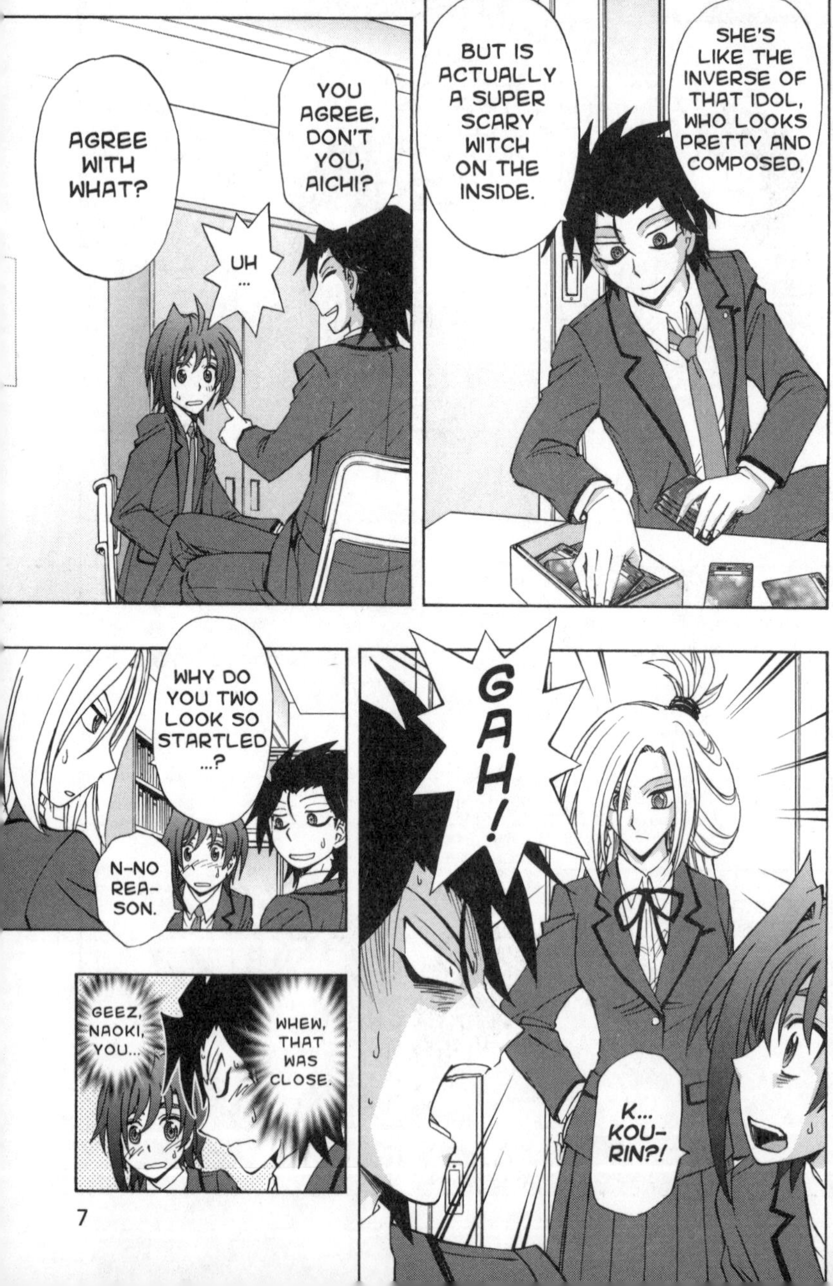
SHE'S LIKE THE INVERSE OF THAT IDOL, WHO LOOKS PRETTY AND COMPOSED,
BUT IS ACTUALLY A SUPER SCARY WITCH ON THE INSIDE.
YOU AGREE, DON'T YOU, AICHI?
AGREE WITH WHAT?
UH ...
GAH!
K... KOU-RIN?!
WHY DO YOU TWO LOOK SO STARTLED ...?
N-NO REA-SON.
WHEW, THAT WAS CLOSE.
GEEZ, NAOKI, YOU...

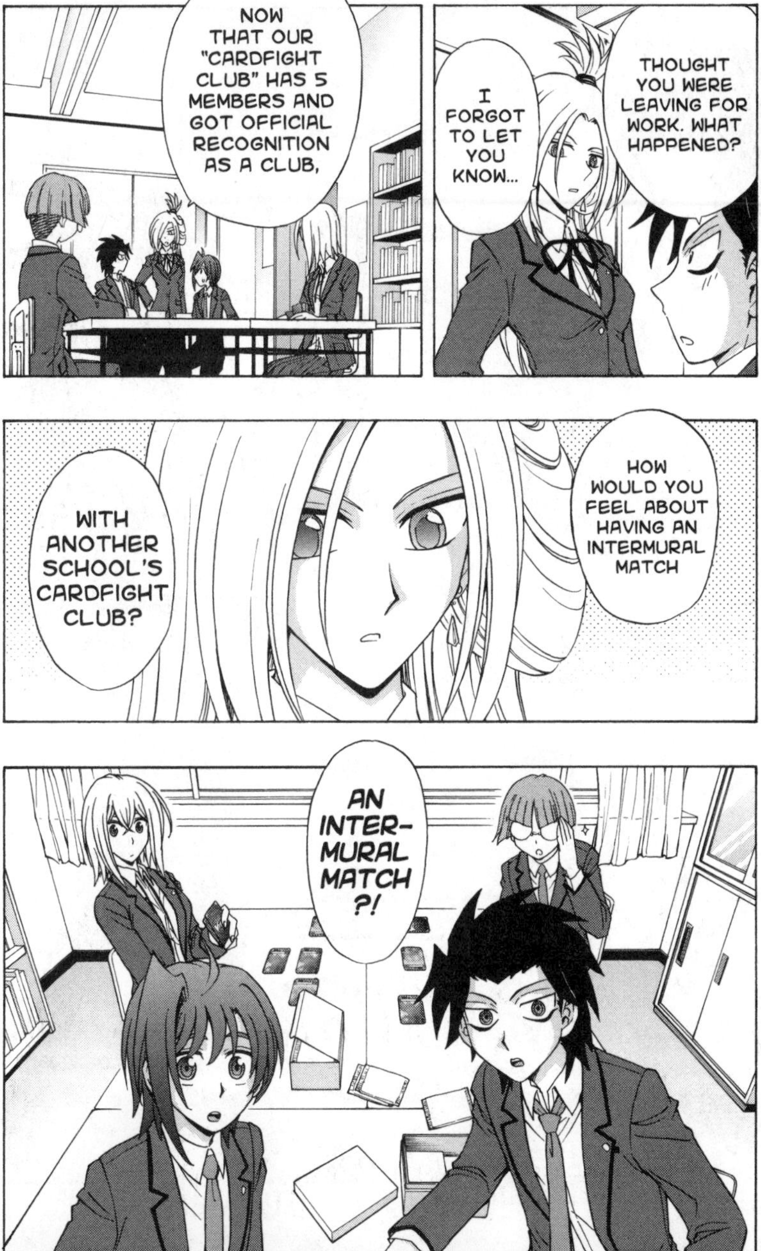
THOUGHT YOU WERE LEAVING FOR WORK. WHAT HAPPENED?
I FORGOT TO LET YOU KNOW...
NOW THAT OUR "CARDFIGHT CLUB" HAS 5 MEMBERS AND GOT OFFICIAL RECOGNITION AS A CLUB,
HOW WOULD YOU FEEL ABOUT HAVING AN INTERMURAL MATCH
WITH ANOTHER SCHOOL'S CARDFIGHT CLUB?
AN INTER-MURAL MATCH?!

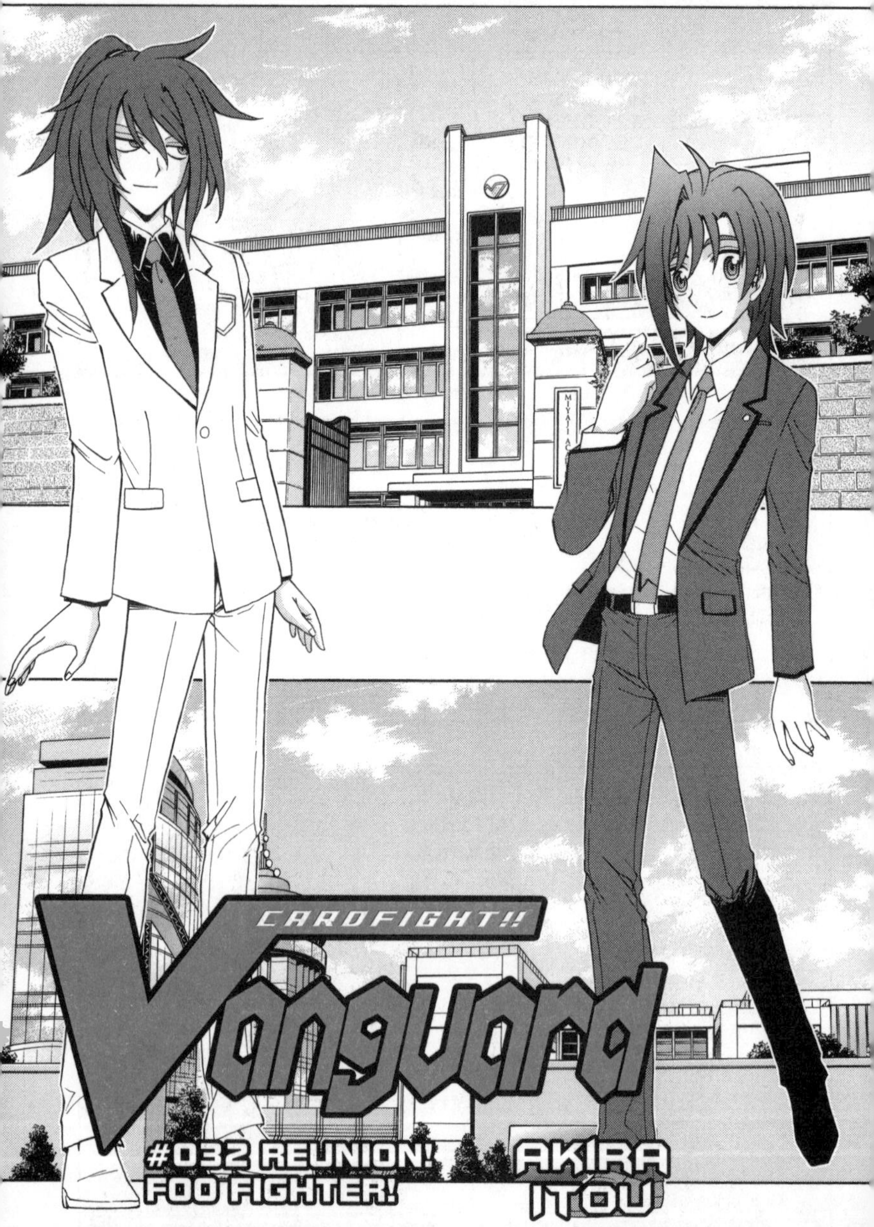
CARDFIGHT!!
Vanguard
#032 REUNION!
FOO FIGHTER!
AKIRA
ITŌU

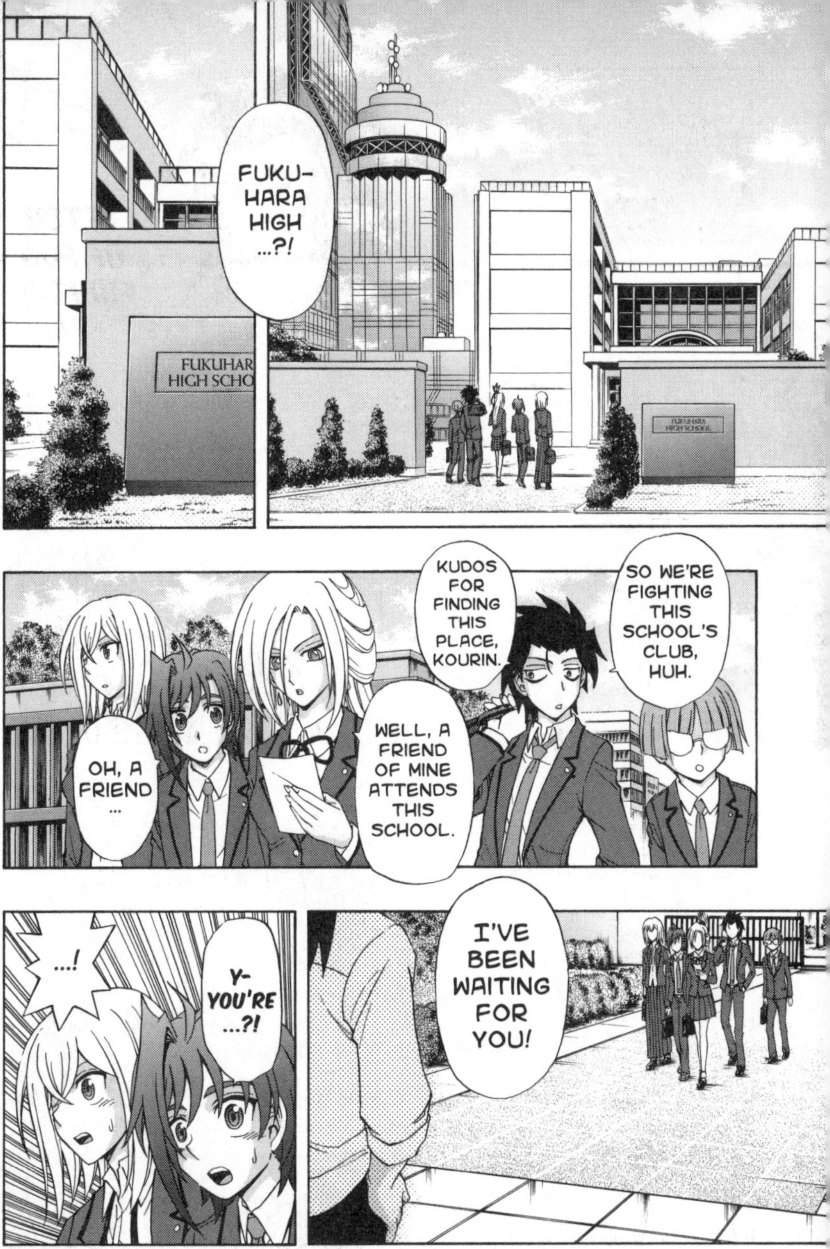
FUKUHARA HIGH SCHOOL
FUKUHARA HIGH SCHO
FUKU-HARA HIGH ...?!
SO WE'RE FIGHTING THIS SCHOOL'S CLUB, HUH.
KUDOS FOR FINDING THIS PLACE, KOURIN.
WELL, A FRIEND OF MINE ATTENDS THIS SCHOOL.
OH, A FRIEND ...
I'VE BEEN WAITING FOR YOU!
Y- YOU'RE ...?!
...!

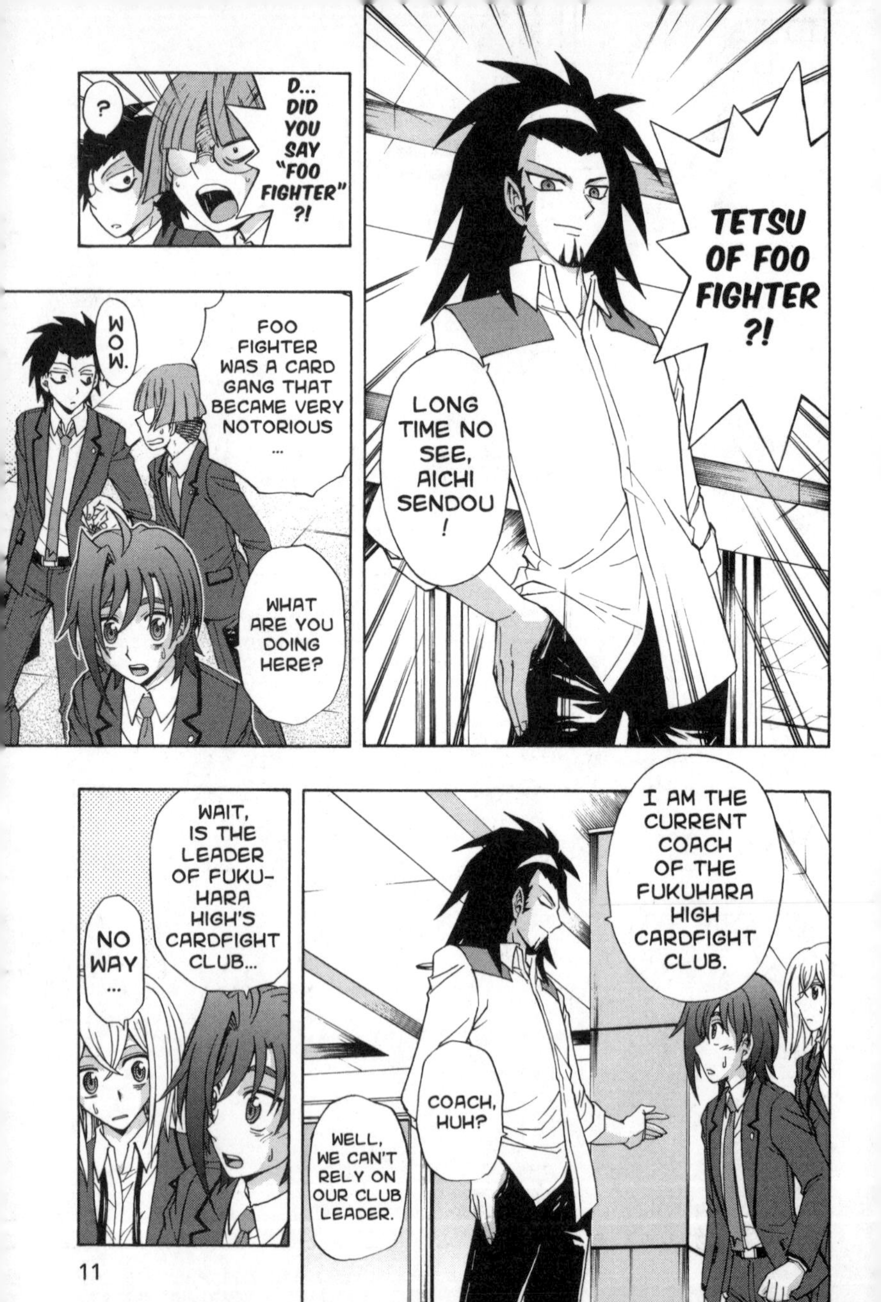
TETSU OF FOO FIGHTER ?!
LONG TIME NO SEE, AICHI SENDOU !
?
D... DID YOU SAY "FOO FIGHTER" ?!
FOO FIGHTER WAS A CARD GANG THAT BECAME VERY NOTORIOUS ...
WOW.
WHAT ARE YOU DOING HERE?
I AM THE CURRENT COACH OF THE FUKUHARA HIGH CARDFIGHT CLUB.
COACH, HUH?
WELL, WE CAN'T RELY ON OUR CLUB LEADER.
WAIT, IS THE LEADER OF FUKU-HARA HIGH'S CARDFIGHT CLUB...
NO WAY ...

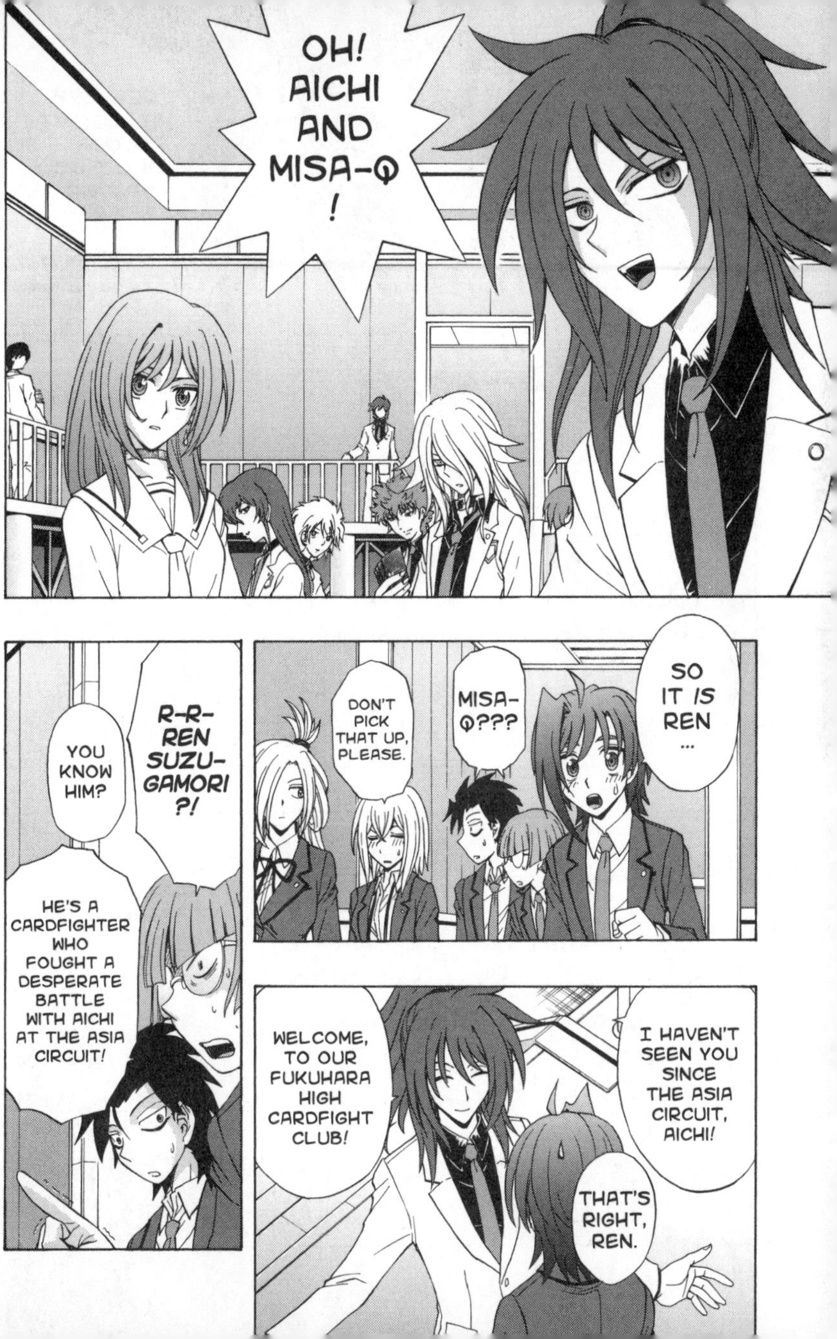
OH! AICHI AND MISA-Q!
SO IT *IS* REN ...
MISA-Q???
DON'T PICK THAT UP, PLEASE.
I HAVEN'T SEEN YOU SINCE THE ASIA CIRCUIT, AICHI!
WELCOME, TO OUR FUKUHARA HIGH CARDFIGHT CLUB!
THAT'S RIGHT, REN.
R-R-REN SUZU-GAMORI?!
YOU KNOW HIM?
HE'S A CARDFIGHTER WHO FOUGHT A DESPERATE BATTLE WITH AICHI AT THE ASIA CIRCUIT!

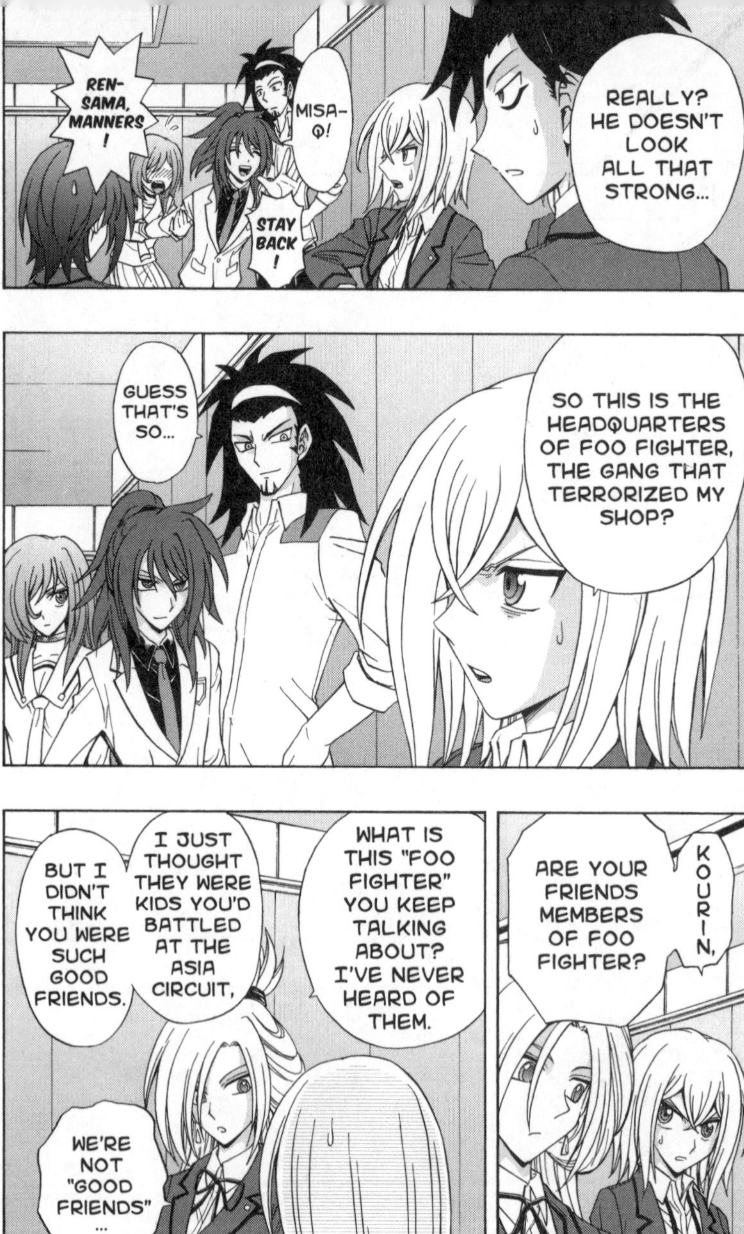
REALLY? HE DOESN'T LOOK ALL THAT STRONG...
MISA-Q!
STAY BACK!
REN-SAMA, MANNERS!
SO THIS IS THE HEADQUARTERS OF FOO FIGHTER, THE GANG THAT TERRORIZED MY SHOP?
GUESS THAT'S SO...
KOURIN,
ARE YOUR FRIENDS MEMBERS OF FOO FIGHTER?
WHAT IS THIS "FOO FIGHTER" YOU KEEP TALKING ABOUT? I'VE NEVER HEARD OF THEM.
I JUST THOUGHT THEY WERE KIDS YOU'D BATTLED AT THE ASIA CIRCUIT,
BUT I DIDN'T THINK YOU WERE SUCH GOOD FRIENDS.
WE'RE NOT "GOOD FRIENDS"...

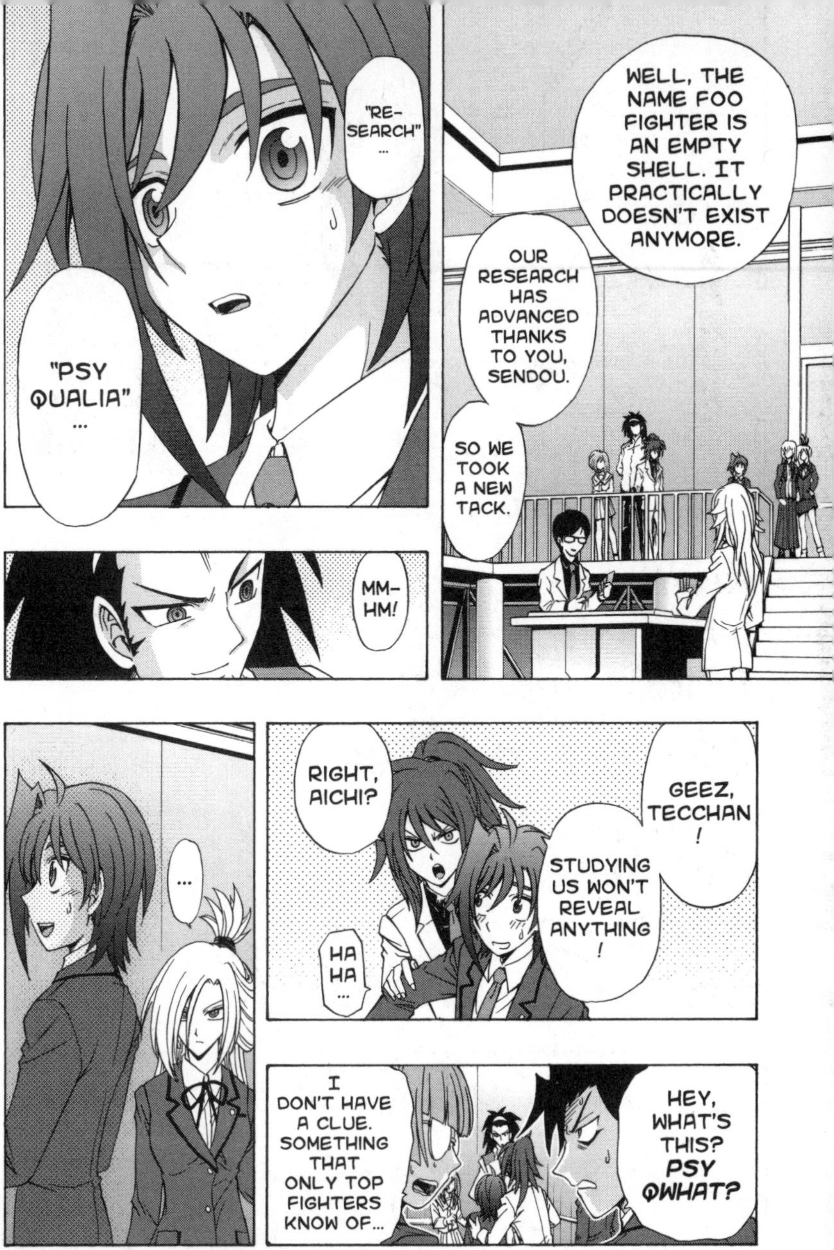
WELL, THE NAME FOO FIGHTER IS AN EMPTY SHELL. IT PRACTICALLY DOESN'T EXIST ANYMORE.
OUR RESEARCH HAS ADVANCED THANKS TO YOU, SENDOU.
SO WE TOOK A NEW TACK.
"RE-SEARCH" ...
"PSY QUALIA" ...
MM-HM!
GEEZ, TECCHAN!
RIGHT, AICHI?
STUDYING US WON'T REVEAL ANYTHING!
HA HA ...
HEY, WHAT'S THIS? PSY QWHAT?
I DON'T HAVE A CLUE. SOMETHING THAT ONLY TOP FIGHTERS KNOW OF...
...

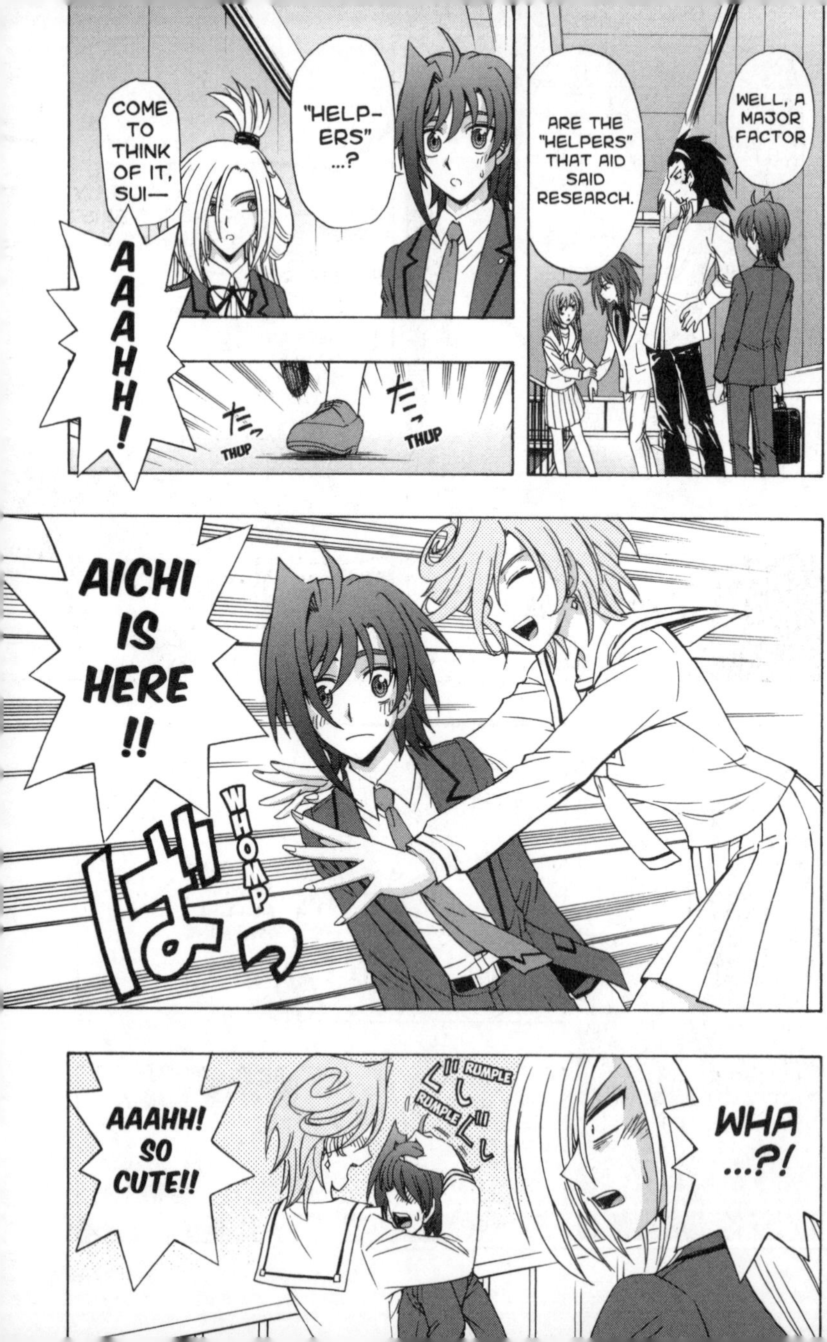
WELL, A MAJOR FACTOR
ARE THE "HELPERS" THAT AID SAID RESEARCH.
"HELPERS" ...?
COME TO THINK OF IT, SUI—
AAAAHH!
たっ THUP
たっ THUP
AICHI IS HERE!!
ばっ
WHOMP
WHA ...?!
くしくし RUMPLE
くしくし RUMPLE
AAAHH! SO CUTE!!

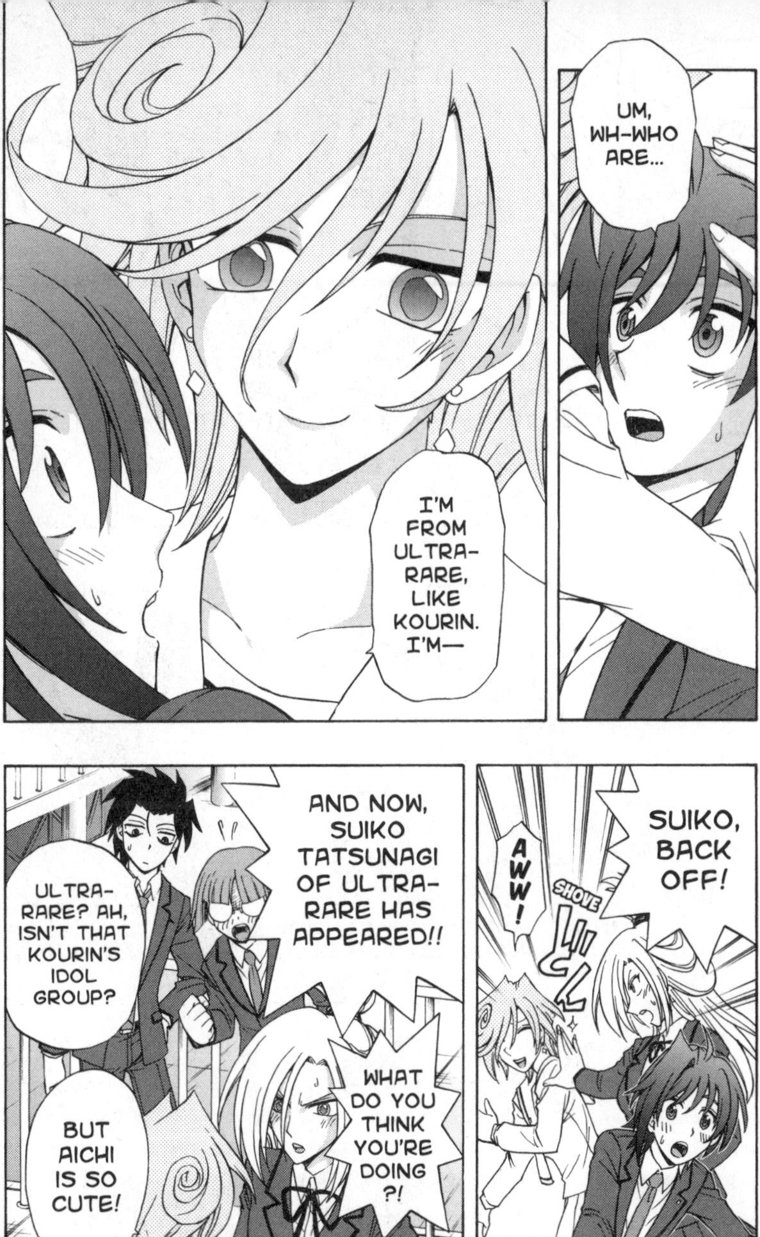
UM, WH-WHO ARE...
I'M FROM ULTRA-RARE, LIKE KOURIN. I'M—
SUIKO, BACK OFF!
AWW!
SHOVE
AND NOW, SUIKO TATSUNAGI OF ULTRA-RARE HAS APPEARED!!
ULTRA-RARE? AH, ISN'T THAT KOURIN'S IDOL GROUP?
WHAT DO YOU THINK YOU'RE DOING?!
BUT AICHI IS SO CUTE!

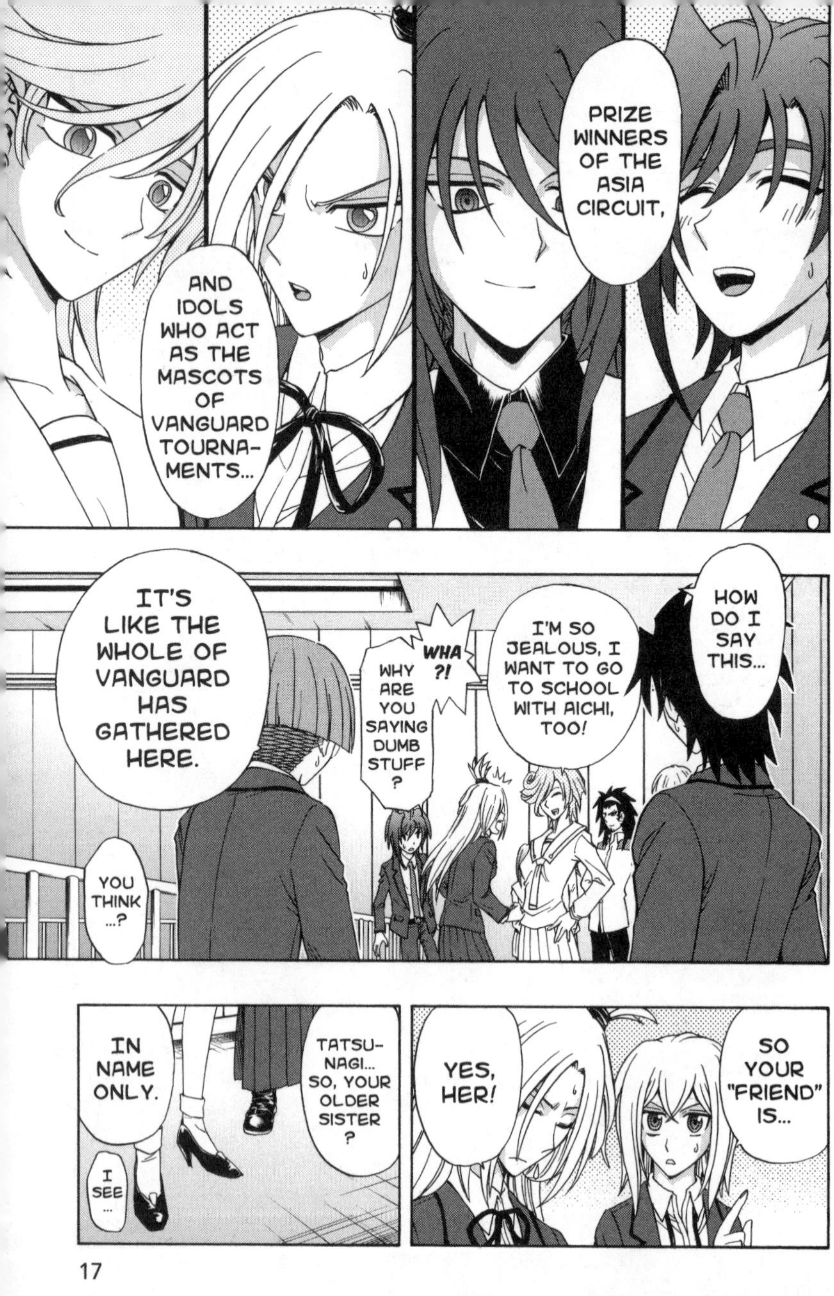
PRIZE WINNERS OF THE ASIA CIRCUIT,
AND IDOLS WHO ACT AS THE MASCOTS OF VANGUARD TOURNA-MENTS...
HOW DO I SAY THIS...
I'M SO JEALOUS, I WANT TO GO TO SCHOOL WITH AICHI, TOO!
WHA?!
WHY ARE YOU SAYING DUMB STUFF?
IT'S LIKE THE WHOLE OF VANGUARD HAS GATHERED HERE.
YOU THINK...?
SO YOUR "FRIEND" IS...
YES, HER!
TATSU-NAGI... SO, YOUR OLDER SISTER?
IN NAME ONLY.
I SEE...

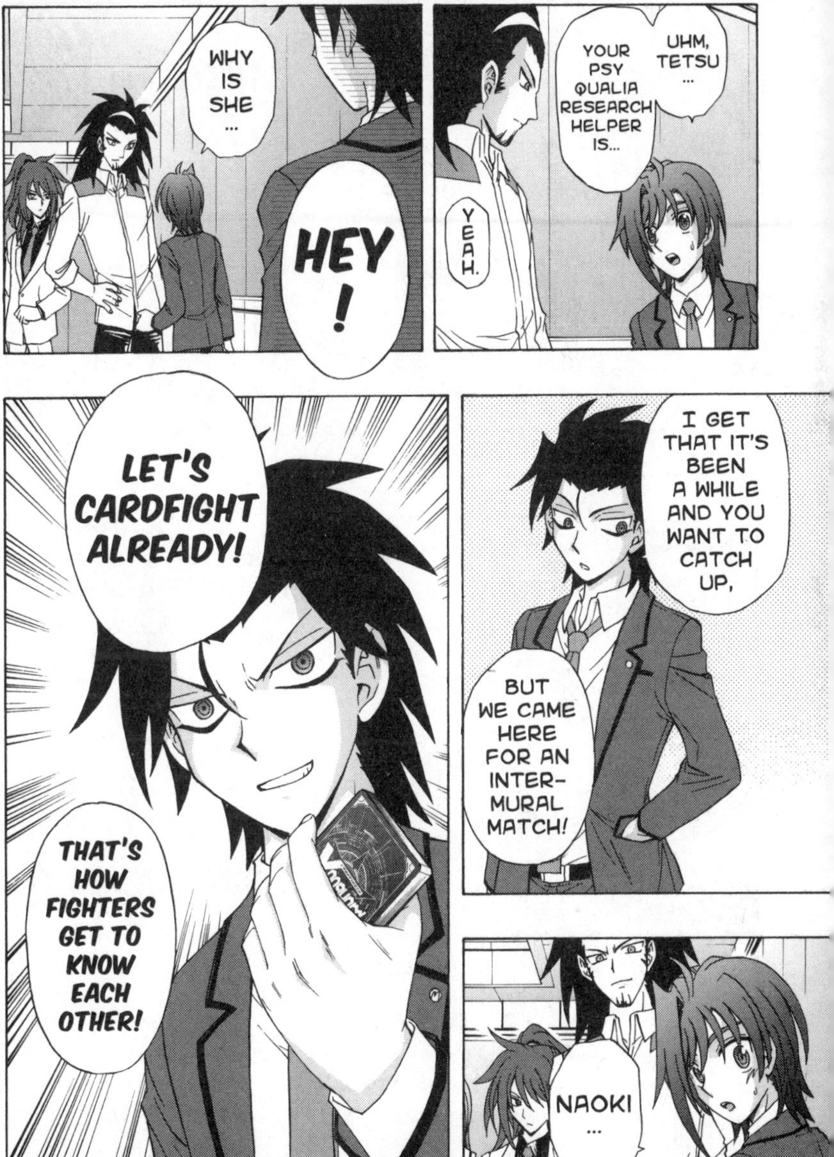
UHM, TETSU ...
YOUR PSY QUALIA RESEARCH HELPER IS...
YEAH.
WHY IS SHE ...
HEY!
I GET THAT IT'S BEEN A WHILE AND YOU WANT TO CATCH UP,
BUT WE CAME HERE FOR AN INTER-MURAL MATCH!
NAOKI ...
LET'S CARDFIGHT ALREADY!
THAT'S HOW FIGHTERS GET TO KNOW EACH OTHER!

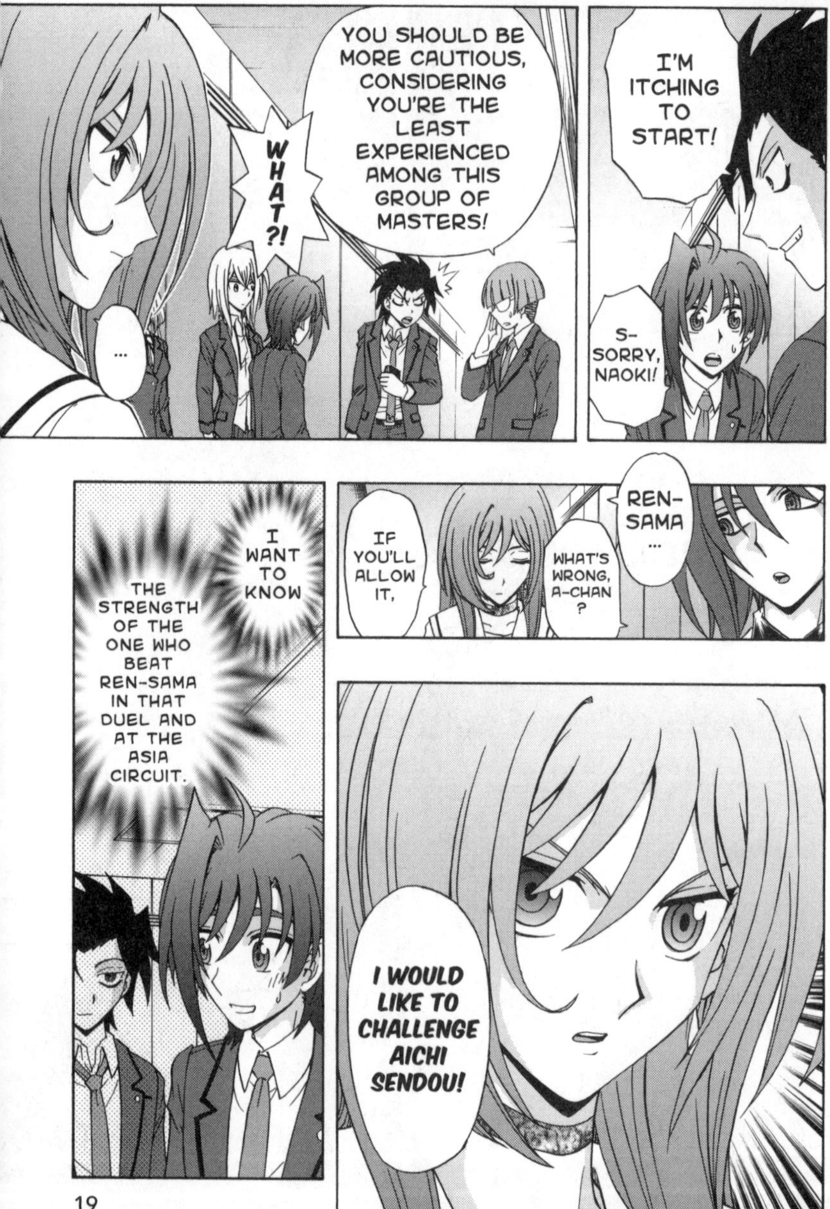
I'M ITCHING TO START!
S-SORRY, NAOKI!
YOU SHOULD BE MORE CAUTIOUS, CONSIDERING YOU'RE THE LEAST EXPERIENCED AMONG THIS GROUP OF MASTERS!
WHAT?!
...
REN-SAMA...
WHAT'S WRONG, A-CHAN?
IF YOU'LL ALLOW IT,
I WOULD LIKE TO CHALLENGE AICHI SENDOU!
I WANT TO KNOW
THE STRENGTH OF THE ONE WHO BEAT REN-SAMA IN THAT DUEL AND AT THE ASIA CIRCUIT.

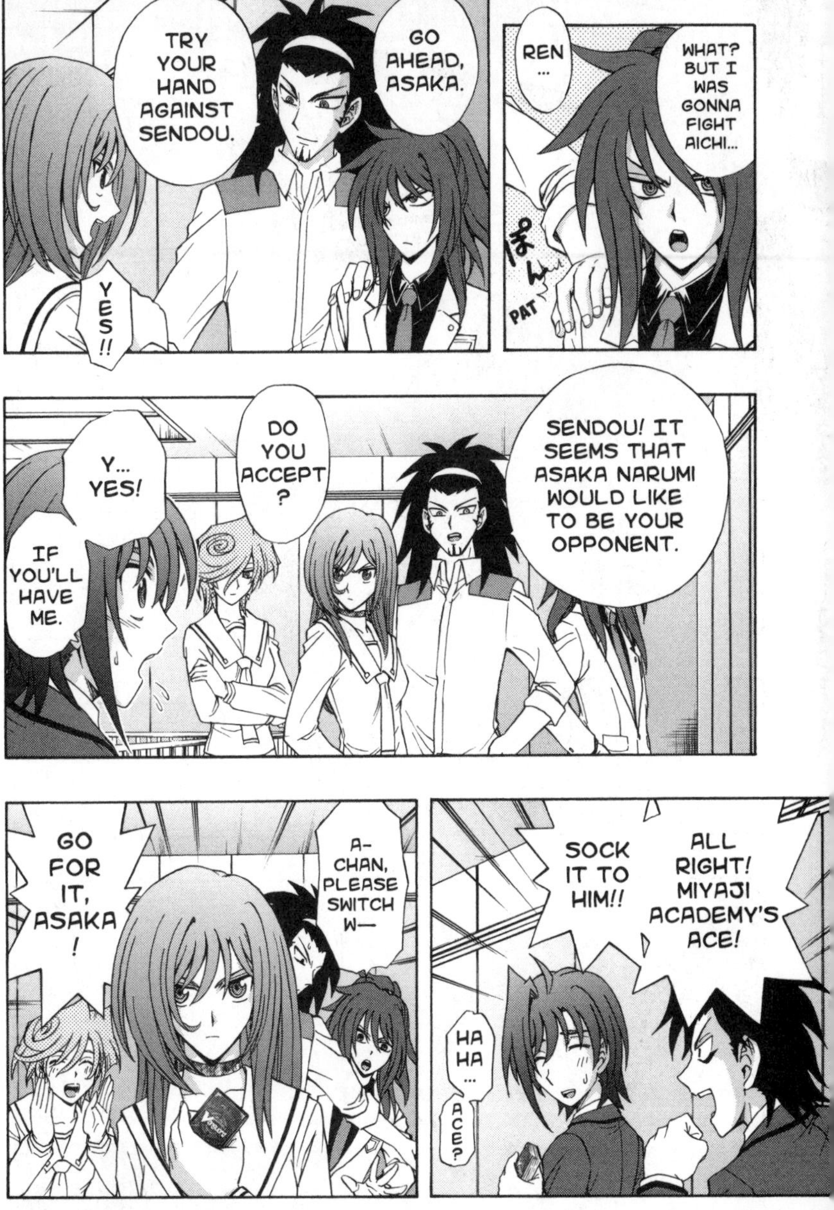
REN ...
WHAT? BUT I WAS GONNA FIGHT AICHI...
ぽん
PAT
GO AHEAD, ASAKA.
TRY YOUR HAND AGAINST SENDOU.
YES!!
SENDOU! IT SEEMS THAT ASAKA NARUMI WOULD LIKE TO BE YOUR OPPONENT.
DO YOU ACCEPT?
Y... YES!
IF YOU'LL HAVE ME.
ALL RIGHT! MIYAJI ACADEMY'S ACE!
SOCK IT TO HIM!!
HA HA ...
ACE?
A-CHAN, PLEASE SWITCH W—
GO FOR IT, ASAKA!

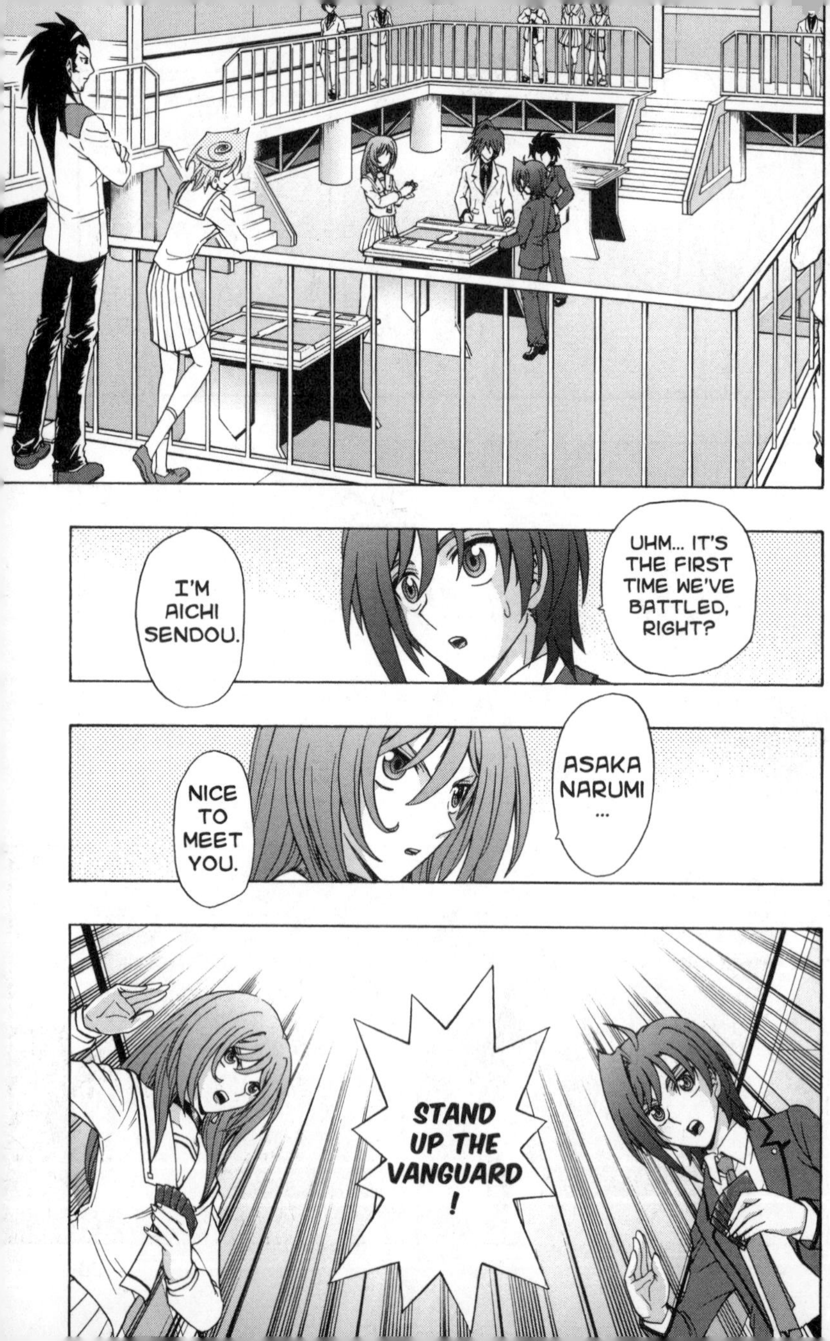
UHM... IT'S THE FIRST TIME WE'VE BATTLED, RIGHT?
I'M AICHI SENDOU.
ASAKA NARUMI ...
NICE TO MEET YOU.
STAND UP THE VANGUARD !

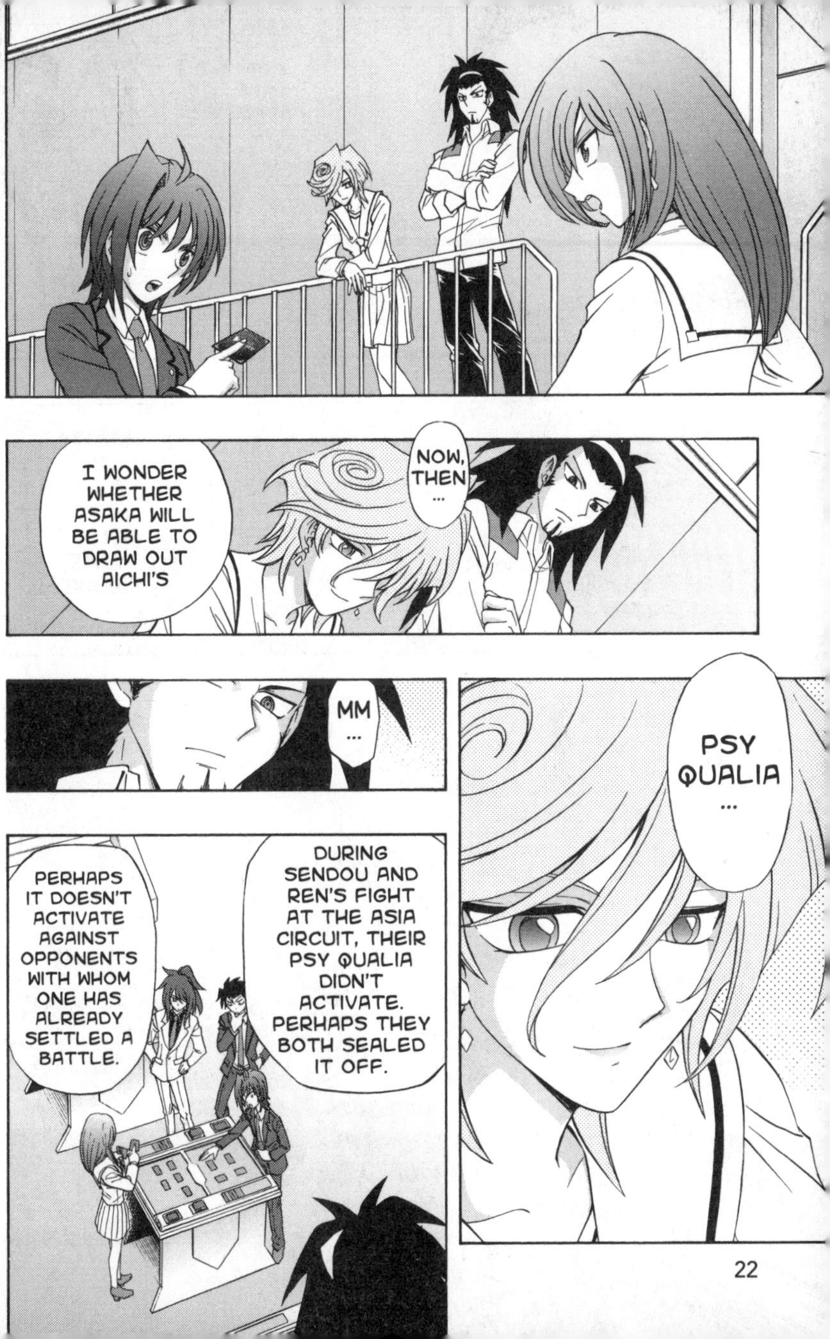
NOW, THEN ...
I WONDER WHETHER ASAKA WILL BE ABLE TO DRAW OUT AICHI'S
PSY QUALIA ...
MM ...
DURING SENDOU AND REN'S FIGHT AT THE ASIA CIRCUIT, THEIR PSY QUALIA DIDN'T ACTIVATE. PERHAPS THEY BOTH SEALED IT OFF.
PERHAPS IT DOESN'T ACTIVATE AGAINST OPPONENTS WITH WHOM ONE HAS ALREADY SETTLED A BATTLE.

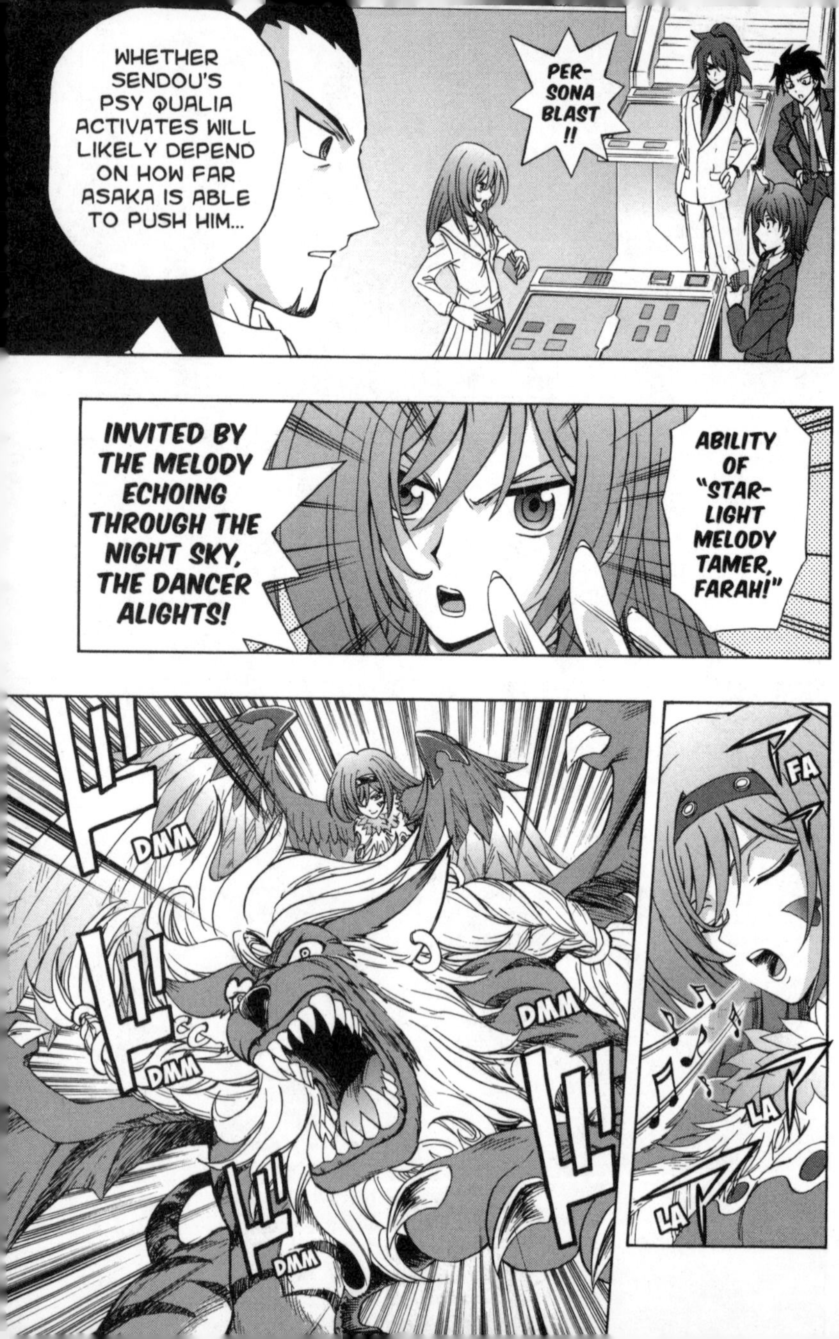
PER-SONA BLAST!!
WHETHER SENDOU'S PSY QUALIA ACTIVATES WILL LIKELY DEPEND ON HOW FAR ASAKA IS ABLE TO PUSH HIM...
ABILITY OF "STAR-LIGHT MELODY TAMER, FARAH!"
INVITED BY THE MELODY ECHOING THROUGH THE NIGHT SKY, THE DANCER ALIGHTS!
FA
LA
LA
DMM
DMM
DMM
DMM

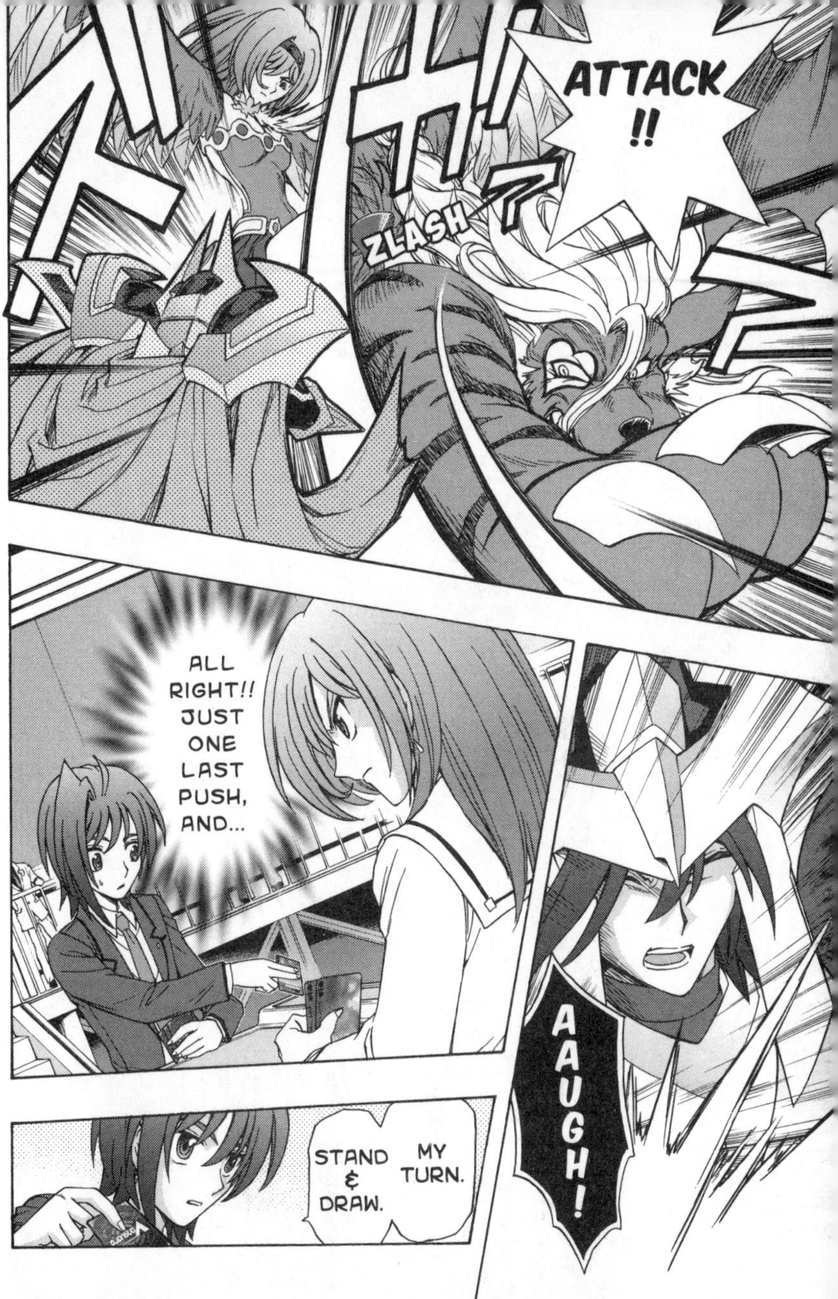
ATTACK!!
ZLASH
AAUGH!
ALL RIGHT!! JUST ONE LAST PUSH, AND...
MY TURN.
STAND & DRAW.

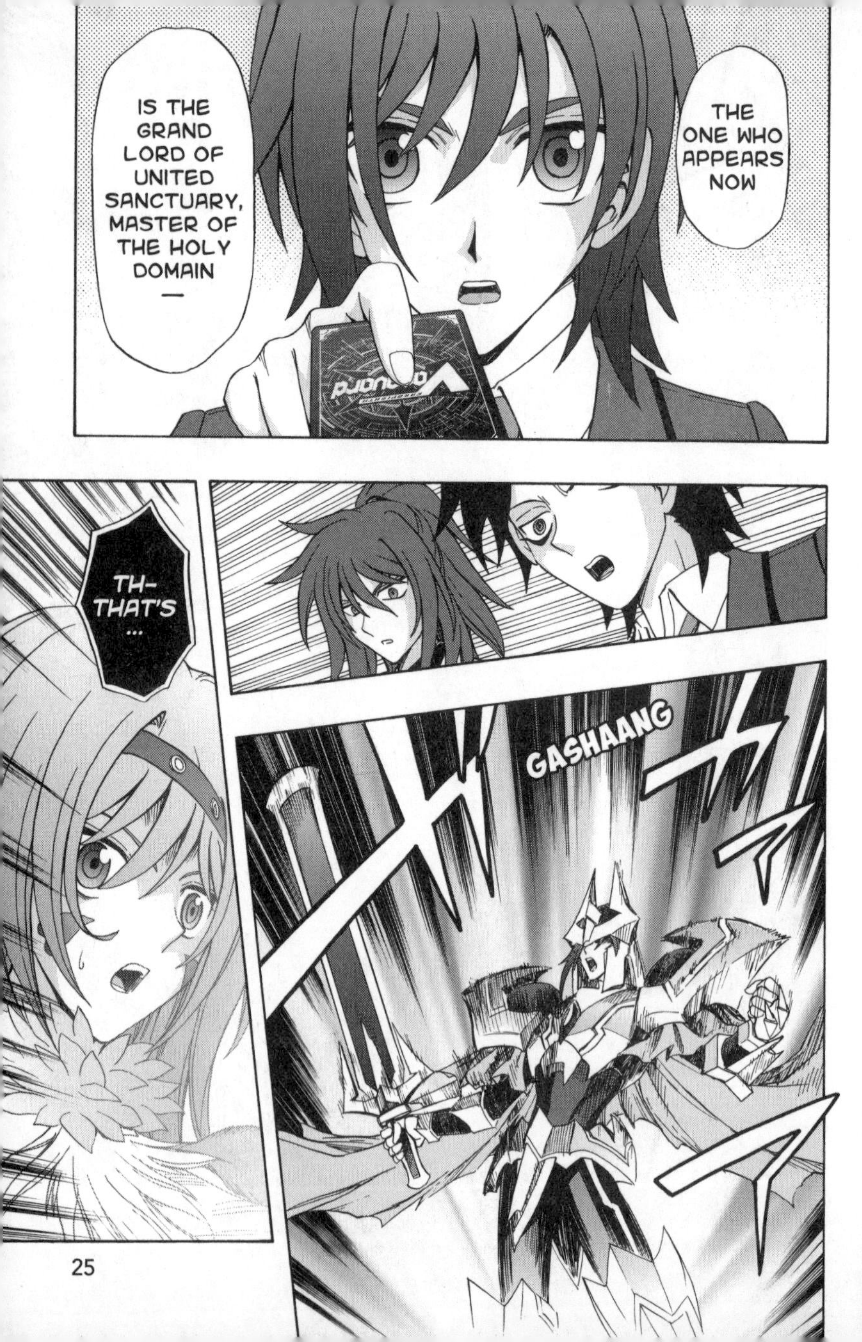
THE ONE WHO APPEARS NOW
IS THE GRAND LORD OF UNITED SANCTUARY, MASTER OF THE HOLY DOMAIN —
GASHAANG
TH-THAT'S ...

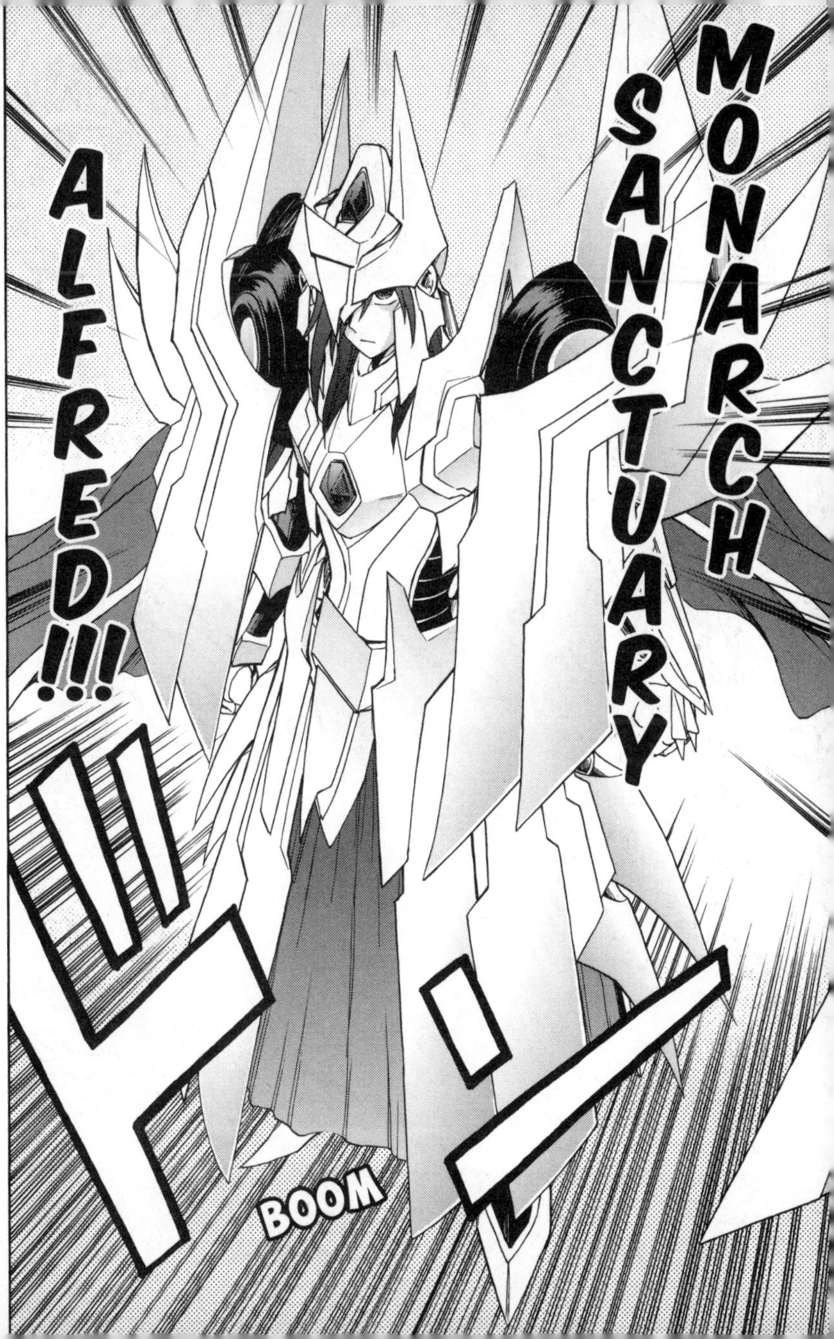
MONARCH
SANCTUARY
ALFRED!!!
BOOM

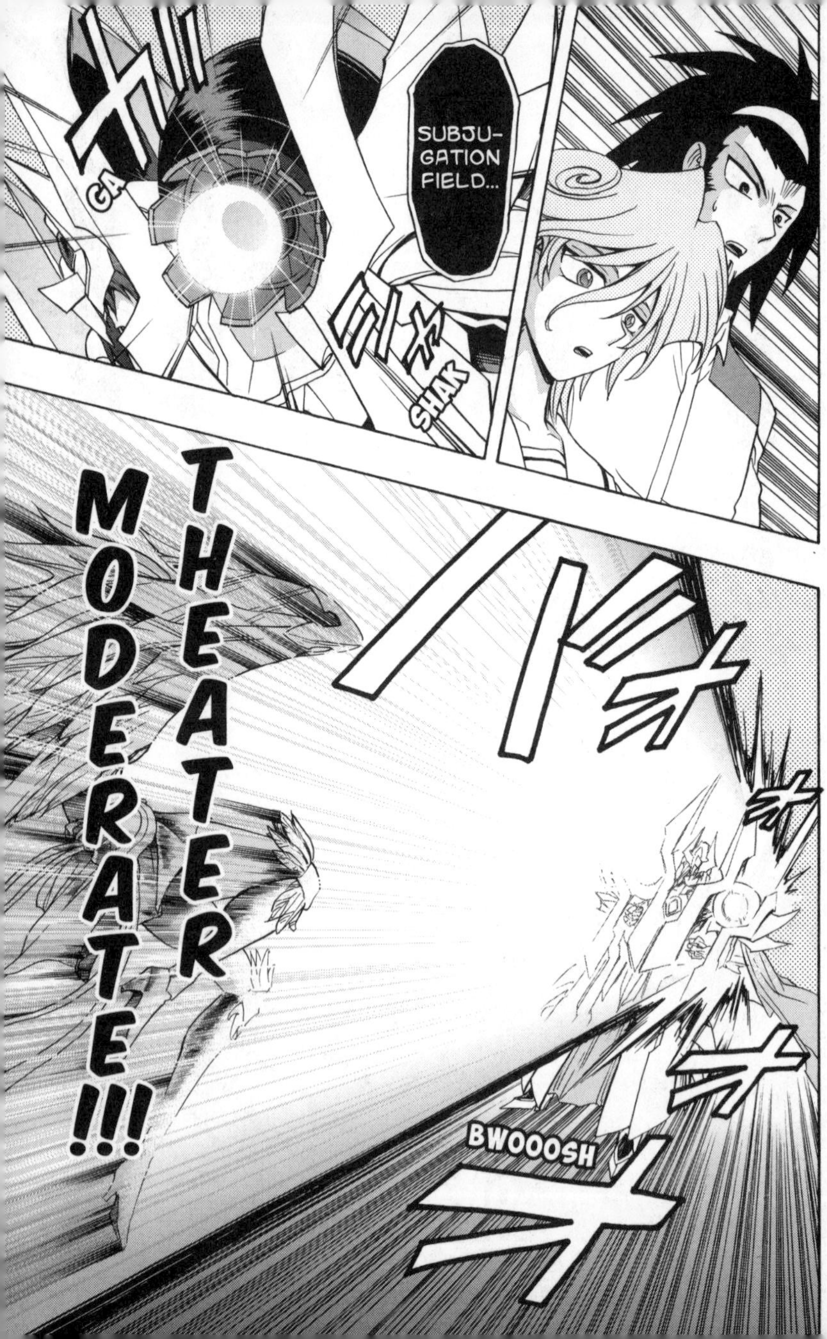
SUBJU-
GATION
FIELD...
GA
SHAK
BWOOOSH
THEATER
MODERATE!!!

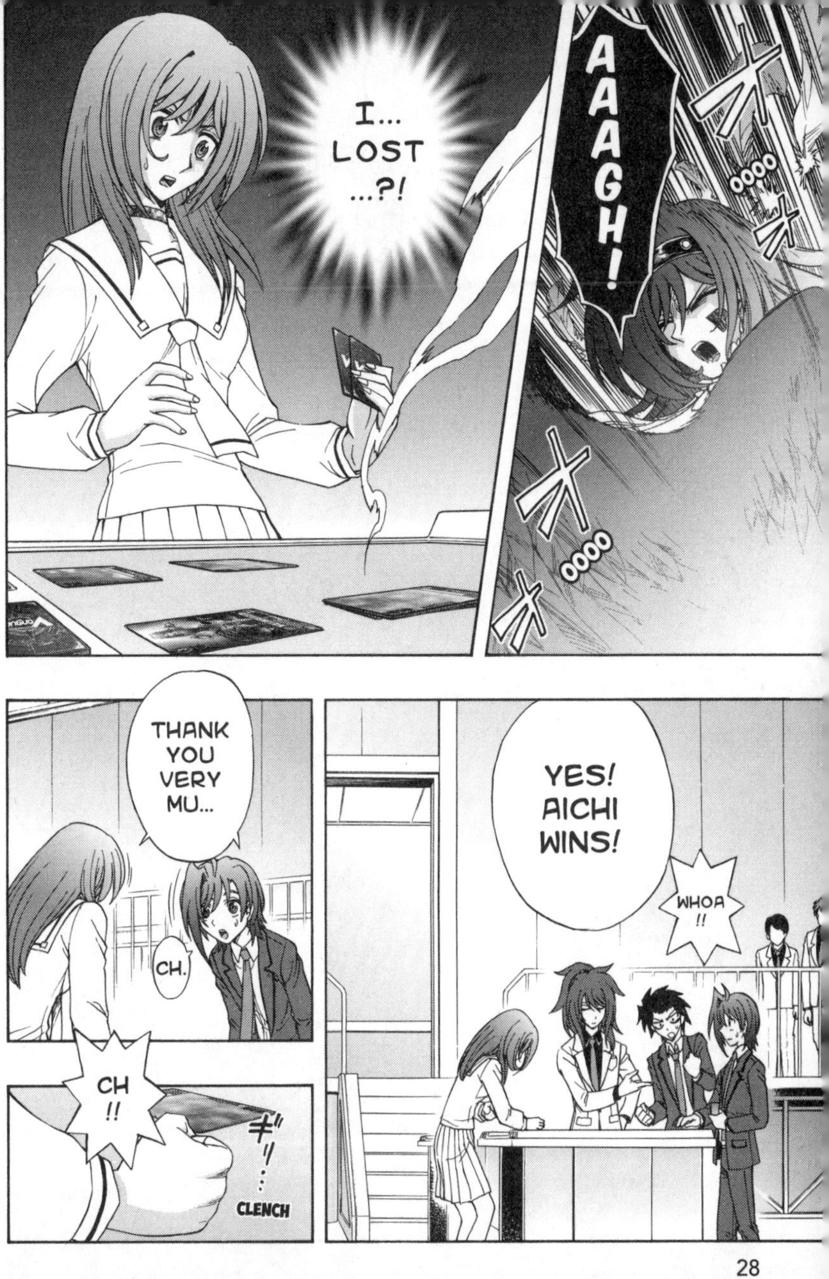
AAAGH!
OOOO
OOOO
I... LOST ...?!
YES! AICHI WINS!
WHOA !!
THANK YOU VERY MU...
CH.
CH !!
CLENCH

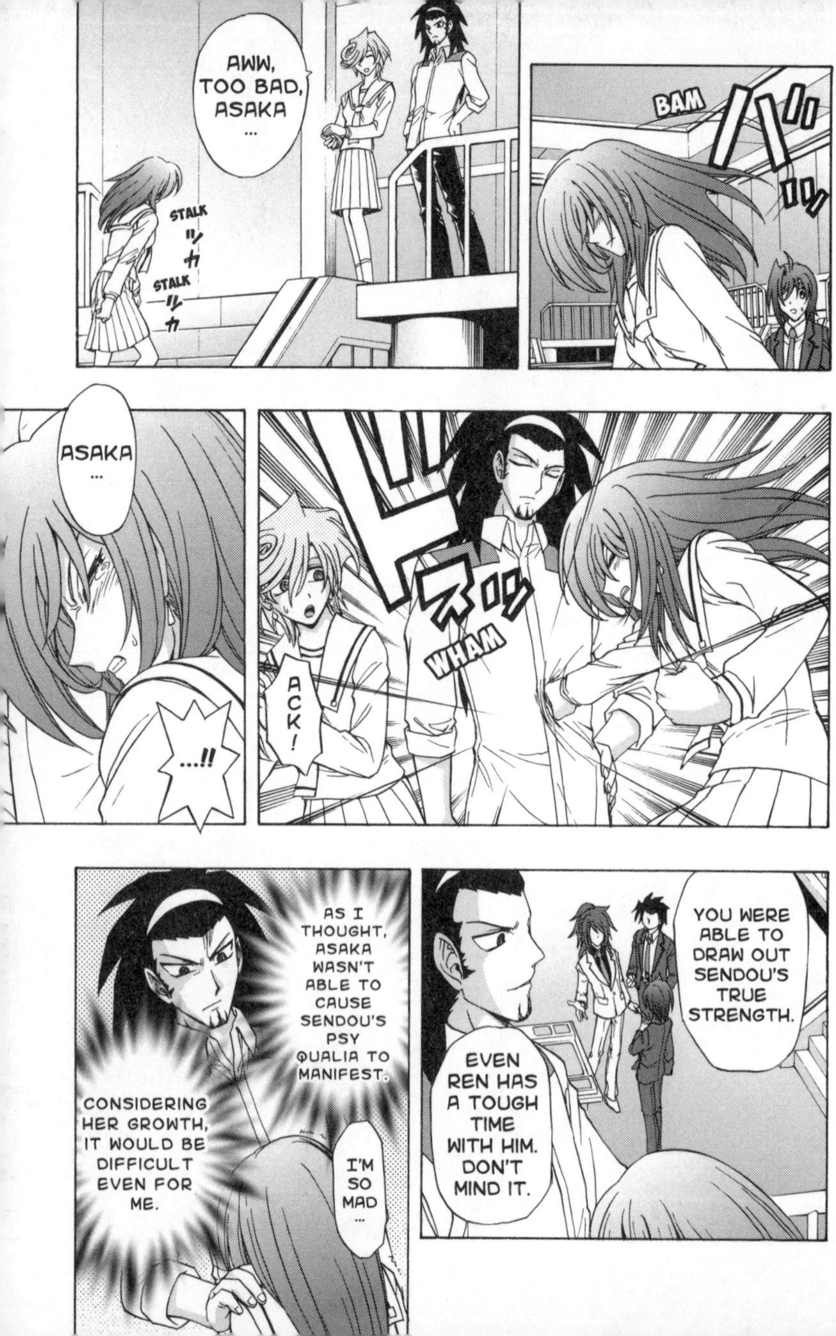
BAM
AWW, TOO BAD, ASAKA ...
STALK
STALK
WHAM
ACK!
ASAKA ...
...!!
YOU WERE ABLE TO DRAW OUT SENDOU'S TRUE STRENGTH.
EVEN REN HAS A TOUGH TIME WITH HIM. DON'T MIND IT.
AS I THOUGHT, ASAKA WASN'T ABLE TO CAUSE SENDOU'S PSY QUALIA TO MANIFEST.
CONSIDERING HER GROWTH, IT WOULD BE DIFFICULT EVEN FOR ME.
I'M SO MAD ...

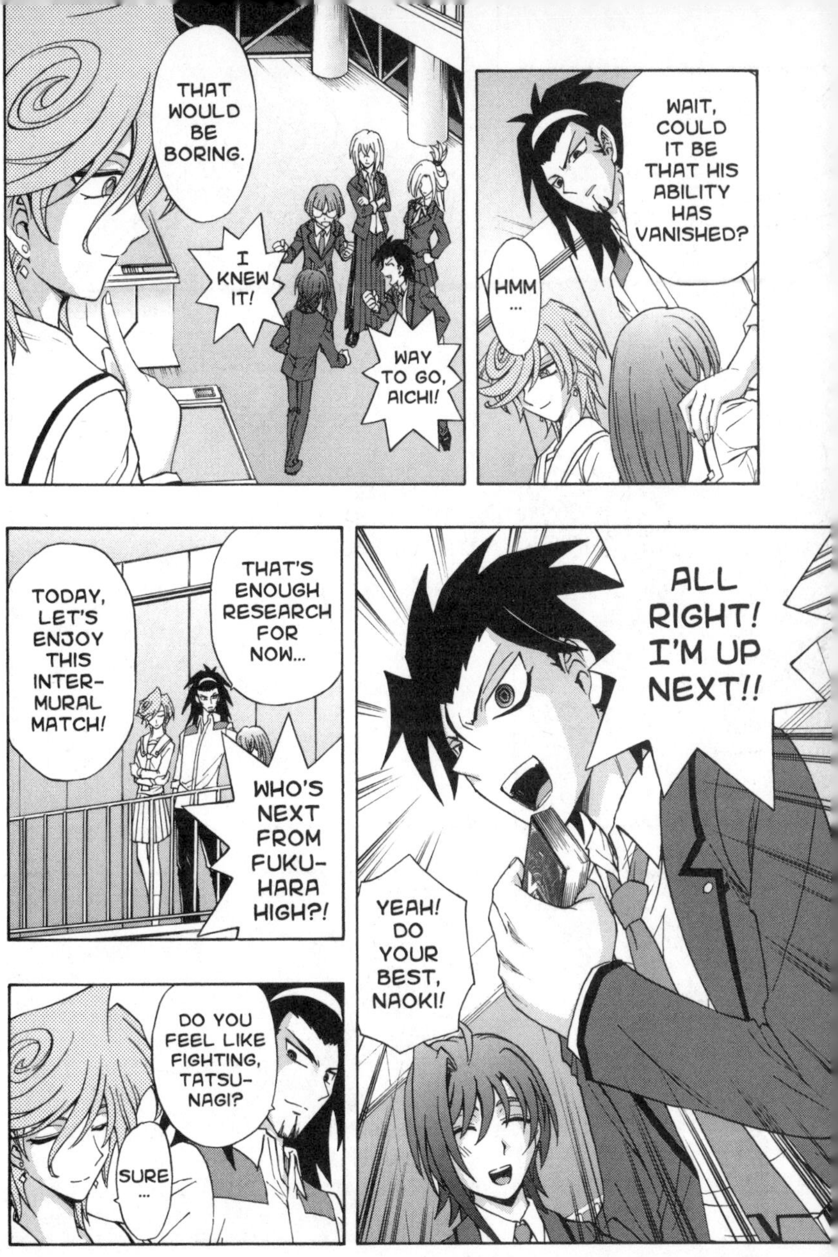
WAIT, COULD IT BE THAT HIS ABILITY HAS VANISHED?
HMM ...
THAT WOULD BE BORING.
I KNEW IT!
WAY TO GO, AICHI!
ALL RIGHT! I'M UP NEXT!!
YEAH! DO YOUR BEST, NAOKI!
THAT'S ENOUGH RESEARCH FOR NOW...
TODAY, LET'S ENJOY THIS INTER-MURAL MATCH!
WHO'S NEXT FROM FUKU-HARA HIGH?!
DO YOU FEEL LIKE FIGHTING, TATSU-NAGI?
SURE ...

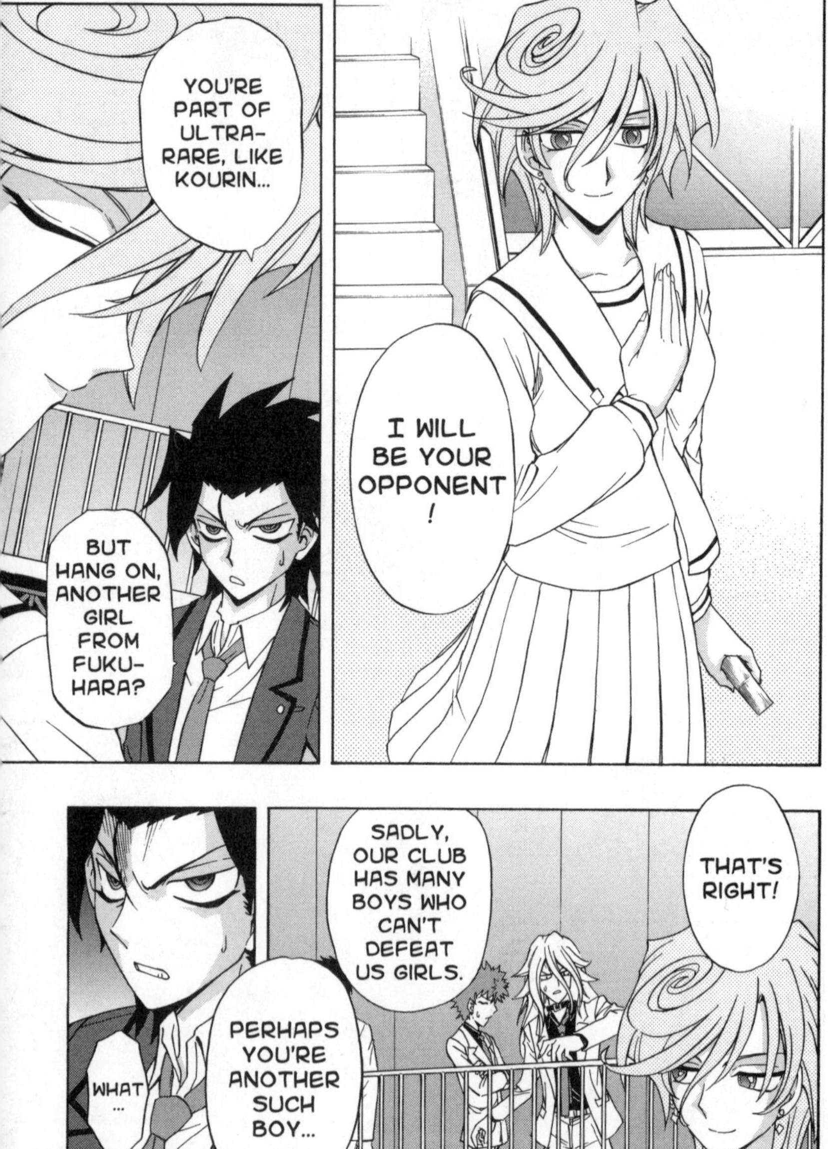
I WILL BE YOUR OPPONENT!
YOU'RE PART OF ULTRA-RARE, LIKE KOURIN...
BUT HANG ON, ANOTHER GIRL FROM FUKU-HARA?
THAT'S RIGHT!
SADLY, OUR CLUB HAS MANY BOYS WHO CAN'T DEFEAT US GIRLS.
PERHAPS YOU'RE ANOTHER SUCH BOY...
WHAT...

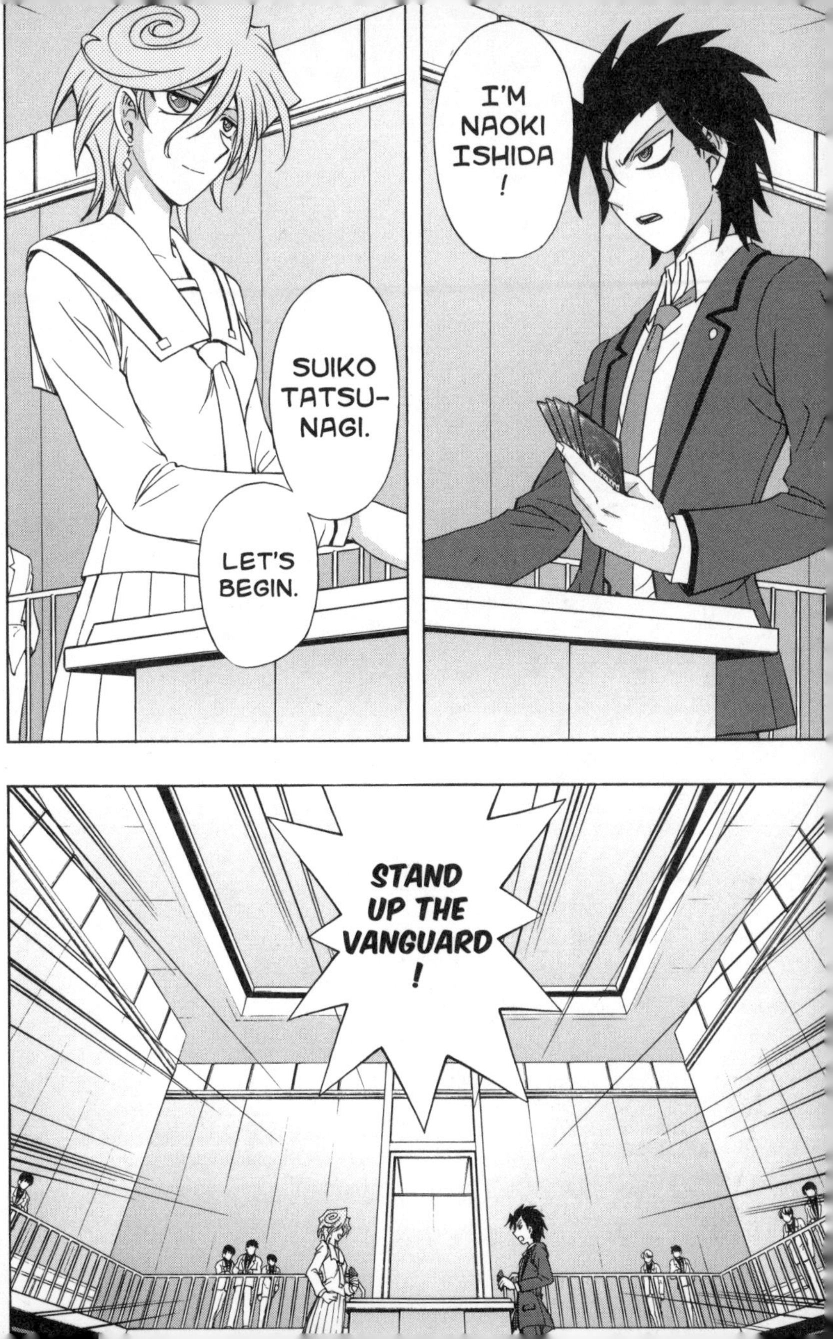
I'M NAOKI ISHIDA!
SUIKO TATSU-NAGI.
LET'S BEGIN.
STAND UP THE VANGUARD!

CARDFIGHT!!
Vanguard

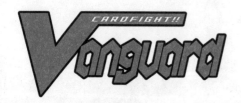

BONUS!

CARDFIGHT!! Vanguard

## VANGUARD LAB

## RIDE THE ORIGINAL DESIGNS!

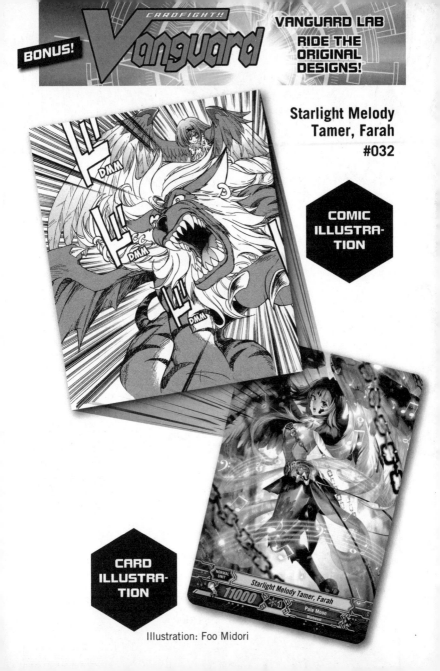

**Starlight Melody Tamer, Farah #032**

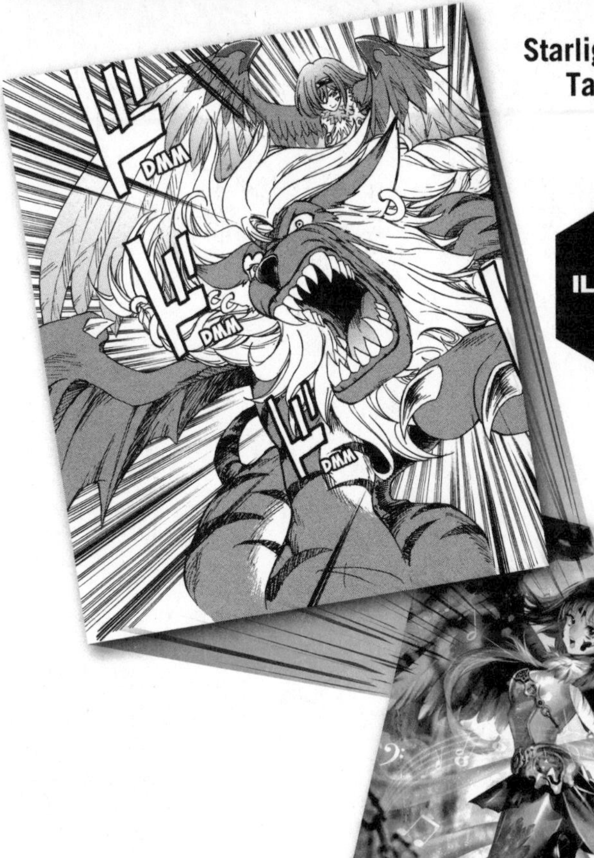
DMM
DMM
DMM

COMIC ILLUSTRATION

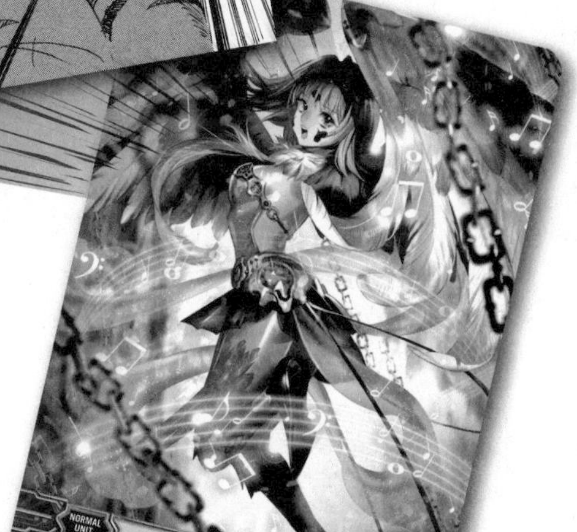
NORMAL UNIT
Starlight Melody Tamer, Farah
11000
1
Pale Moon
Warbeast

CARD ILLUSTRATION

Illustration: Foo Midori

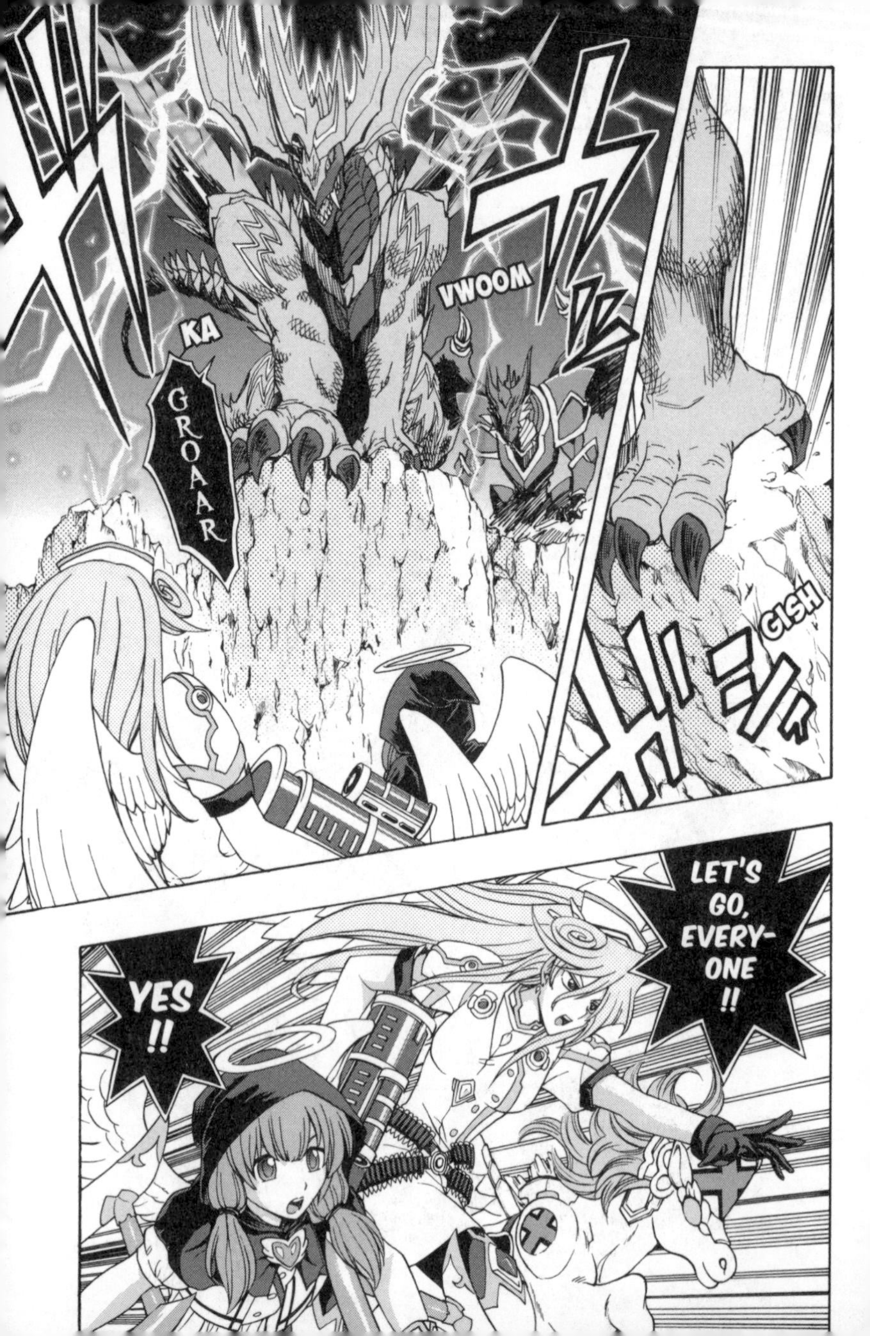
GISH
VWOOM
KA
GROAAR
LET'S GO, EVERYONE!!
YES!!

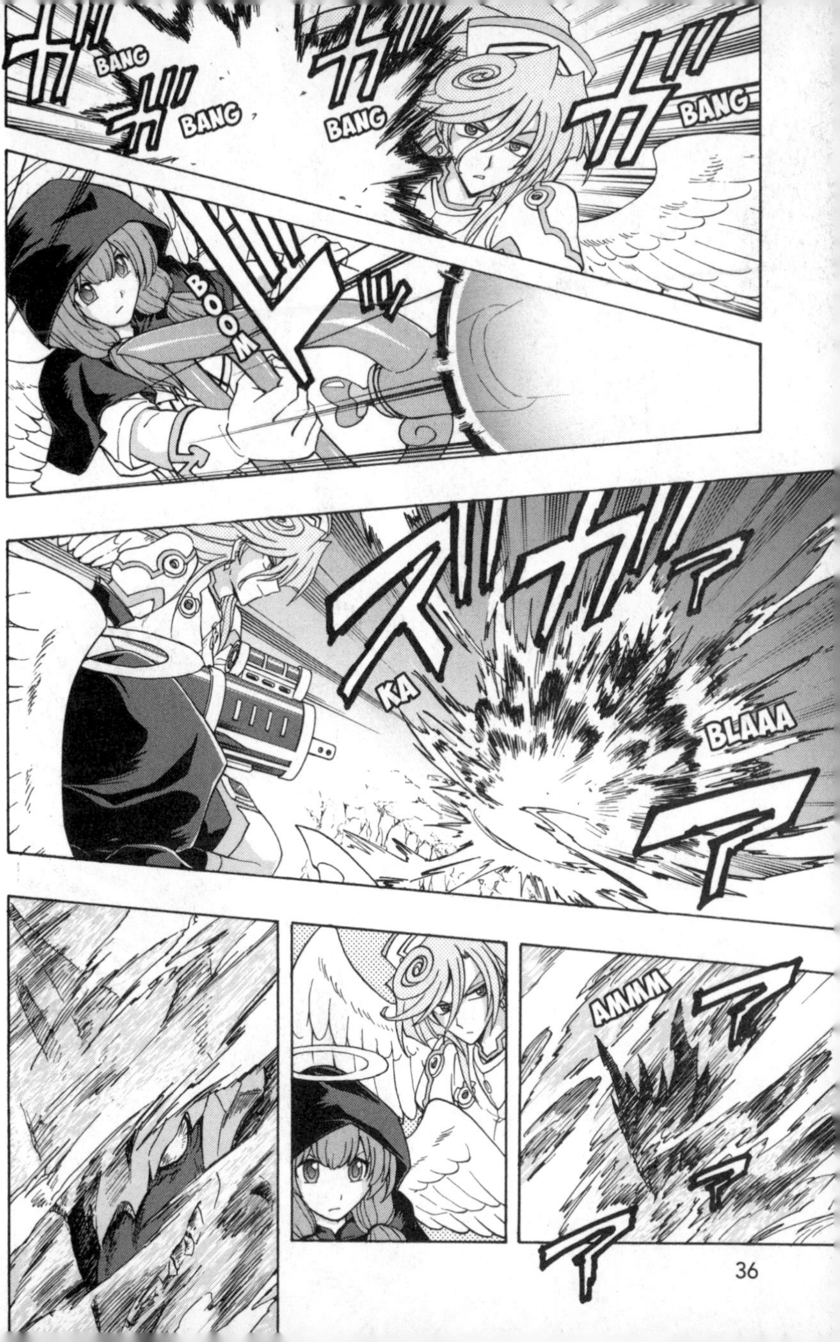
BANG
BANG
BANG
BANG
BOOM
KA
BLAAA
AMMM

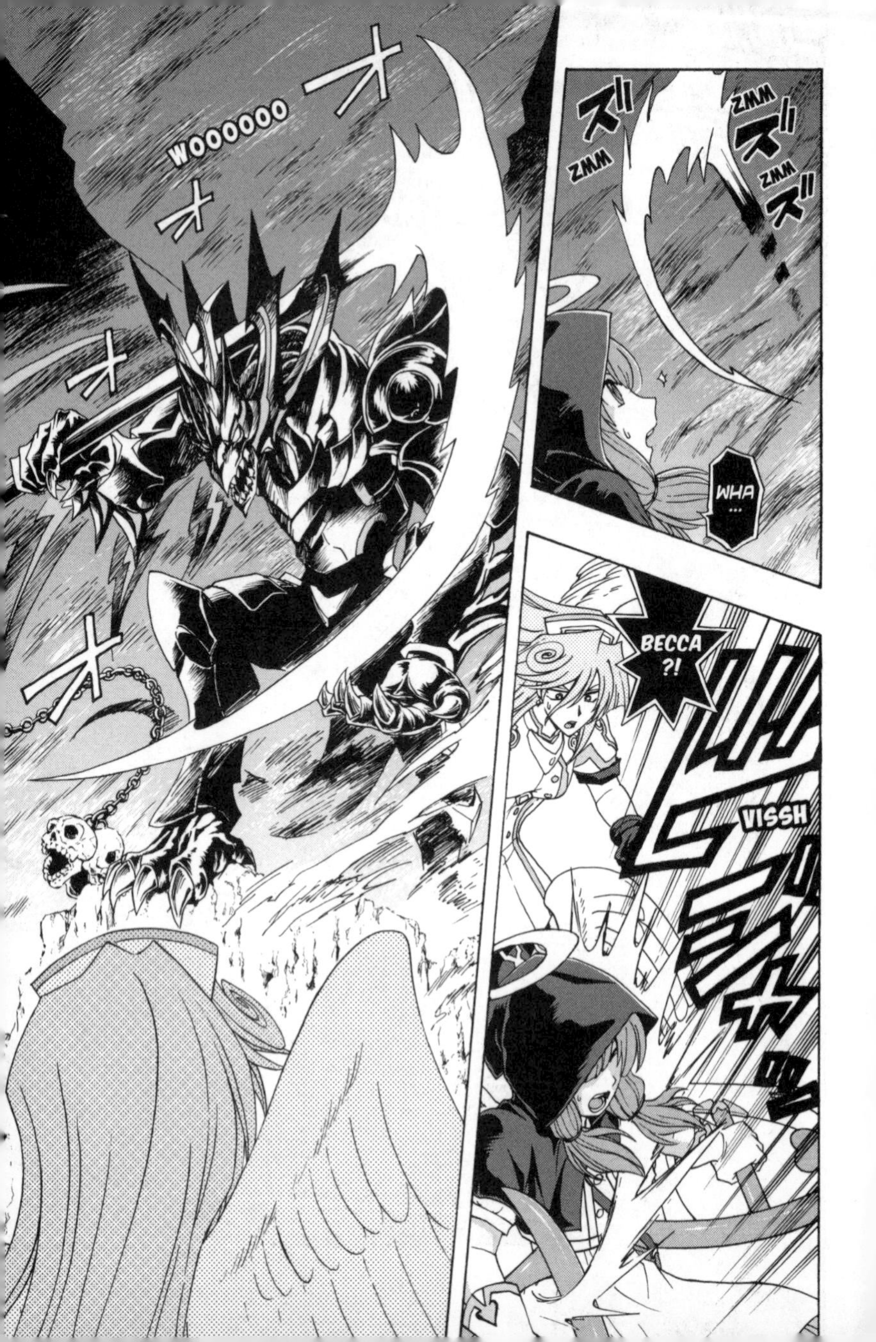

ZMM
ZMM
ZMM
WHA...
BECCA?!
VISSH
WOOOOOO

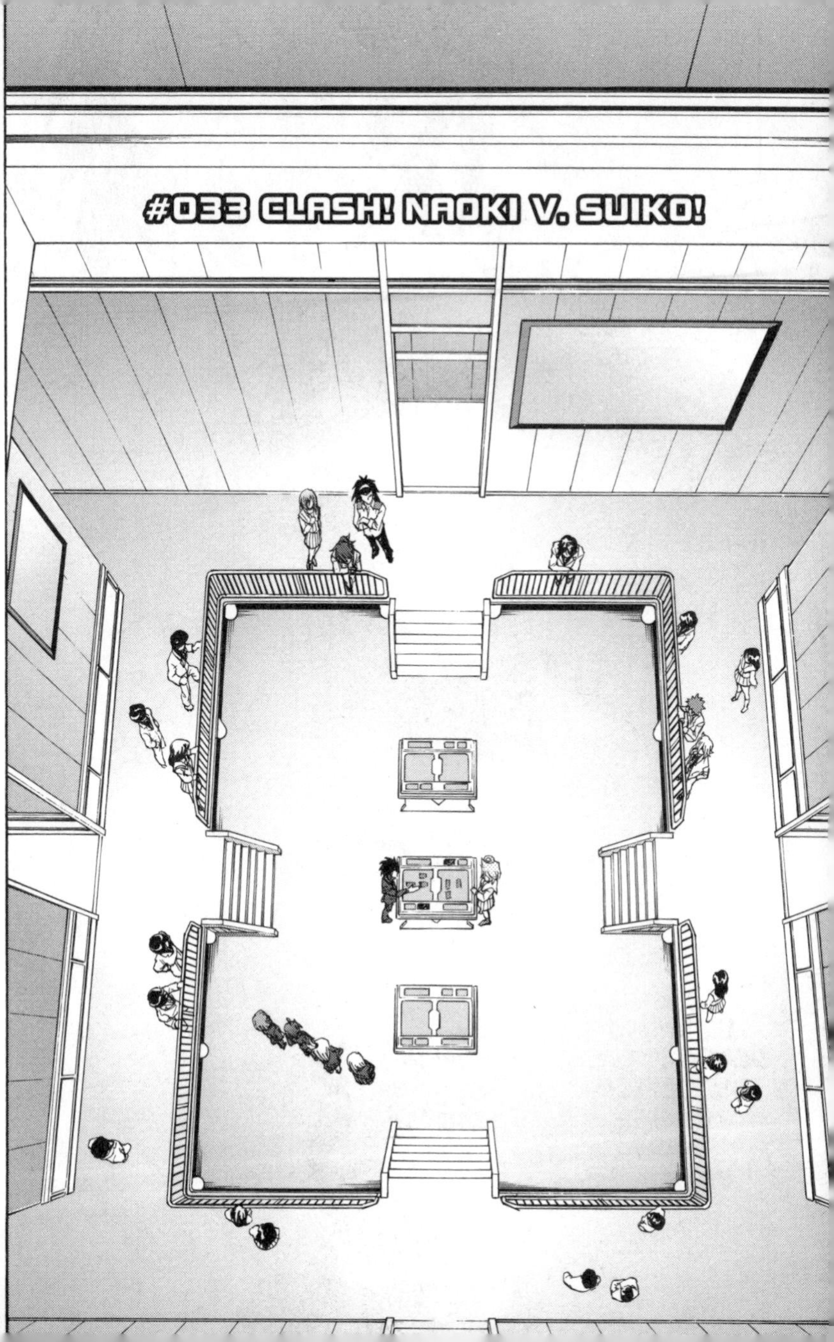
#033 CLASH! NAOKI V. SUIKO!

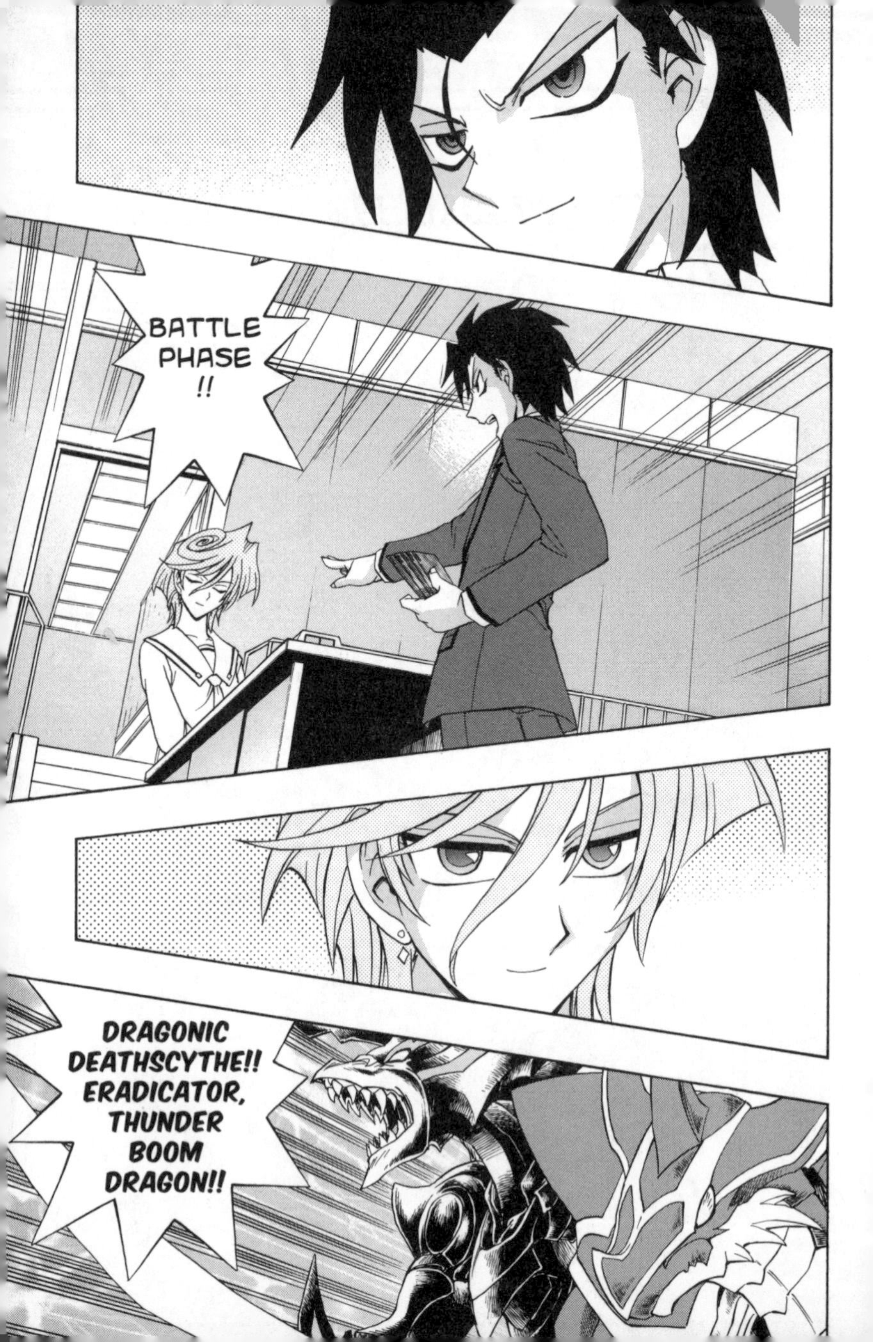
BATTLE PHASE !!
DRAGONIC DEATHSCYTHE!! ERADICATOR, THUNDER BOOM DRAGON!!

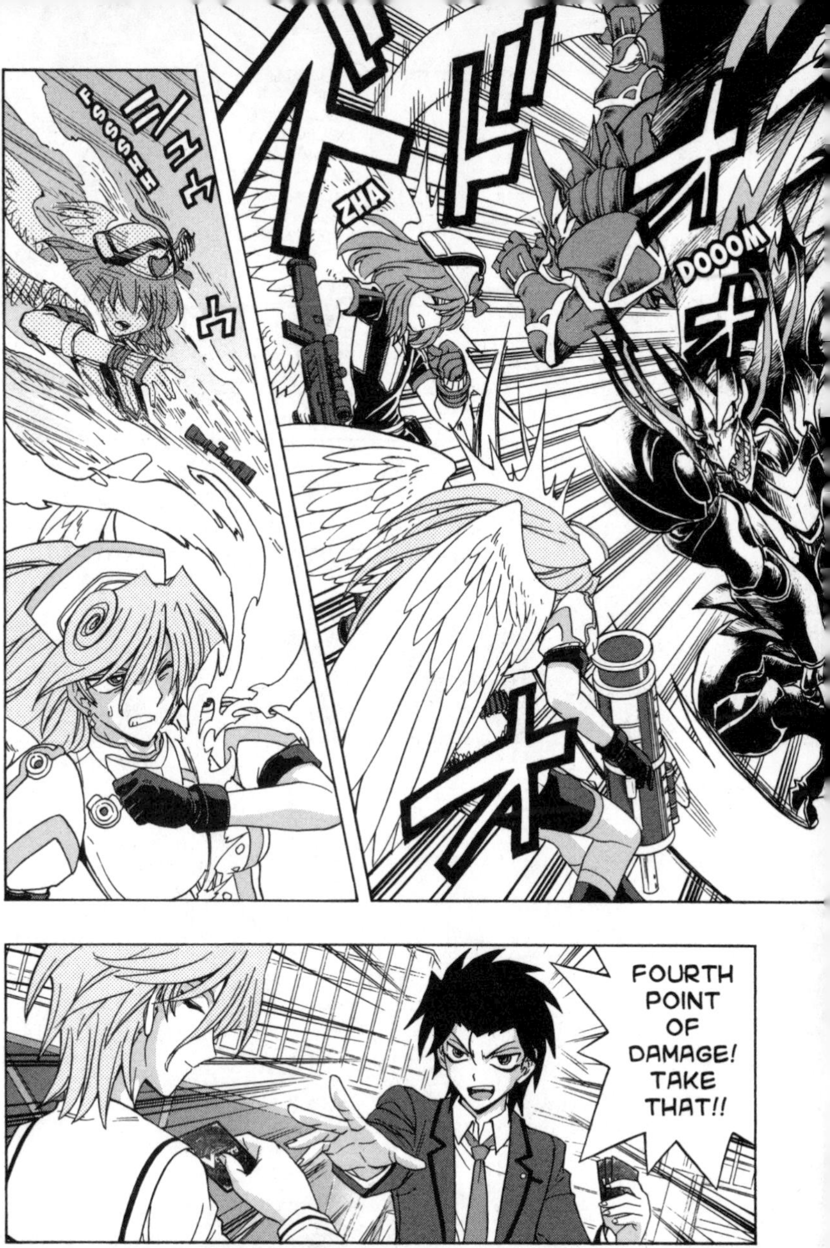
ZHA
DOOOM
FSSSHH
FOURTH POINT OF DAMAGE! TAKE THAT!!

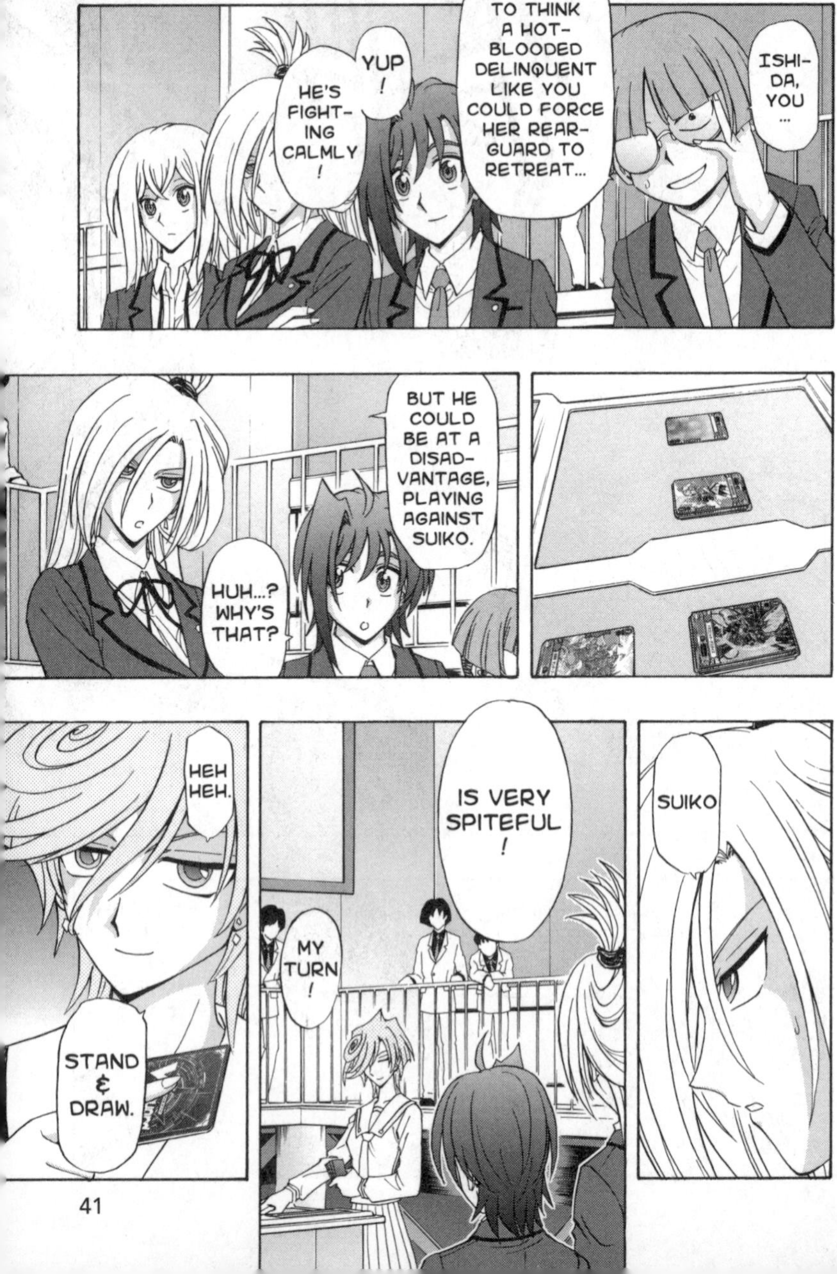
ISHI-DA, YOU ...
TO THINK A HOT-BLOODED DELINQUENT LIKE YOU COULD FORCE HER REAR-GUARD TO RETREAT...
YUP!
HE'S FIGHTING CALMLY!
BUT HE COULD BE AT A DISAD-VANTAGE, PLAYING AGAINST SUIKO.
HUH...? WHY'S THAT?
SUIKO
IS VERY SPITEFUL!
MY TURN!
HEH HEH.
STAND & DRAW.

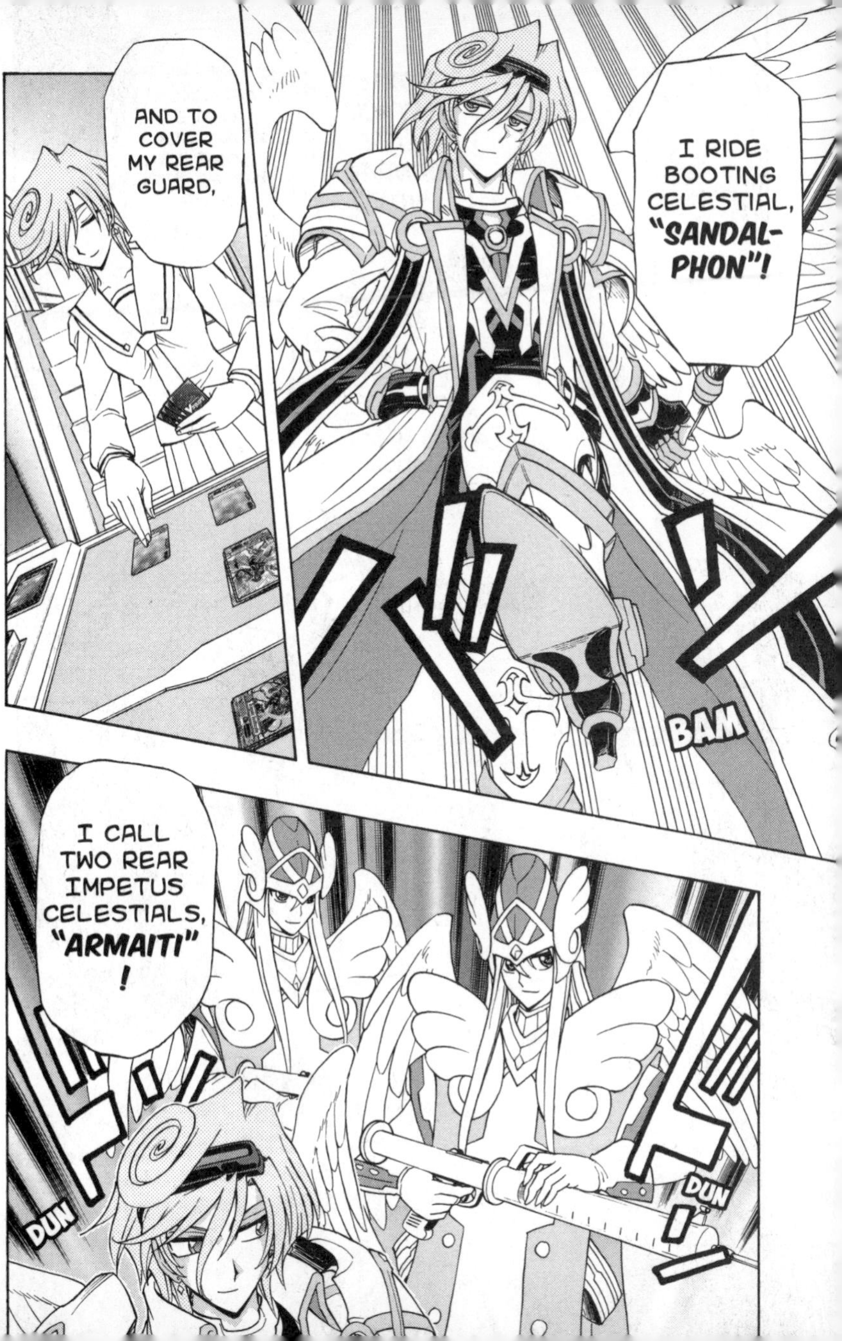
I RIDE BOOTING CELESTIAL, "SANDAL-PHON"!
BAM
AND TO COVER MY REAR GUARD,
I CALL TWO REAR IMPETUS CELESTIALS, "ARMAITI"!
DUN
DUN

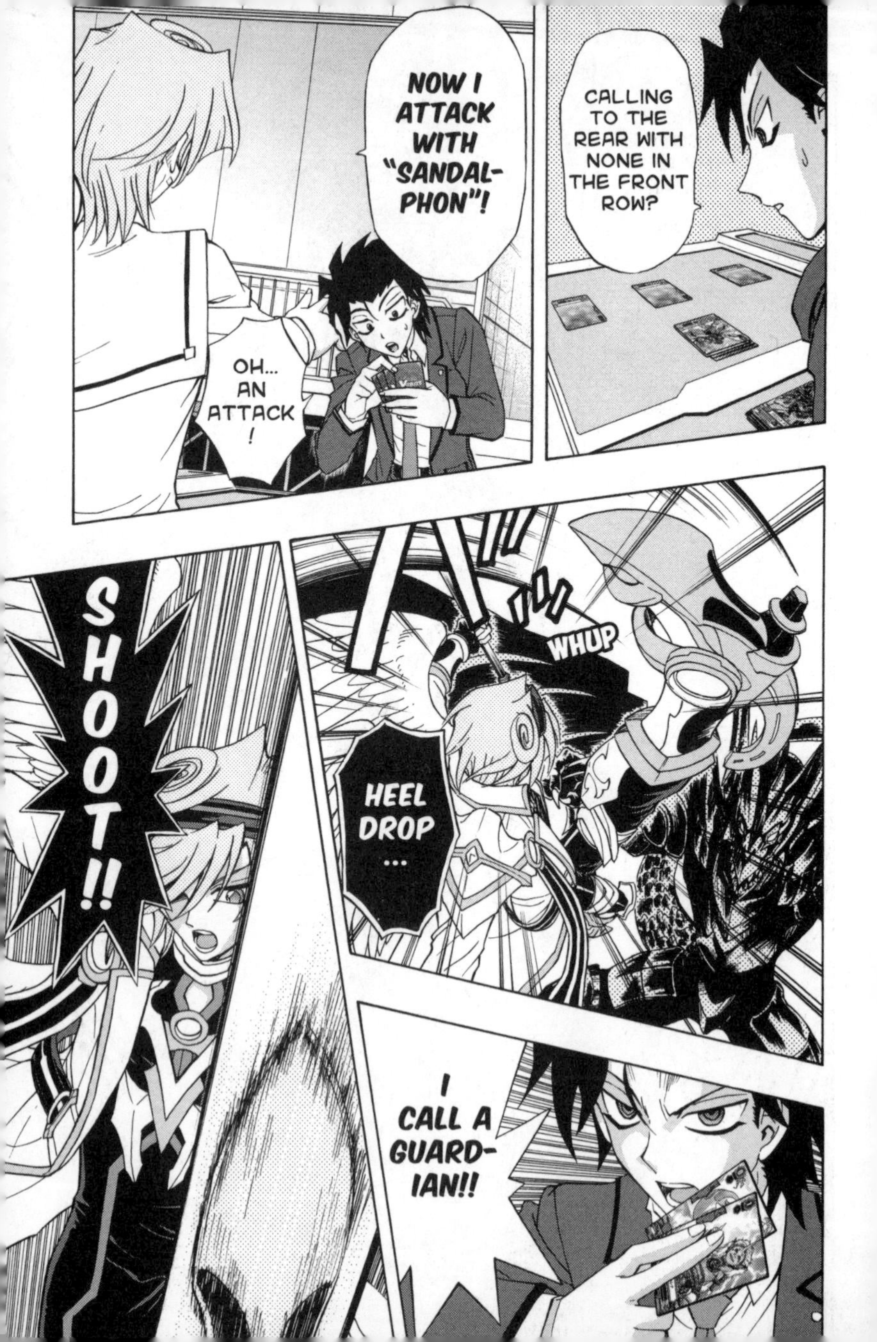
CALLING TO THE REAR WITH NONE IN THE FRONT ROW?
NOW I ATTACK WITH "SANDALPHON"!
OH... AN ATTACK!
WHUP
HEEL DROP ...
I CALL A GUARDIAN!!
SHOOT!!

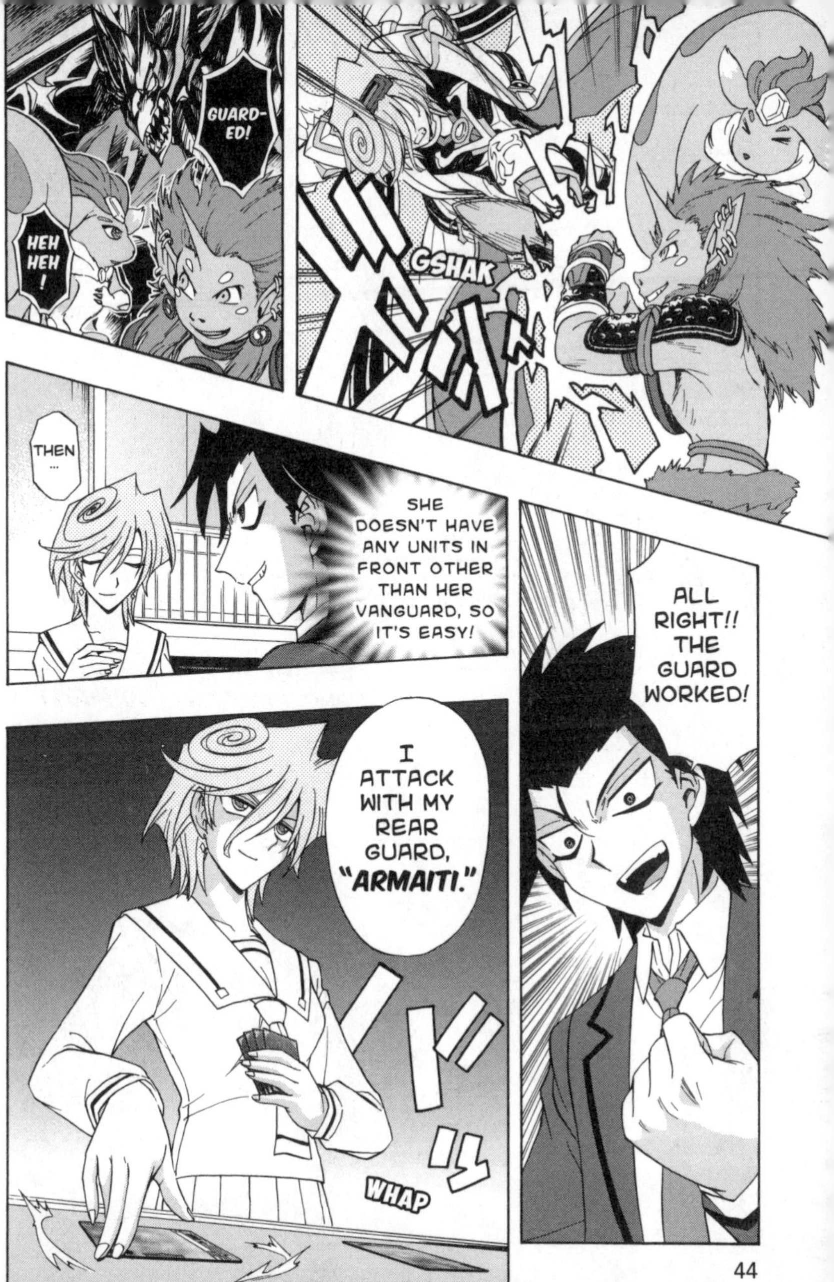
GSHAK
GUARD-ED!
HEH HEH!
ALL RIGHT!! THE GUARD WORKED!
THEN...
SHE DOESN'T HAVE ANY UNITS IN FRONT OTHER THAN HER VANGUARD, SO IT'S EASY!
I ATTACK WITH MY REAR GUARD, "ARMAITI."
WHAP

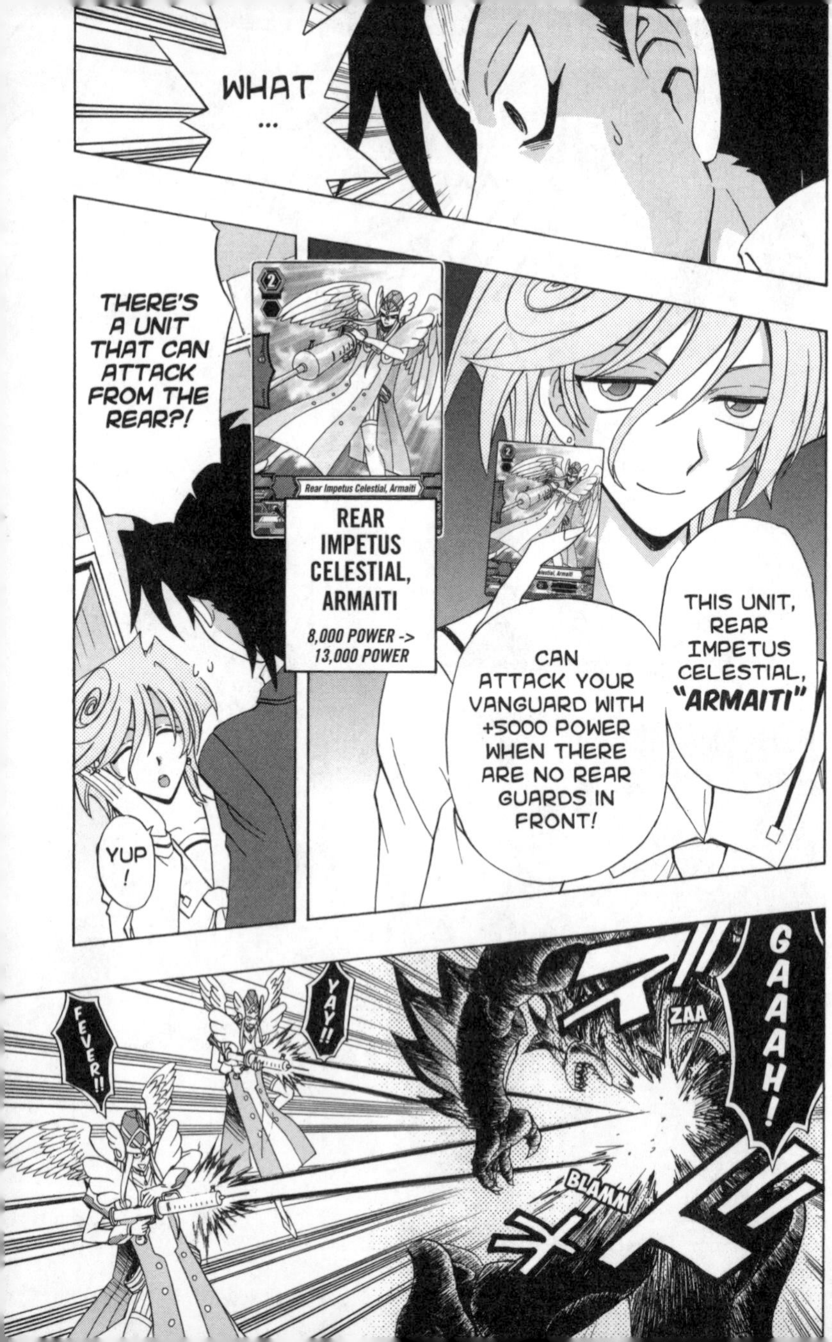
WHAT ...
THIS UNIT, REAR IMPETUS CELESTIAL, "ARMAITI"
CAN ATTACK YOUR VANGUARD WITH +5000 POWER WHEN THERE ARE NO REAR GUARDS IN FRONT!
Rear Impetus Celestial, Armaiti
REAR IMPETUS CELESTIAL, ARMAITI
8,000 POWER -> 13,000 POWER
THERE'S A UNIT THAT CAN ATTACK FROM THE REAR?!
YUP!
GAAAH!
ZAA
BLAMM
YAY!!
FEVER!!

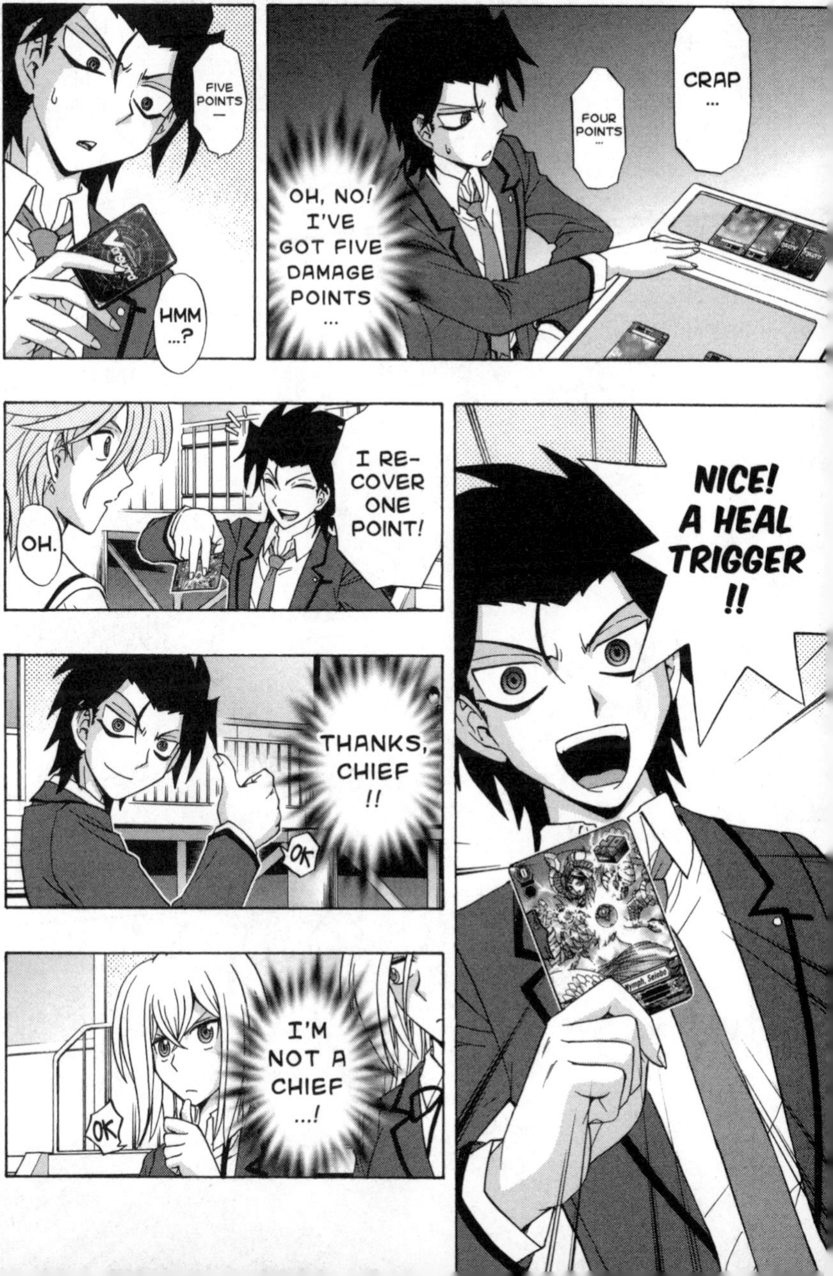
CRAP ...
FOUR POINTS ...
OH, NO! I'VE GOT FIVE DAMAGE POINTS ...
FIVE POINTS —
HMM ...?
NICE! A HEAL TRIGGER !!
I RE-COVER ONE POINT!
OH.
THANKS, CHIEF !!
OK
I'M NOT A CHIEF ...!
OK

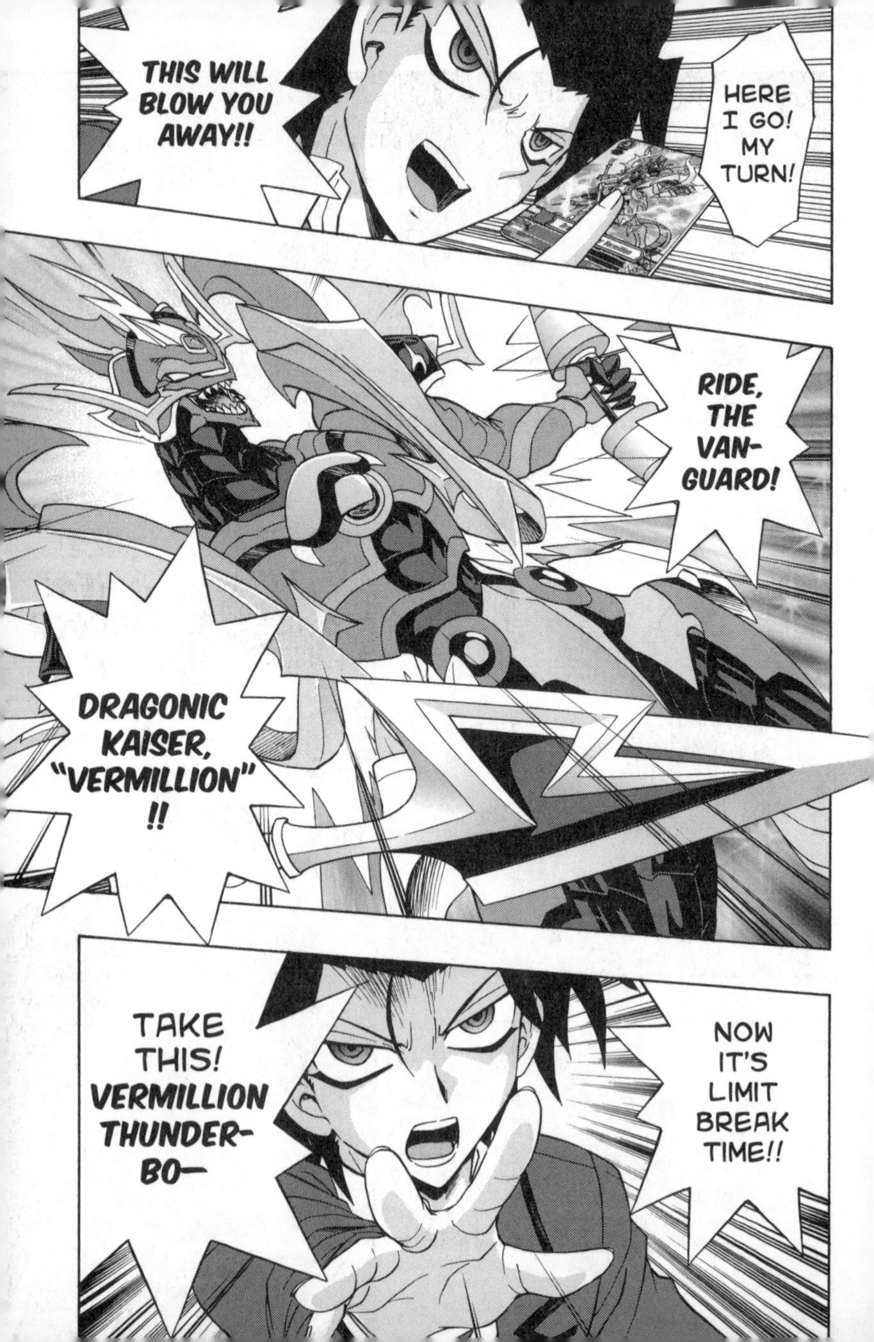
HERE I GO! MY TURN!
THIS WILL BLOW YOU AWAY!!
RIDE, THE VAN-GUARD!
DRAGONIC KAISER, "VERMILLION" !!
NOW IT'S LIMIT BREAK TIME!!
TAKE THIS! VERMILLION THUNDER-BO—

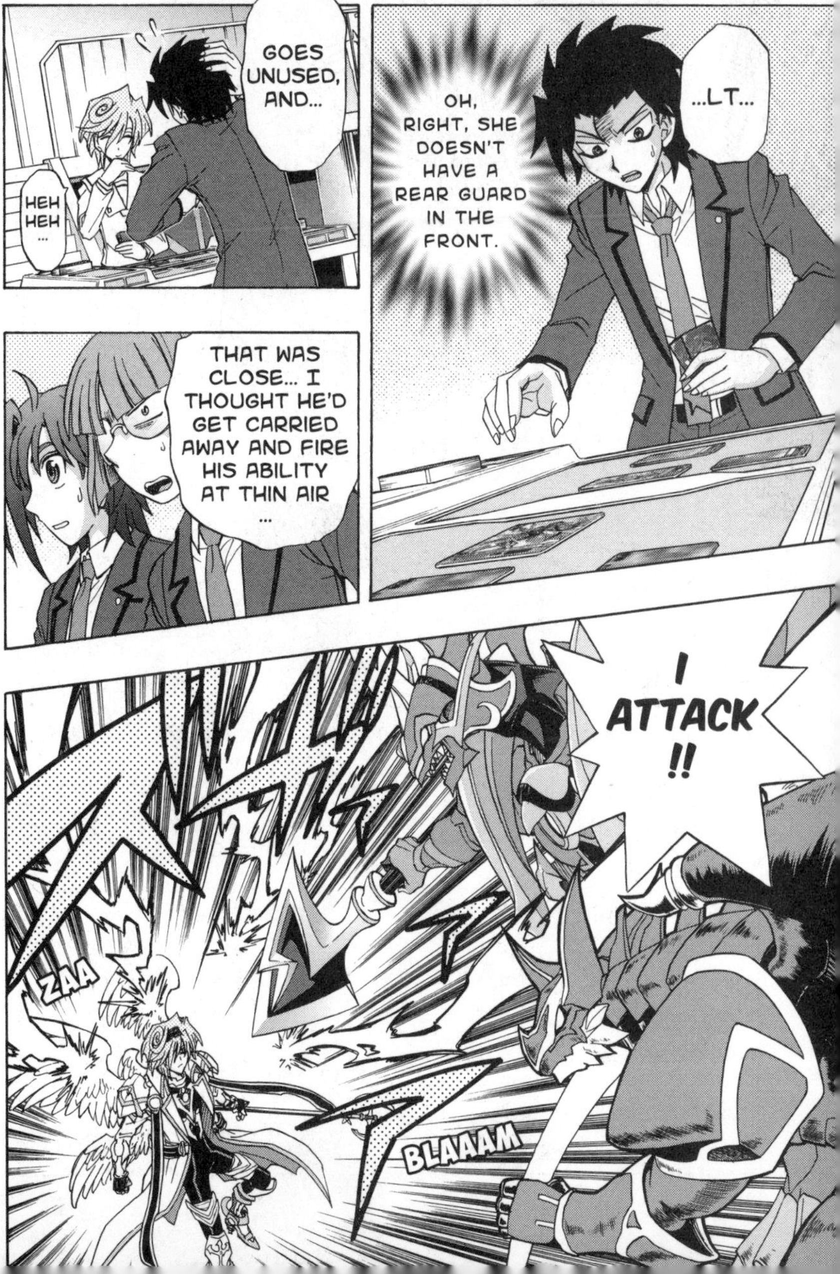
...LT...
OH, RIGHT, SHE DOESN'T HAVE A REAR GUARD IN THE FRONT.
GOES UNUSED, AND...
HEH HEH ...
THAT WAS CLOSE... I THOUGHT HE'D GET CARRIED AWAY AND FIRE HIS ABILITY AT THIN AIR ...
I ATTACK !!
ZAA
BLAAAM

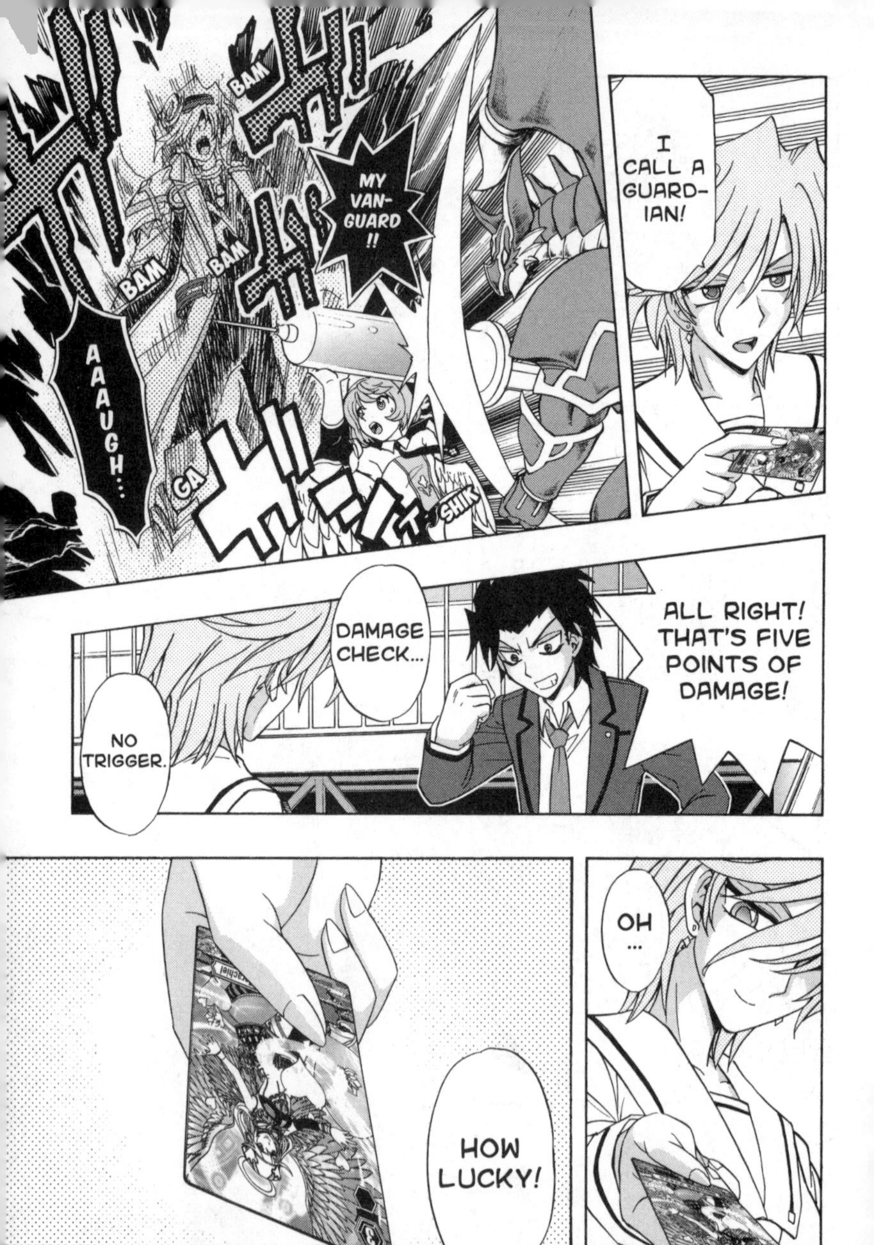
I CALL A GUARD-IAN!
BAM
MY VAN-GUARD!!
BAM
BAM
AAAUGH...
GA
SHIK
ALL RIGHT! THAT'S FIVE POINTS OF DAMAGE!
DAMAGE CHECK...
NO TRIGGER.
OH ...
HOW LUCKY!

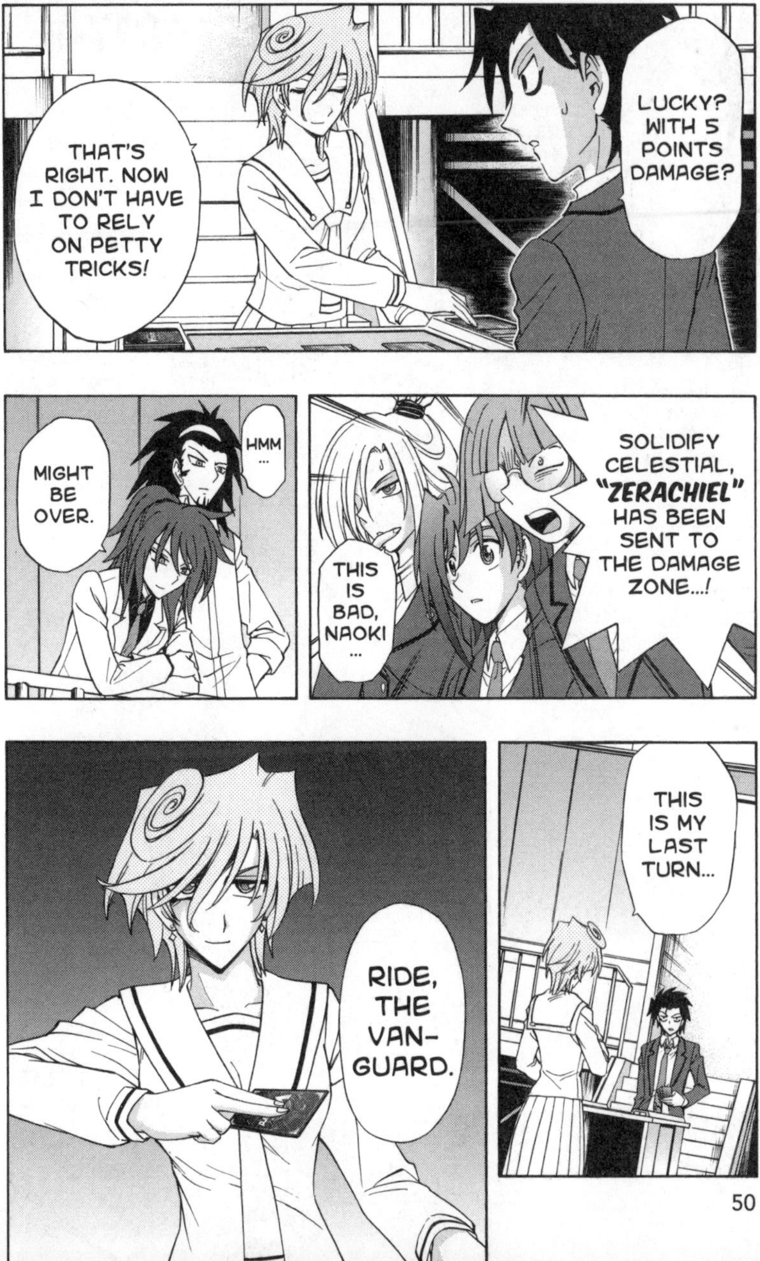
LUCKY? WITH 5 POINTS DAMAGE?
THAT'S RIGHT. NOW I DON'T HAVE TO RELY ON PETTY TRICKS!
SOLIDIFY CELESTIAL, "ZERACHIEL" HAS BEEN SENT TO THE DAMAGE ZONE...!
THIS IS BAD, NAOKI...
HMM...
MIGHT BE OVER.
THIS IS MY LAST TURN...
RIDE, THE VAN-GUARD.

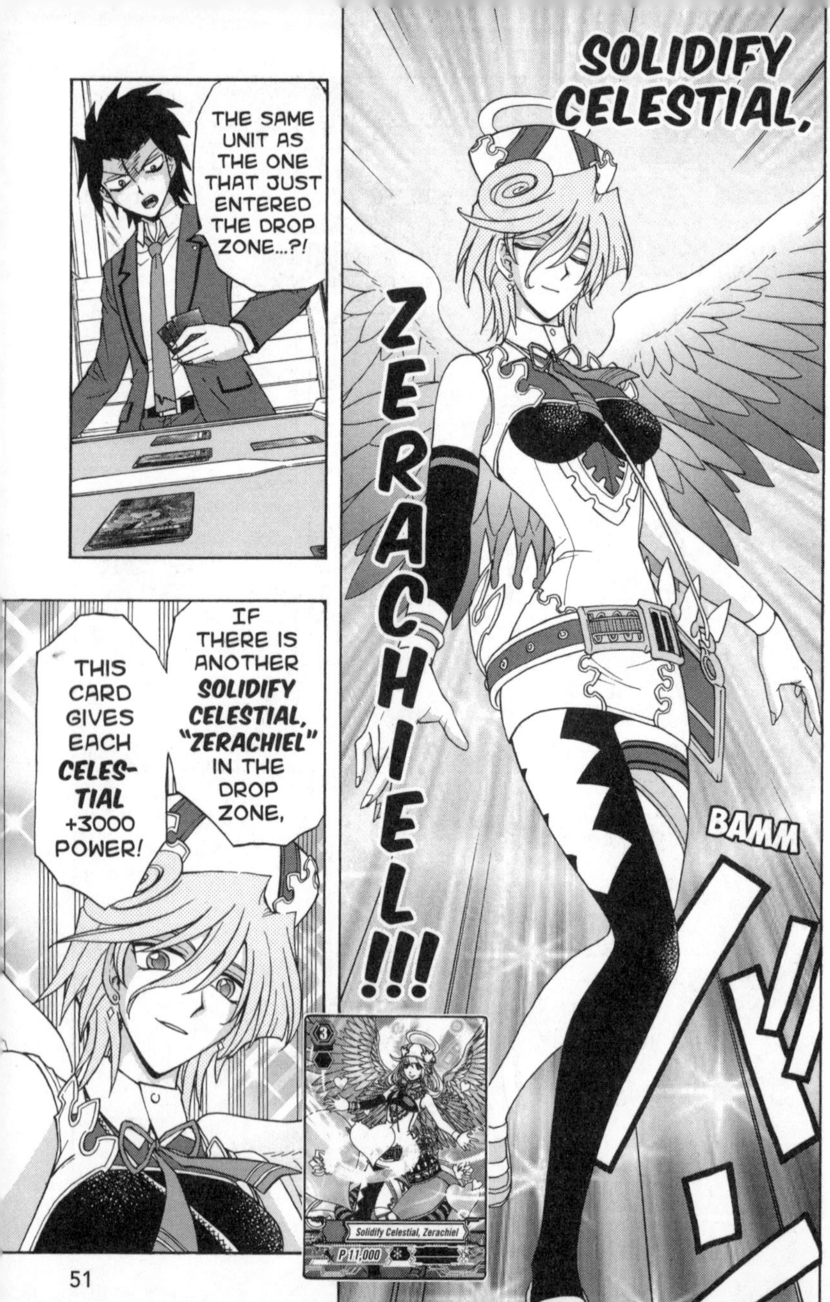
SOLIDIFY CELESTIAL,
ZERACHIEL!!!
BAMM
THE SAME UNIT AS THE ONE THAT JUST ENTERED THE DROP ZONE...?!
IF THERE IS ANOTHER SOLIDIFY CELESTIAL, "ZERACHIEL" IN THE DROP ZONE,
THIS CARD GIVES EACH CELES-TIAL +3000 POWER!
Solidify Celestial, Zerachiel
P 11,000

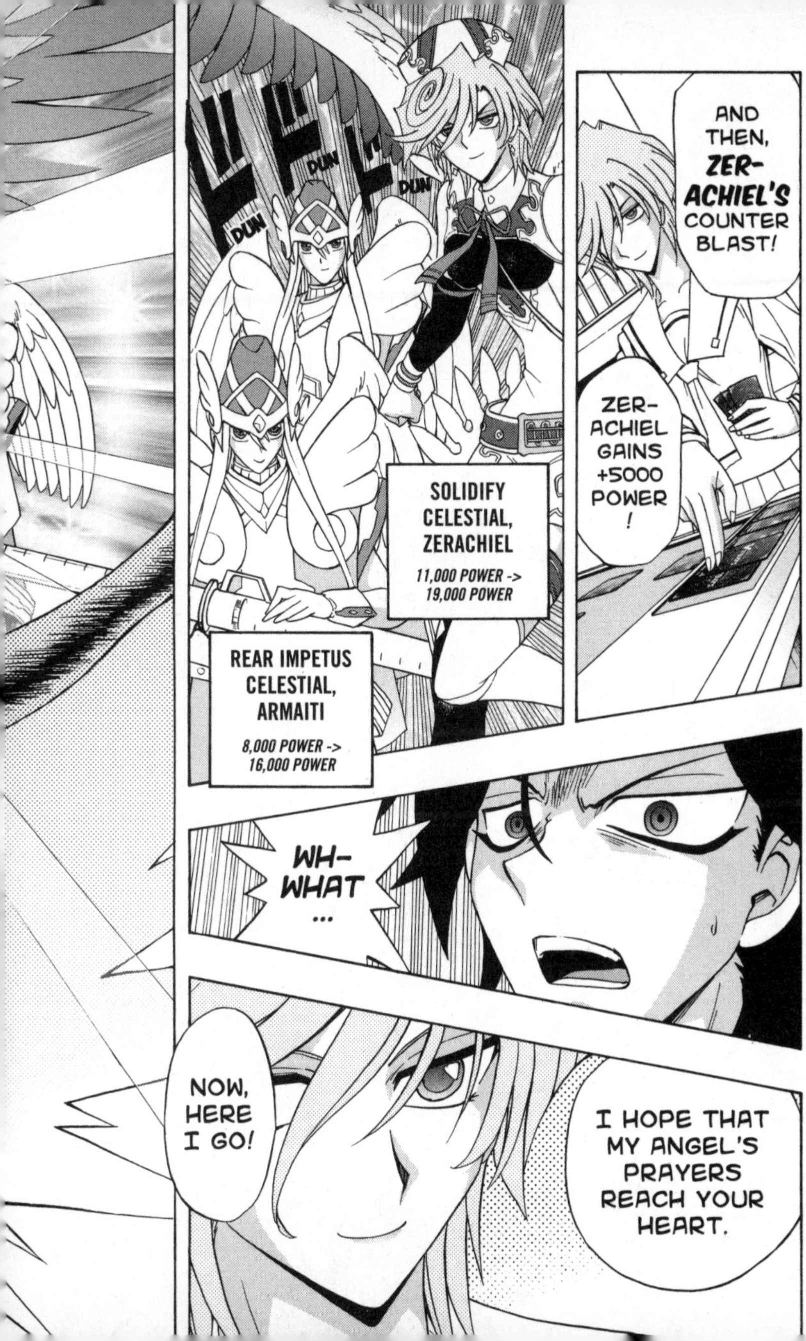
AND THEN, **ZER-ACHIEL'S** COUNTER BLAST!
ZER-ACHIEL GAINS +5000 POWER!
DUN
DUN
DUN
SOLIDIFY CELESTIAL, ZERACHIEL
*11,000 POWER -> 19,000 POWER*
REAR IMPETUS CELESTIAL, ARMAITI
*8,000 POWER -> 16,000 POWER*
WH-WHAT ...
I HOPE THAT MY ANGEL'S PRAYERS REACH YOUR HEART.
NOW, HERE I GO!

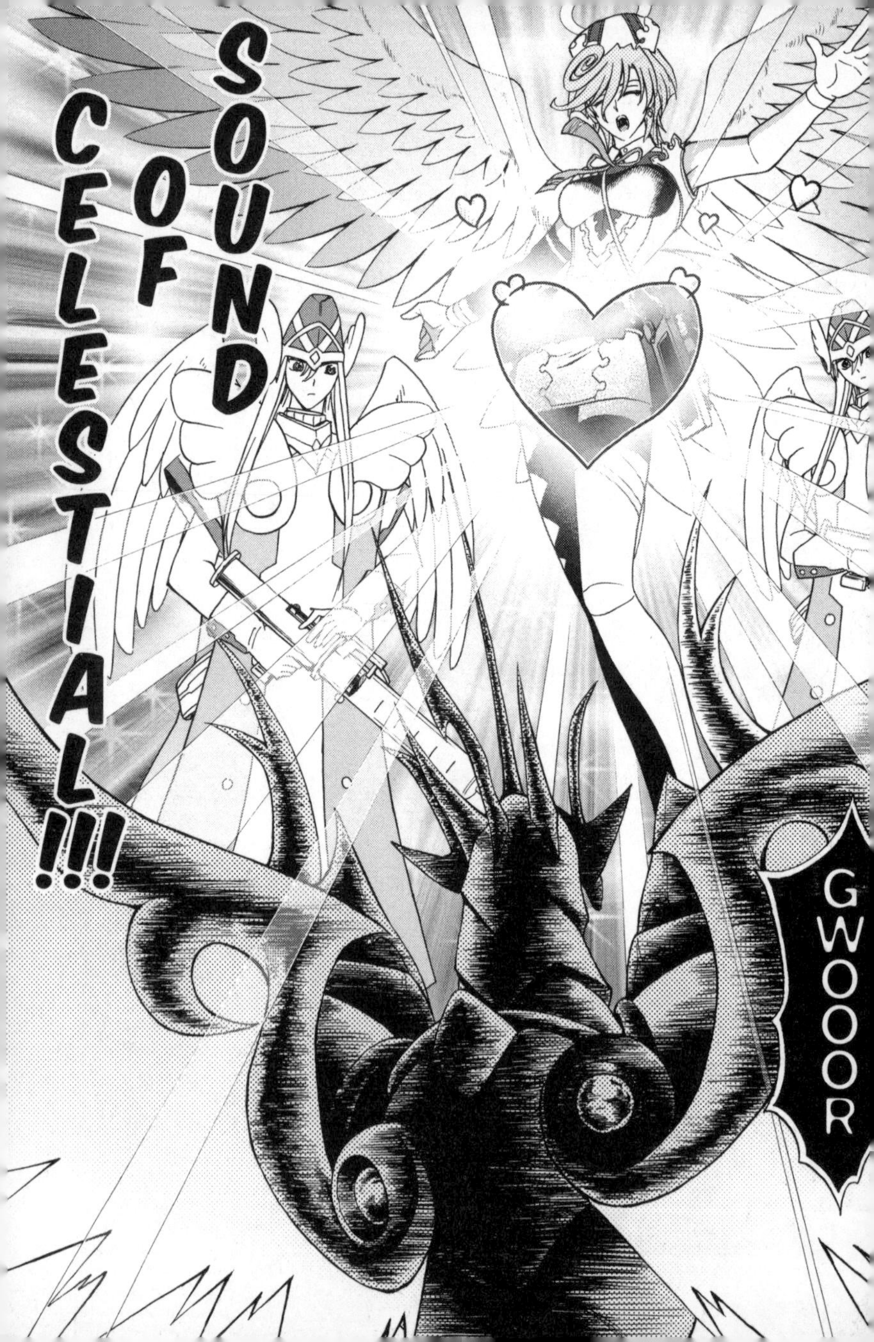
CELESTIAL SOUND OF
GWOOOR

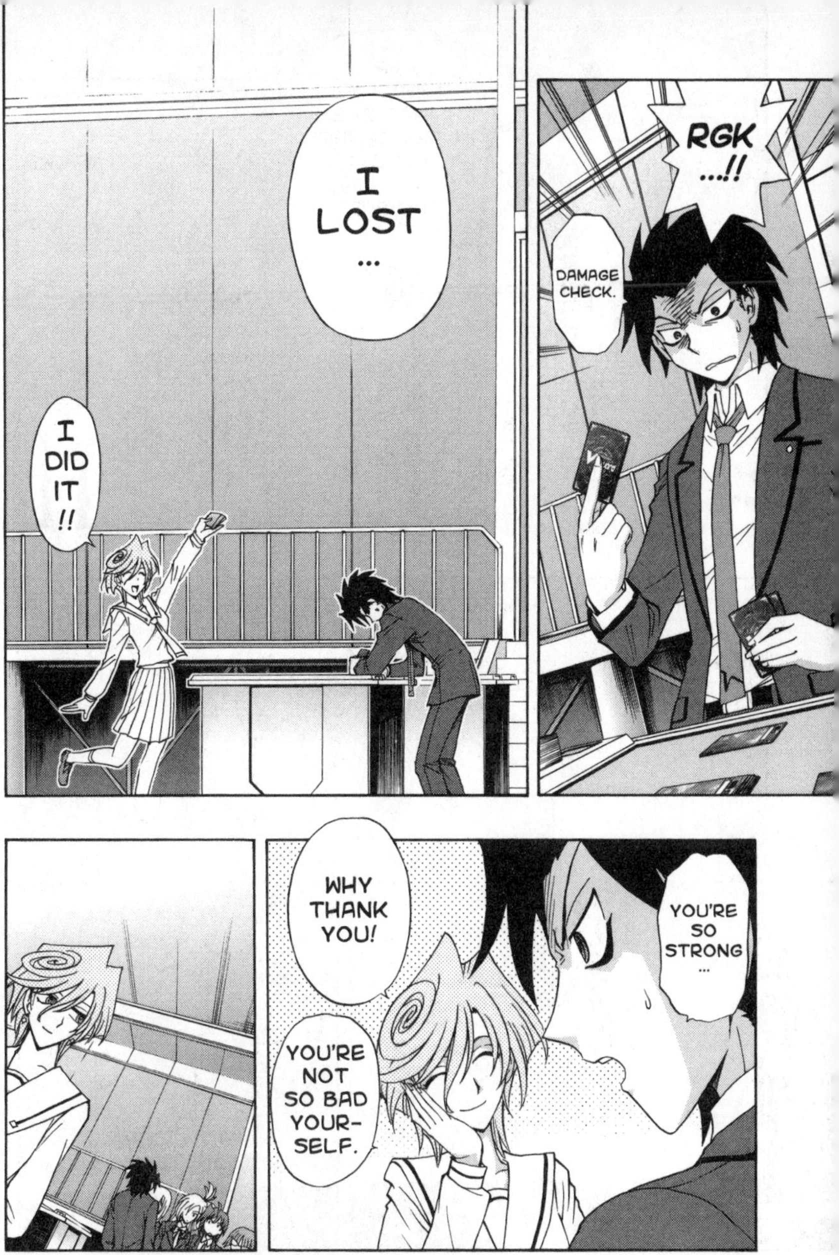
RGK ...!!
DAMAGE CHECK.
I LOST ...
I DID IT !!
YOU'RE SO STRONG ...
WHY THANK YOU!
YOU'RE NOT SO BAD YOUR-SELF.

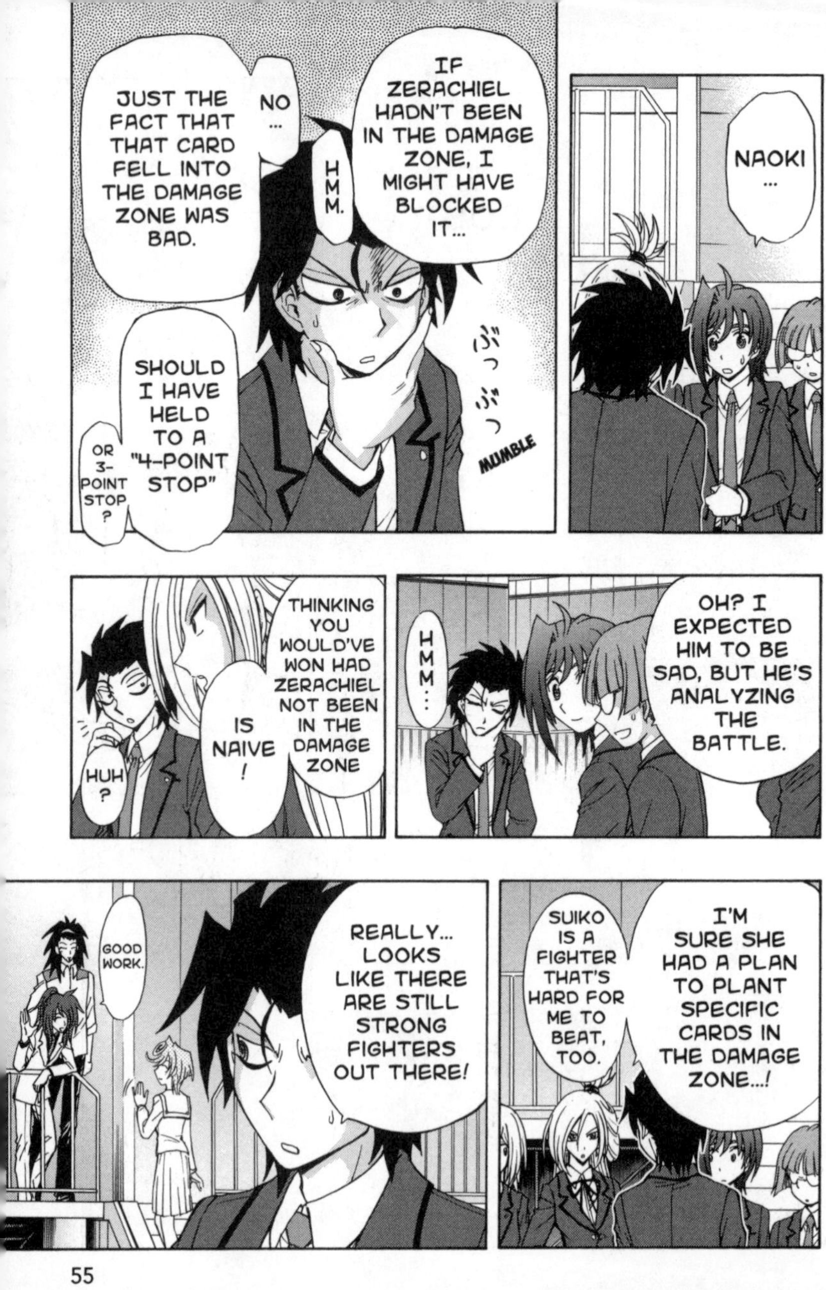
NAOKI ...
IF ZERACHIEL HADN'T BEEN IN THE DAMAGE ZONE, I MIGHT HAVE BLOCKED IT...
HMM.
NO ...
JUST THE FACT THAT THAT CARD FELL INTO THE DAMAGE ZONE WAS BAD.
ぶつぶつ
MUMBLE
SHOULD I HAVE HELD TO A "4-POINT STOP"
OR 3-POINT STOP?
OH? I EXPECTED HIM TO BE SAD, BUT HE'S ANALYZING THE BATTLE.
HMM...
THINKING YOU WOULD'VE WON HAD ZERACHIEL NOT BEEN IN THE DAMAGE ZONE
IS NAIVE!
HUH?
I'M SURE SHE HAD A PLAN TO PLANT SPECIFIC CARDS IN THE DAMAGE ZONE...!
SUIKO IS A FIGHTER THAT'S HARD FOR ME TO BEAT, TOO.
REALLY... LOOKS LIKE THERE ARE STILL STRONG FIGHTERS OUT THERE!
GOOD WORK.

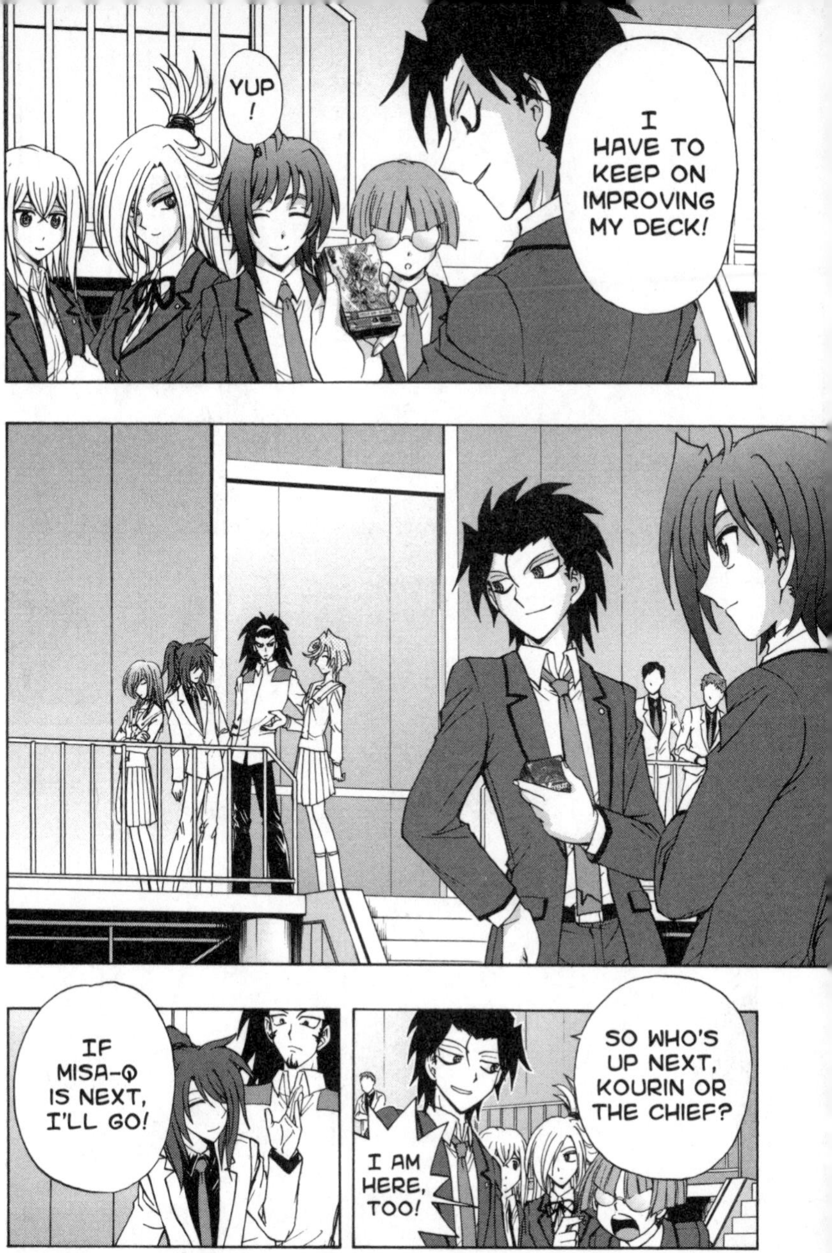
I HAVE TO KEEP ON IMPROVING MY DECK!
YUP!
SO WHO'S UP NEXT, KOURIN OR THE CHIEF?
I AM HERE, TOO!
IF MISA-Q IS NEXT, I'LL GO!

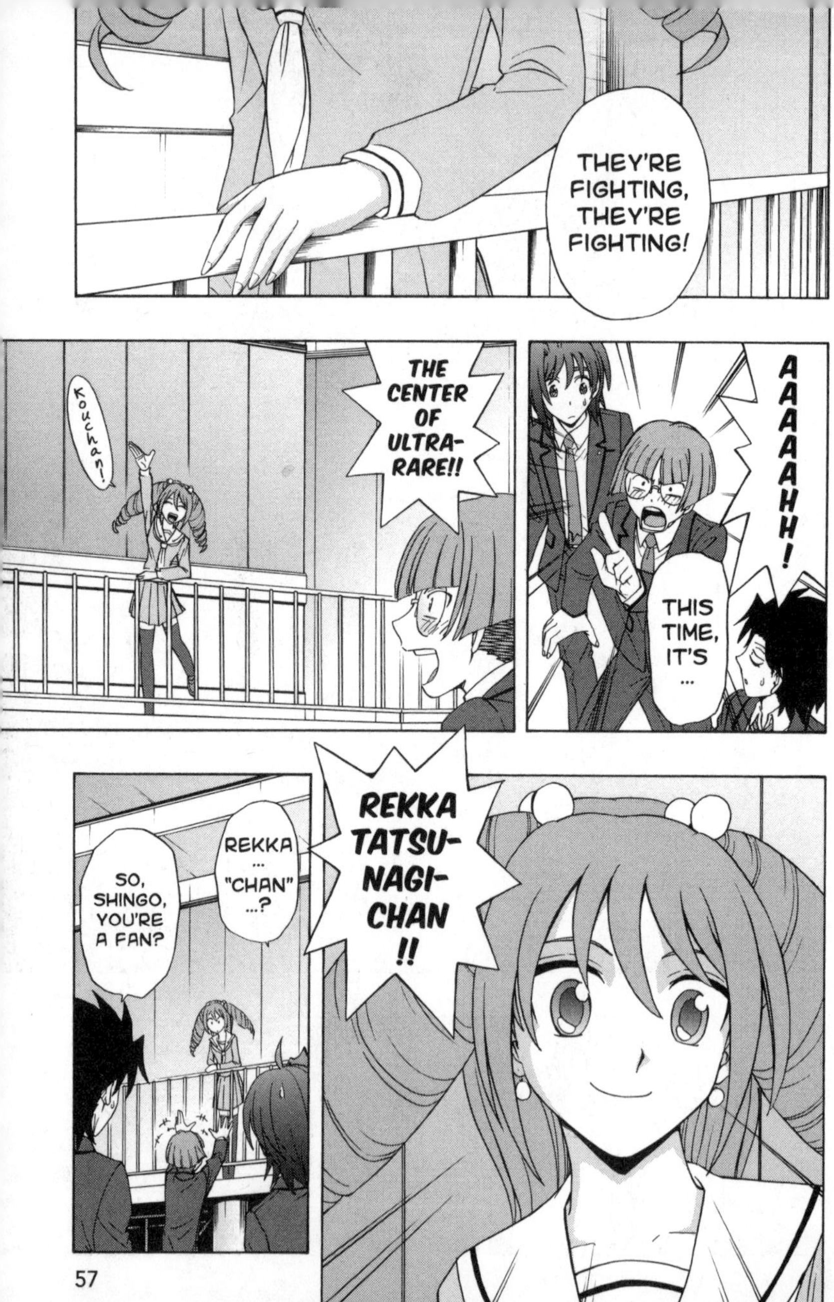
THEY'RE FIGHTING, THEY'RE FIGHTING!
AAAAAAAH!
THIS TIME, IT'S ...
THE CENTER OF ULTRA-RARE!!
Kouchan!
REKKA TATSUNAGI-CHAN !!
REKKA ... "CHAN" ...?
SO, SHINGO, YOU'RE A FAN?

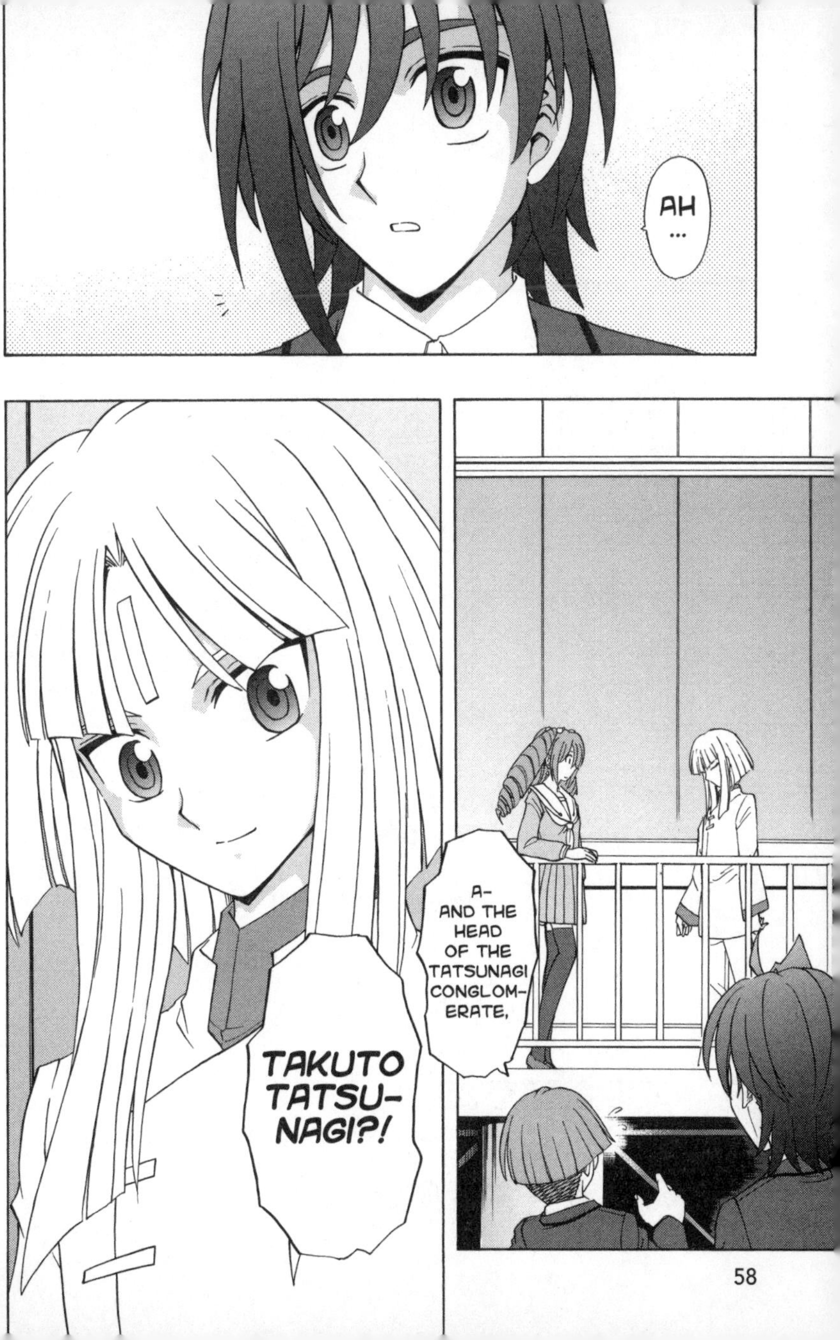
AH ...
A- AND THE HEAD OF THE TATSUNAGI CONGLOM- ERATE,
TAKUTO TATSU- NAGI?!

CARDFIGHT!!
Vanguard

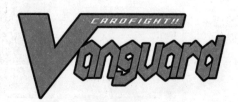

BONUS!

CARDFIGHT!! Vanguard

VANGUARD LAB

RIDE THE ORIGINAL DESIGNS!

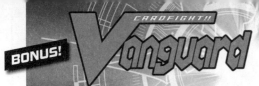

**Booting Celestial, Sandalphon**
**#033**

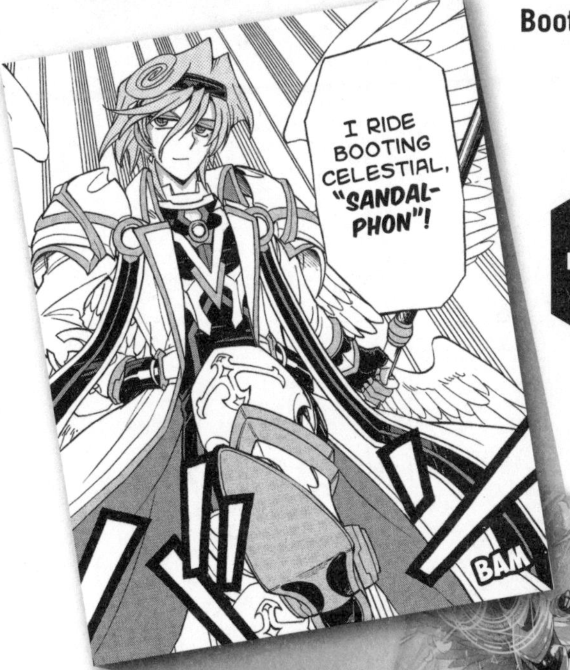
I RIDE BOOTING CELESTIAL, "SANDAL-PHON"!
BAM

COMIC ILLUSTRA-TION

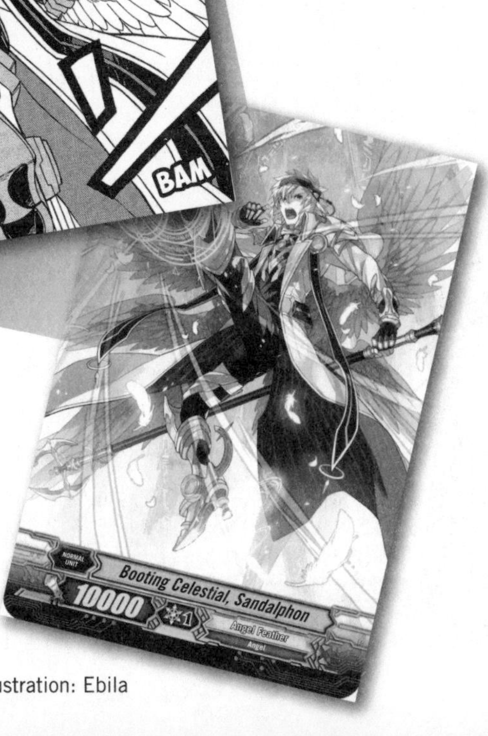
NORMAL UNIT
Booting Celestial, Sandalphon
10000
1
Angel Feather
Angel

CARD ILLUSTRA-TION

Illustration: Ebila

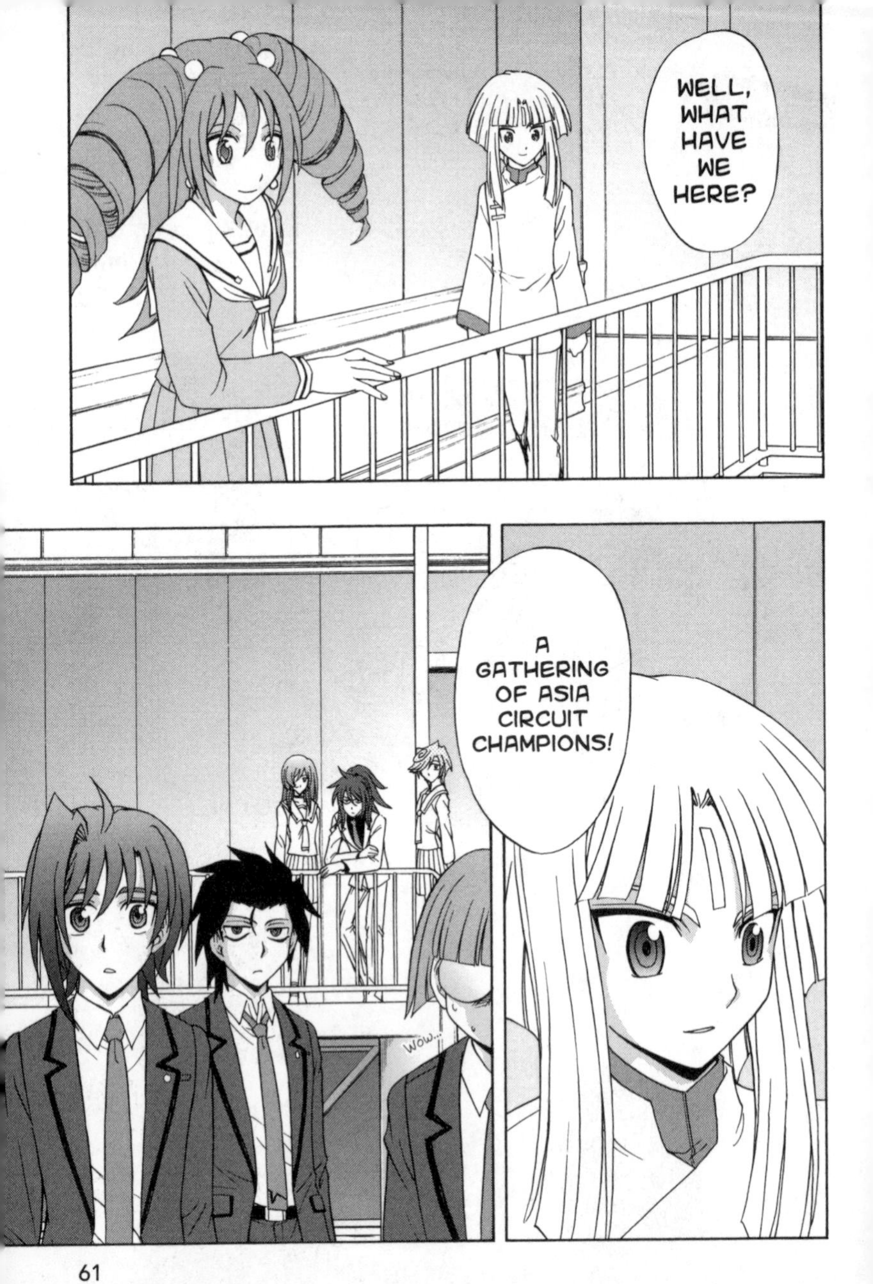
WELL, WHAT HAVE WE HERE?
A GATHERING OF ASIA CIRCUIT CHAMPIONS!
Wow...

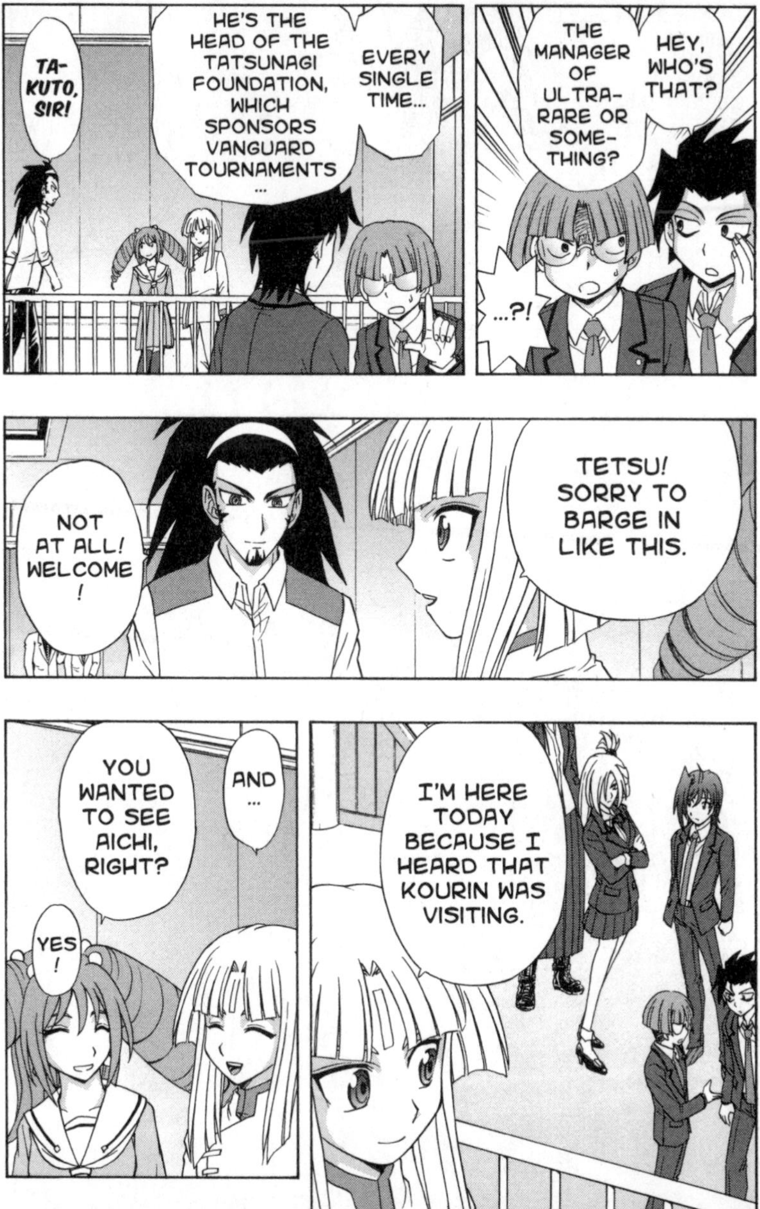
HEY, WHO'S THAT?
THE MANAGER OF ULTRA-RARE OR SOME-THING?
...?!
EVERY SINGLE TIME...
HE'S THE HEAD OF THE TATSUNAGI FOUNDATION, WHICH SPONSORS VANGUARD TOURNAMENTS...
TA-KUTO, SIR!
TETSU! SORRY TO BARGE IN LIKE THIS.
NOT AT ALL! WELCOME!
I'M HERE TODAY BECAUSE I HEARD THAT KOURIN WAS VISITING.
AND ...
YOU WANTED TO SEE AICHI, RIGHT?
YES!

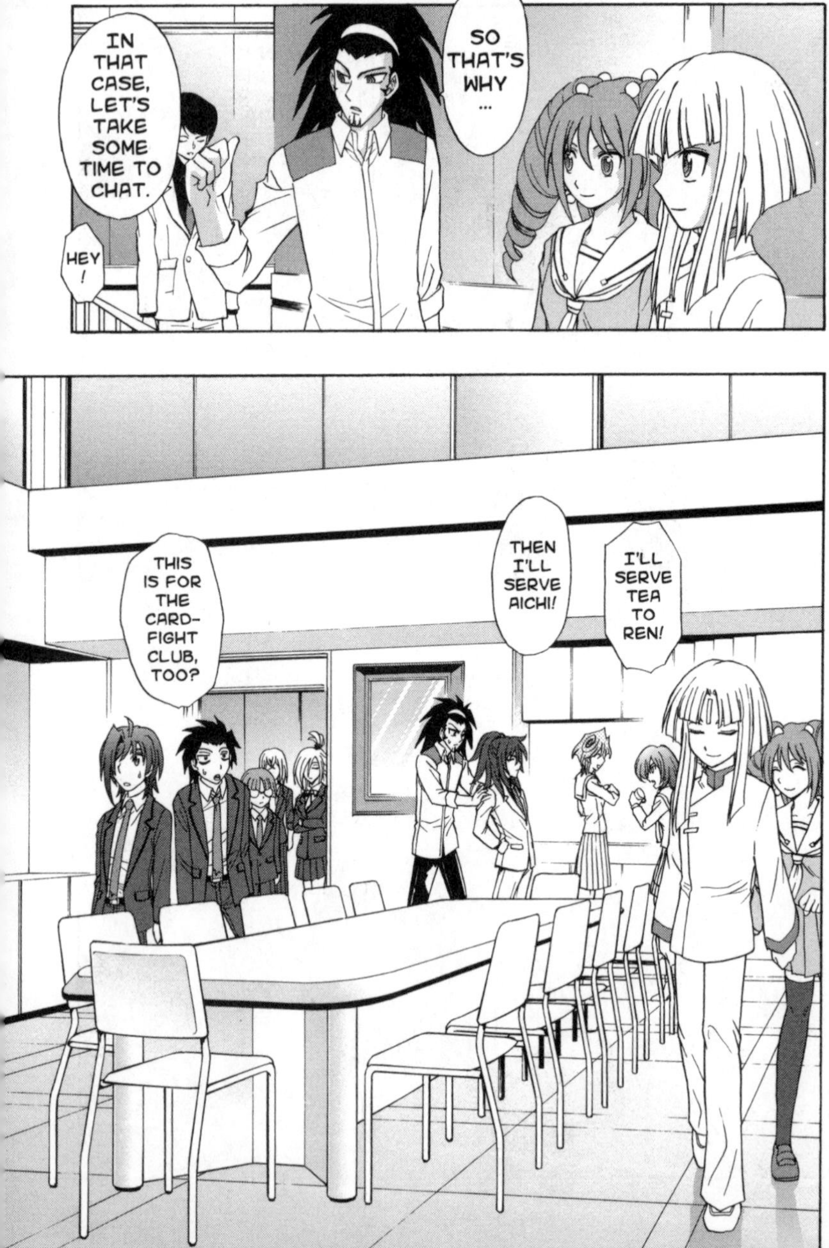
SO THAT'S WHY ...
IN THAT CASE, LET'S TAKE SOME TIME TO CHAT.
HEY!
I'LL SERVE TEA TO REN!
THEN I'LL SERVE AICHI!
THIS IS FOR THE CARD-FIGHT CLUB, TOO?

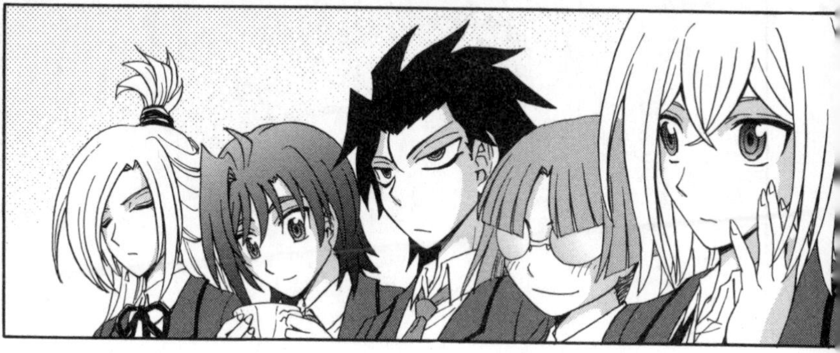

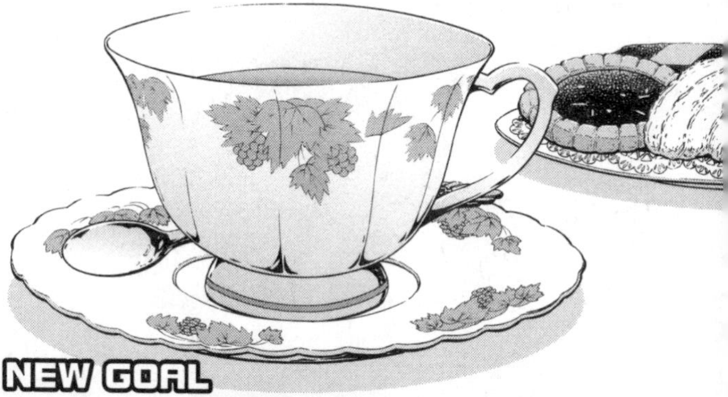

## #034 A NEW GOAL

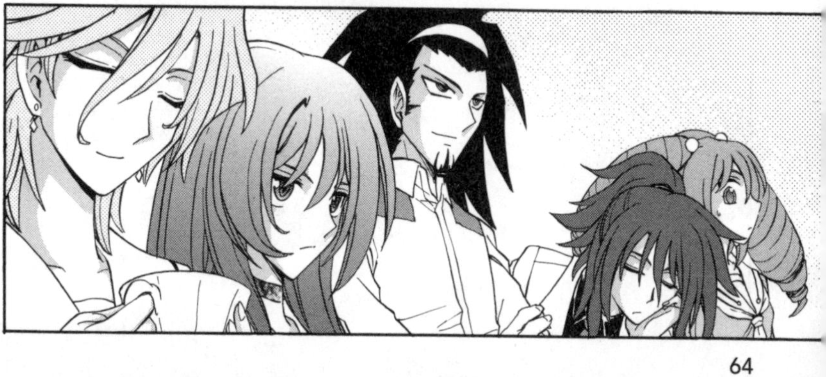

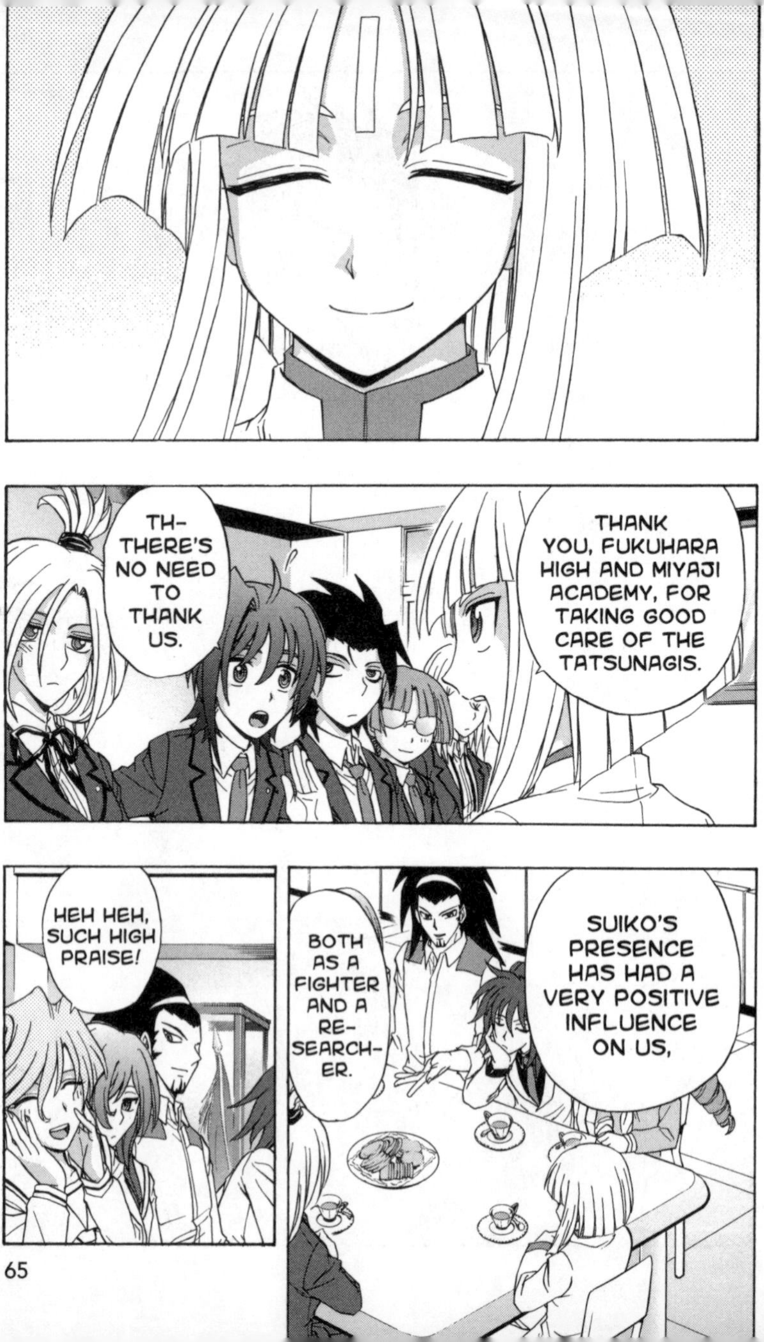
THANK YOU, FUKUHARA HIGH AND MIYAJI ACADEMY, FOR TAKING GOOD CARE OF THE TATSUNAGIS.
TH-THERE'S NO NEED TO THANK US.
SUIKO'S PRESENCE HAS HAD A VERY POSITIVE INFLUENCE ON US,
BOTH AS A FIGHTER AND A RE-SEARCH-ER.
HEH HEH, SUCH HIGH PRAISE!

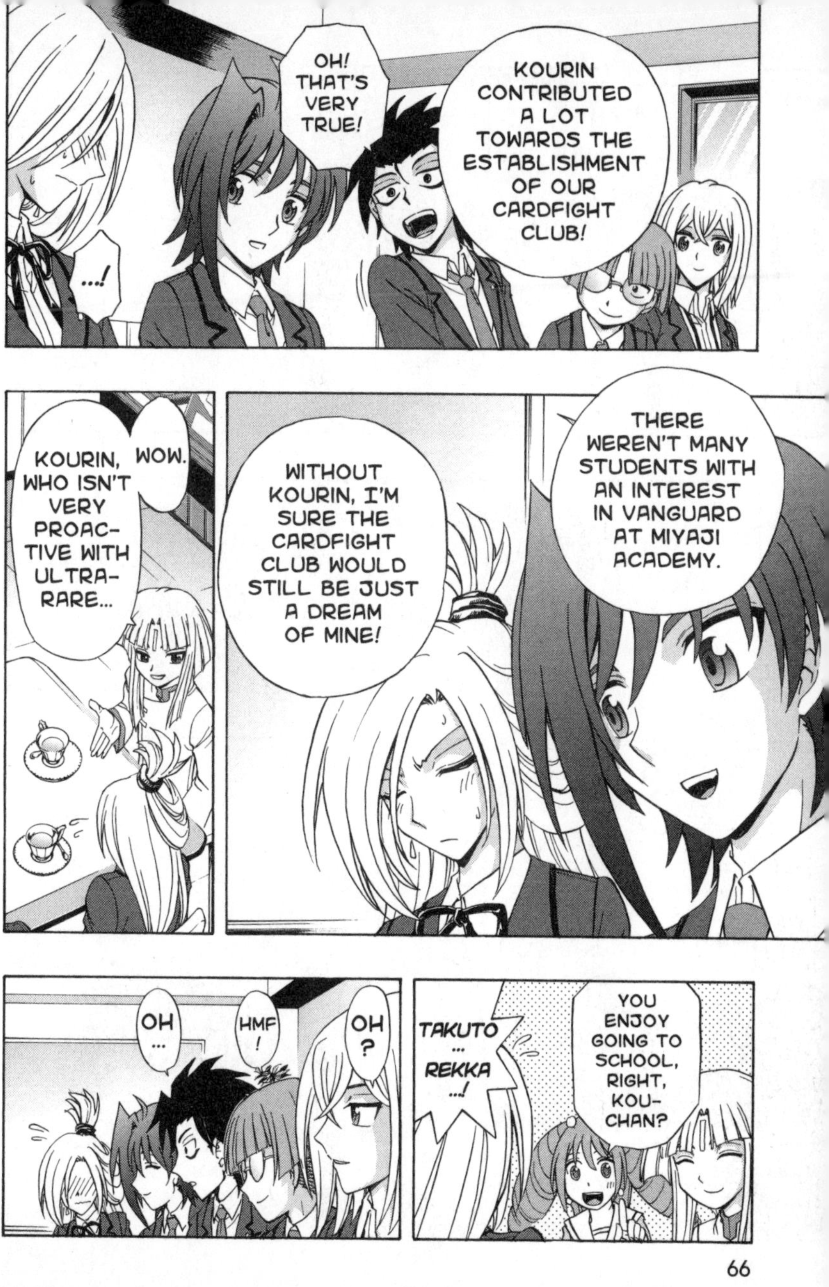
KOURIN CONTRIBUTED A LOT TOWARDS THE ESTABLISHMENT OF OUR CARDFIGHT CLUB!
OH! THAT'S VERY TRUE!
...!
THERE WEREN'T MANY STUDENTS WITH AN INTEREST IN VANGUARD AT MIYAJI ACADEMY.
WITHOUT KOURIN, I'M SURE THE CARDFIGHT CLUB WOULD STILL BE JUST A DREAM OF MINE!
WOW.
KOURIN, WHO ISN'T VERY PROAC-TIVE WITH ULTRA-RARE...
YOU ENJOY GOING TO SCHOOL, RIGHT, KOU-CHAN?
TAKUTO ... REKKA ...!
OH ?
HMF !
OH ...

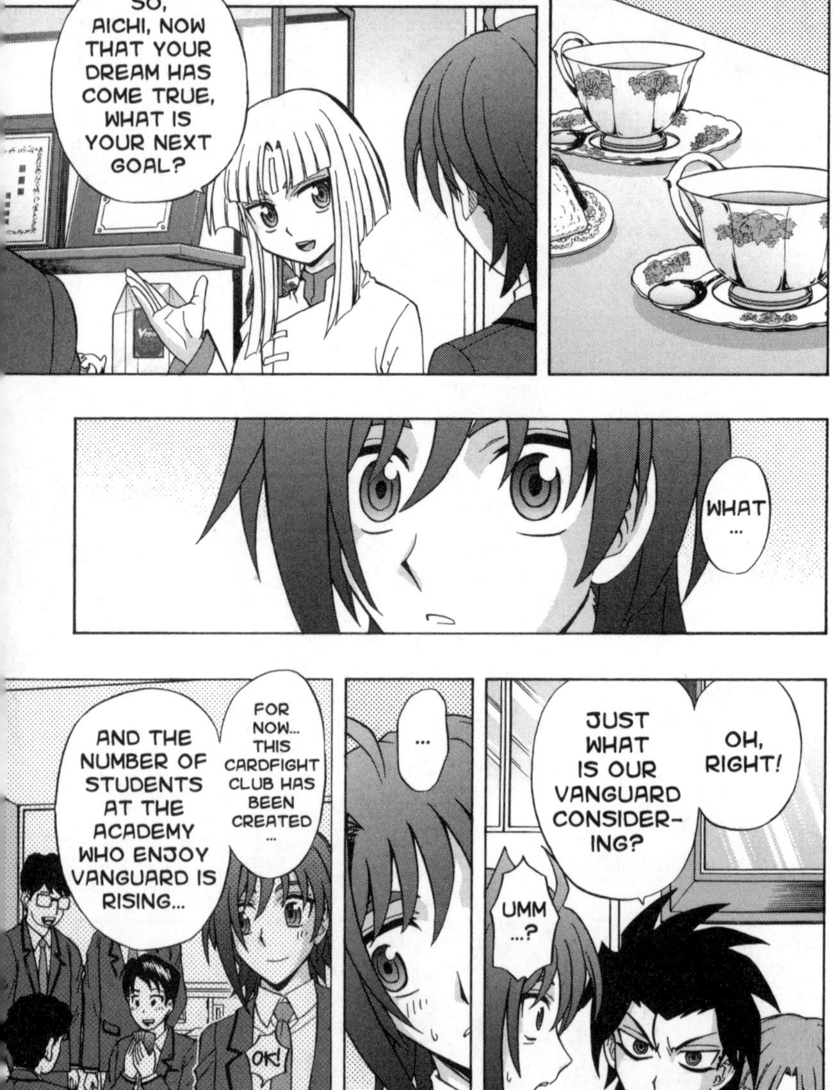
SO, AICHI, NOW THAT YOUR DREAM HAS COME TRUE, WHAT IS YOUR NEXT GOAL?
WHAT ...
OH, RIGHT!
JUST WHAT IS OUR VANGUARD CONSIDER-ING?
UMM ...?
...
FOR NOW... THIS CARDFIGHT CLUB HAS BEEN CREATED ...
AND THE NUMBER OF STUDENTS AT THE ACADEMY WHO ENJOY VANGUARD IS RISING...
OK!

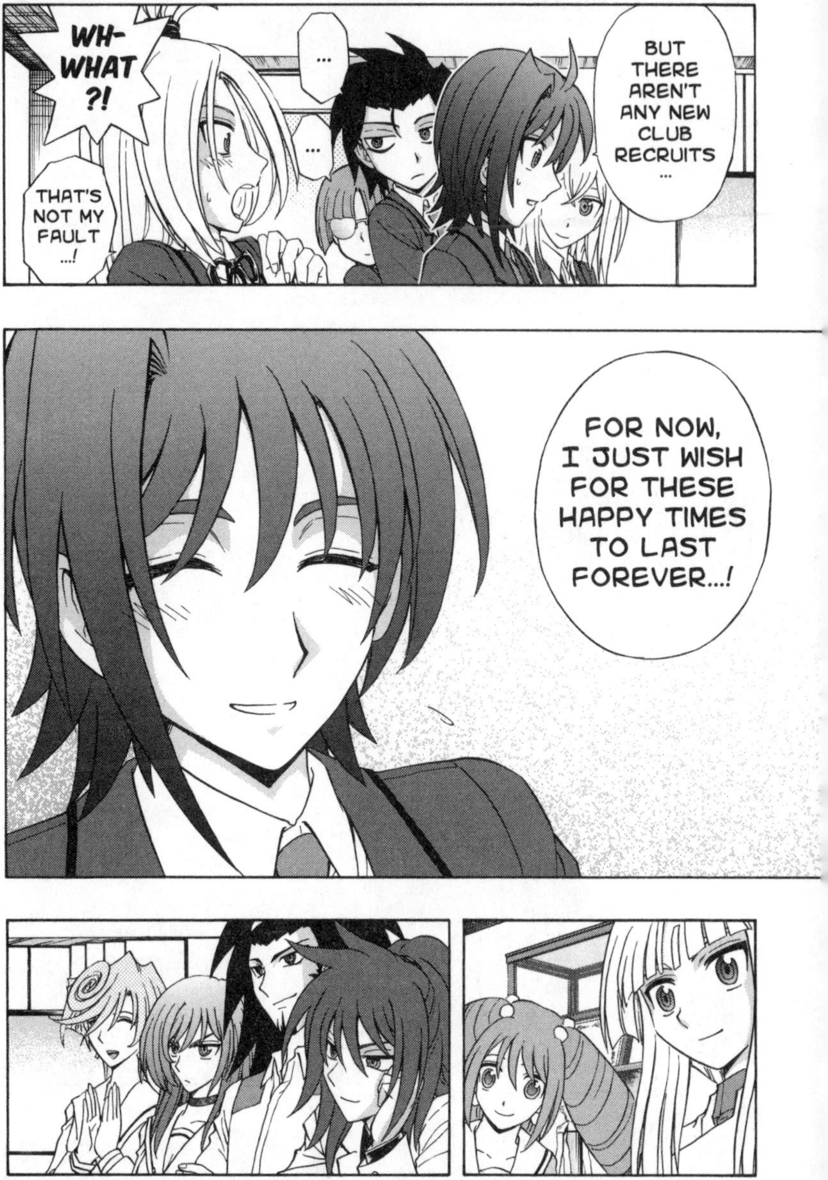
BUT THERE AREN'T ANY NEW CLUB RECRUITS ...
...
...
WH- WHAT ?!
THAT'S NOT MY FAULT ...!
FOR NOW, I JUST WISH FOR THESE HAPPY TIMES TO LAST FOREVER...!

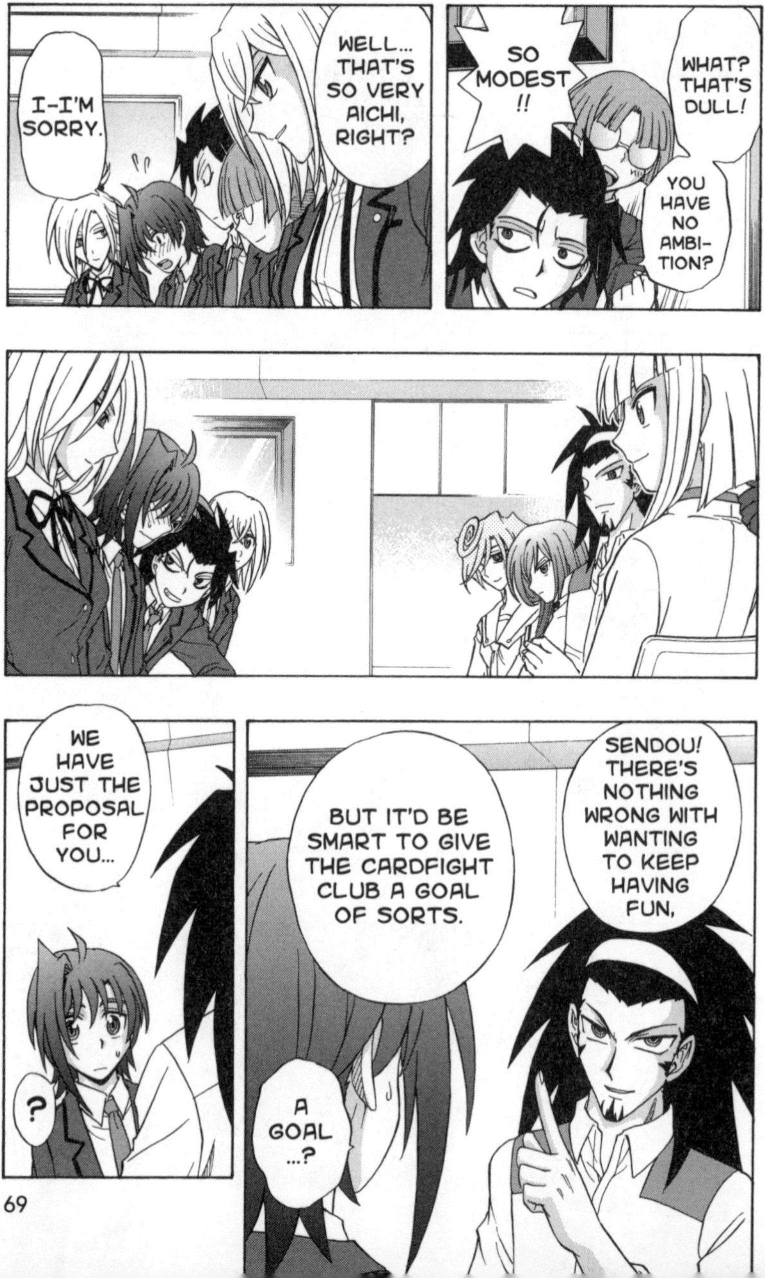
WHAT? THAT'S DULL!
SO MODEST !!
YOU HAVE NO AMBI-TION?
WELL... THAT'S SO VERY AICHI, RIGHT?
I-I'M SORRY.
SENDOU! THERE'S NOTHING WRONG WITH WANTING TO KEEP HAVING FUN,
BUT IT'D BE SMART TO GIVE THE CARDFIGHT CLUB A GOAL OF SORTS.
A GOAL ...?
WE HAVE JUST THE PROPOSAL FOR YOU...
?

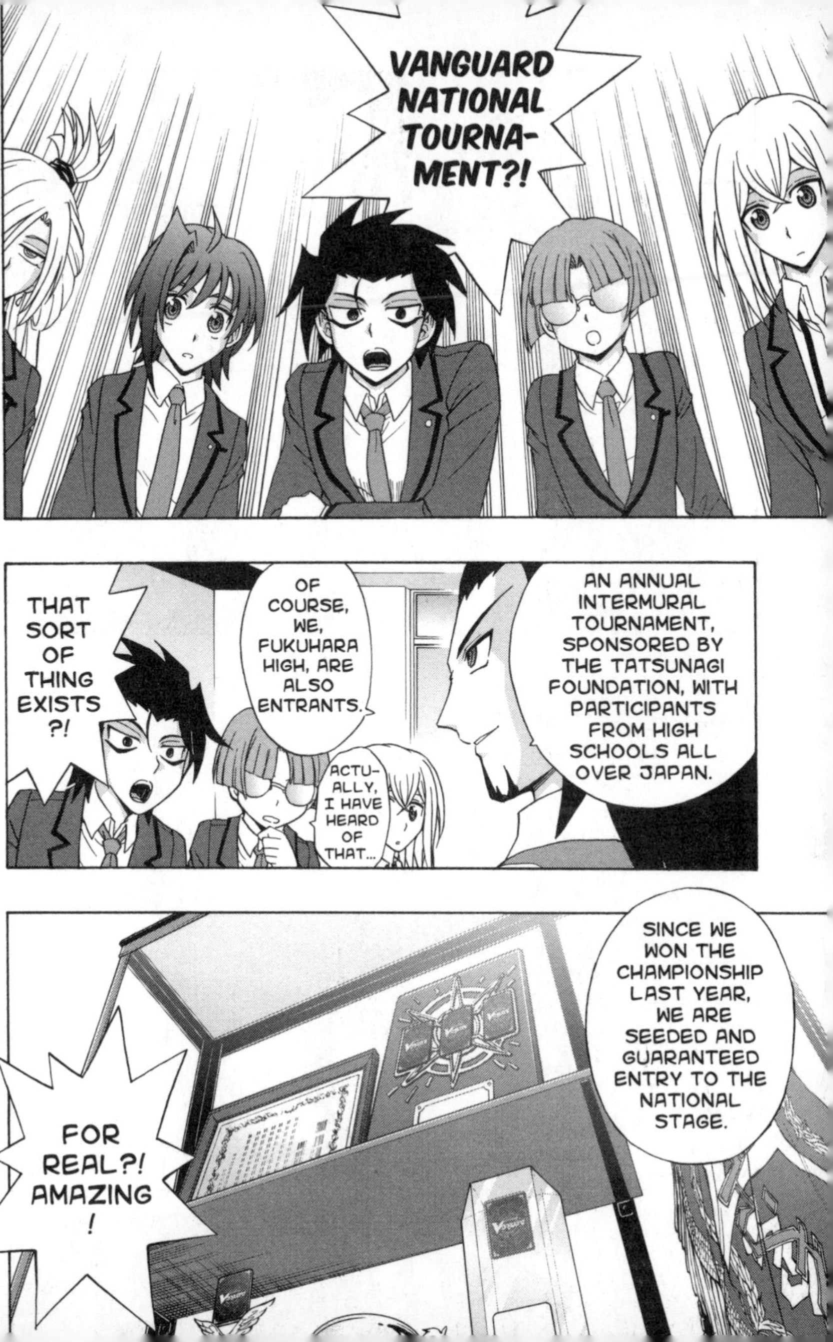
VANGUARD NATIONAL TOURNAMENT?!
AN ANNUAL INTERMURAL TOURNAMENT, SPONSORED BY THE TATSUNAGI FOUNDATION, WITH PARTICIPANTS FROM HIGH SCHOOLS ALL OVER JAPAN.
OF COURSE, WE, FUKUHARA HIGH, ARE ALSO ENTRANTS.
THAT SORT OF THING EXISTS?!
ACTUALLY, I HAVE HEARD OF THAT...
SINCE WE WON THE CHAMPIONSHIP LAST YEAR, WE ARE SEEDED AND GUARANTEED ENTRY TO THE NATIONAL STAGE.
FOR REAL?! AMAZING!

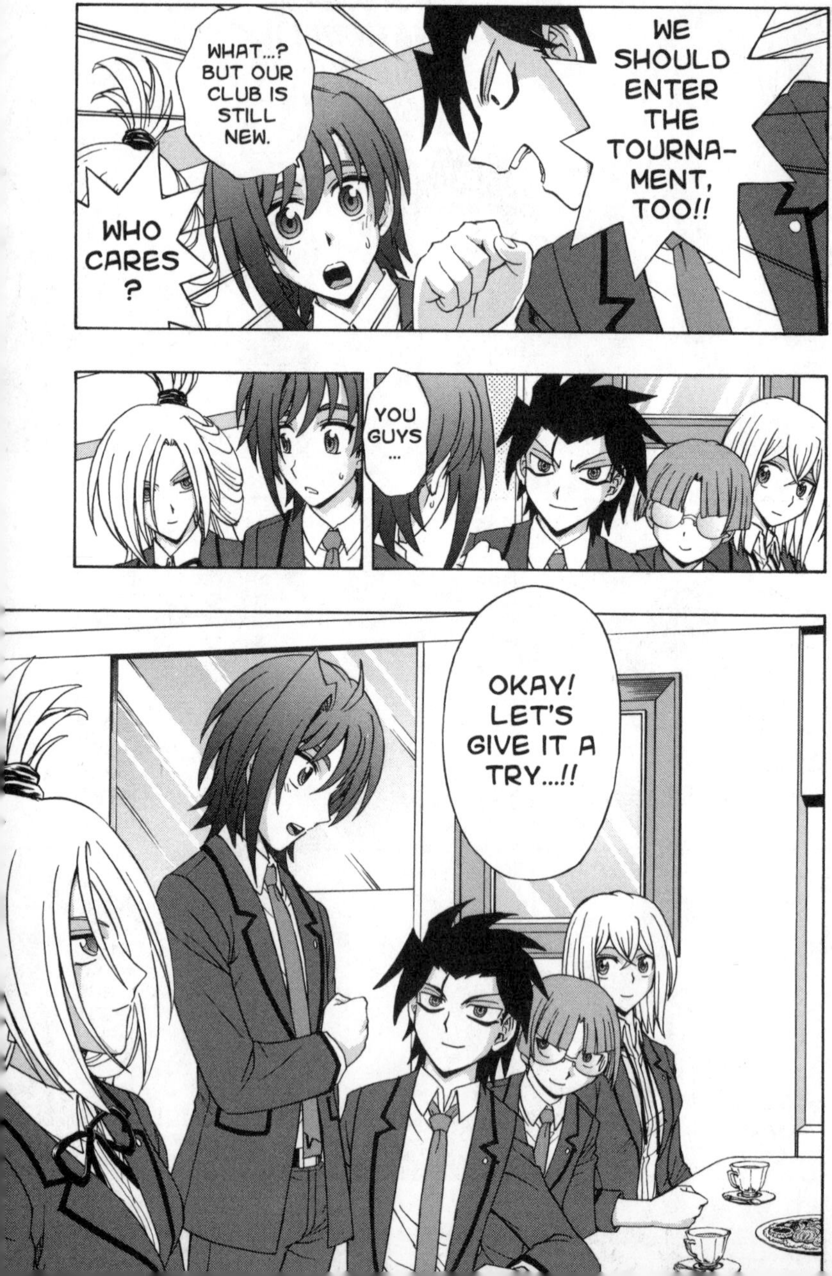
WE SHOULD ENTER THE TOURNA-MENT, TOO!!
WHAT...? BUT OUR CLUB IS STILL NEW.
WHO CARES?
YOU GUYS...
OKAY! LET'S GIVE IT A TRY...!!

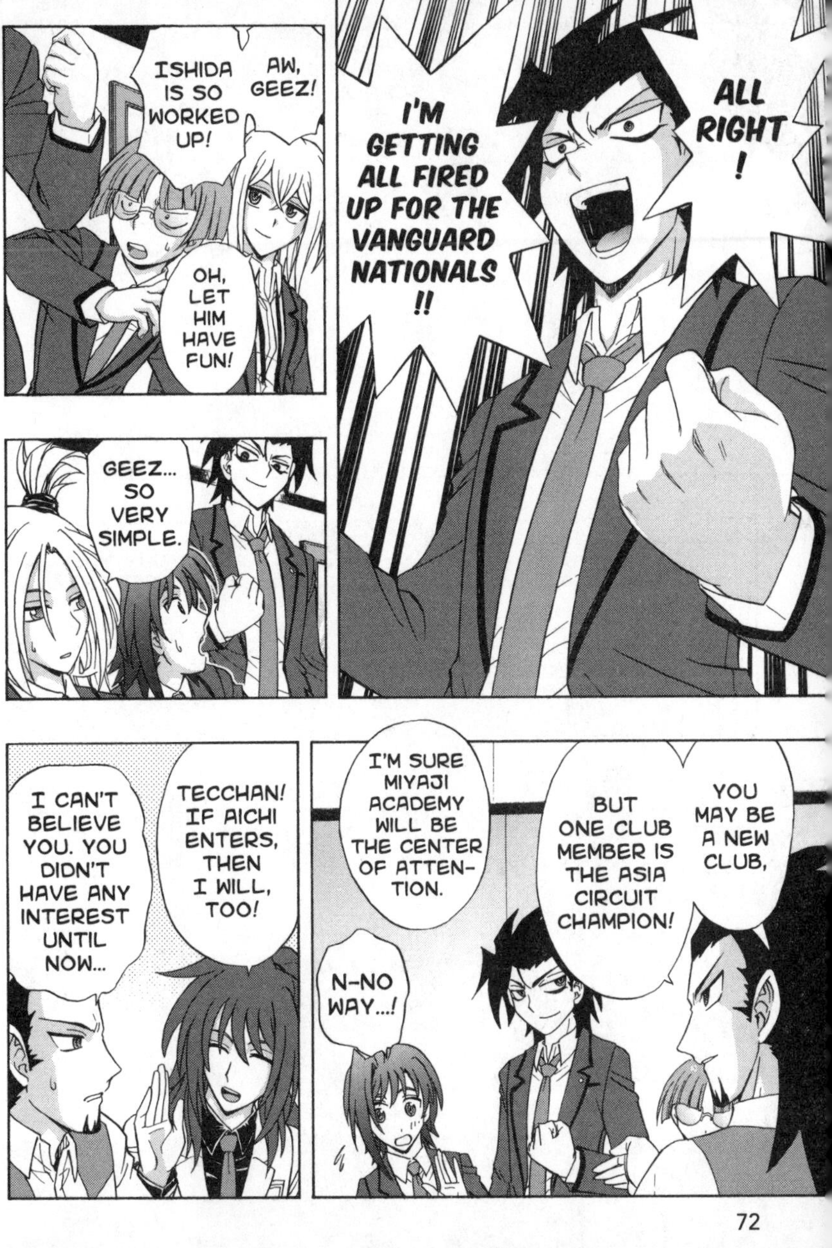
ALL RIGHT!
I'M GETTING ALL FIRED UP FOR THE VANGUARD NATIONALS!!
AW, GEEZ!
ISHIDA IS SO WORKED UP!
OH, LET HIM HAVE FUN!
GEEZ... SO VERY SIMPLE.
YOU MAY BE A NEW CLUB,
BUT ONE CLUB MEMBER IS THE ASIA CIRCUIT CHAMPION!
I'M SURE MIYAJI ACADEMY WILL BE THE CENTER OF ATTEN-TION.
N-NO WAY...!
TECCHAN! IF AICHI ENTERS, THEN I WILL, TOO!
I CAN'T BELIEVE YOU. YOU DIDN'T HAVE ANY INTEREST UNTIL NOW...

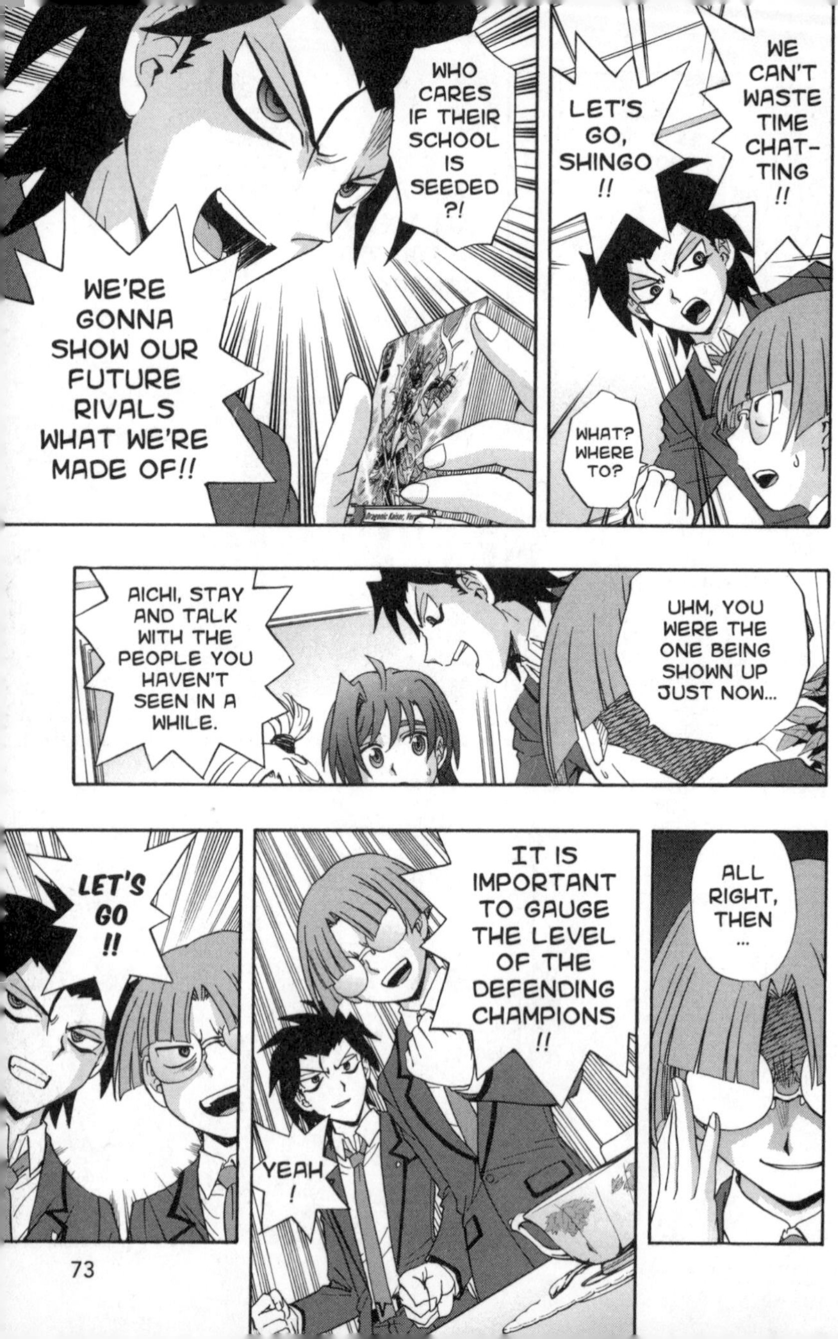

WE CAN'T WASTE TIME CHAT-TING!!
LET'S GO, SHINGO!!
WHAT? WHERE TO?
WHO CARES IF THEIR SCHOOL IS SEEDED?!
WE'RE GONNA SHOW OUR FUTURE RIVALS WHAT WE'RE MADE OF!!
UHM, YOU WERE THE ONE BEING SHOWN UP JUST NOW...
AICHI, STAY AND TALK WITH THE PEOPLE YOU HAVEN'T SEEN IN A WHILE.
ALL RIGHT, THEN ...
IT IS IMPORTANT TO GAUGE THE LEVEL OF THE DEFENDING CHAMPIONS!!
YEAH!
LET'S GO!!

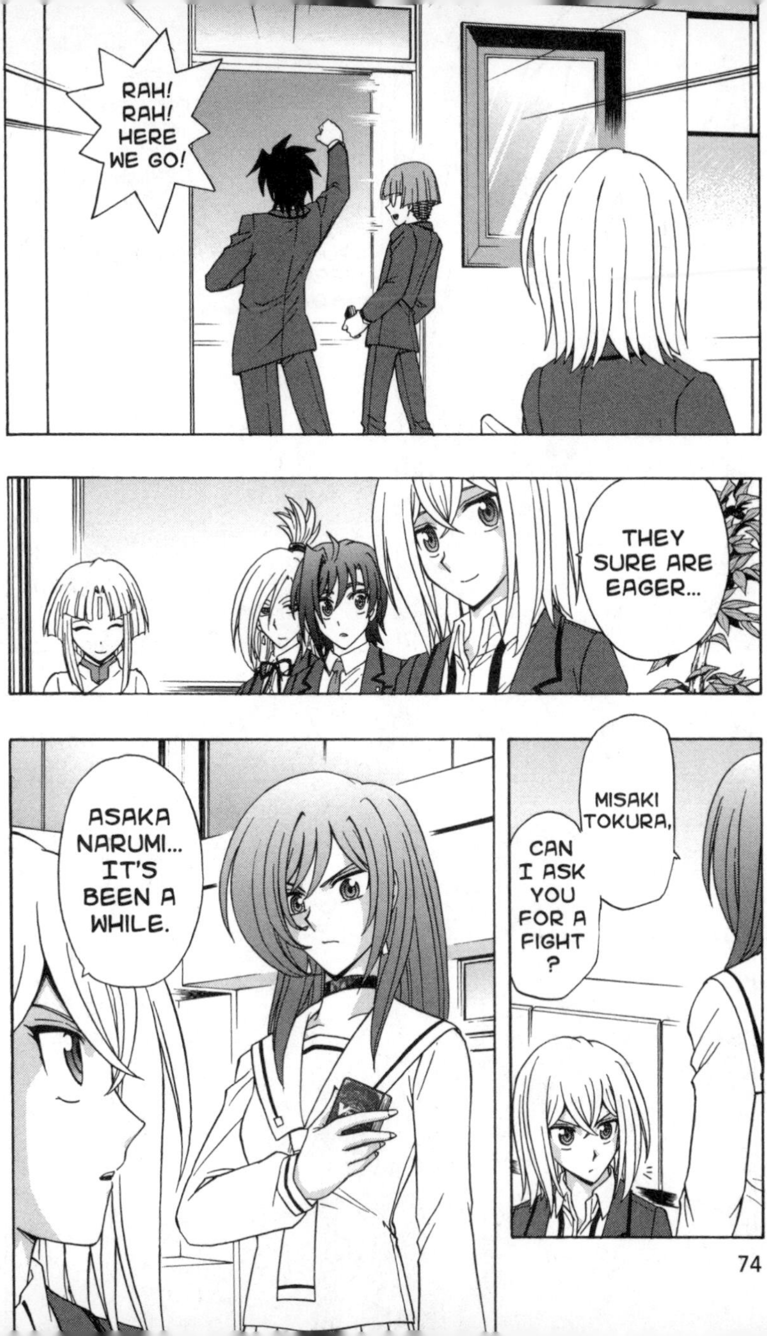
RAH! RAH! HERE WE GO!
THEY SURE ARE EAGER...
MISAKI TOKURA,
CAN I ASK YOU FOR A FIGHT?
ASAKA NARUMI... IT'S BEEN A WHILE.

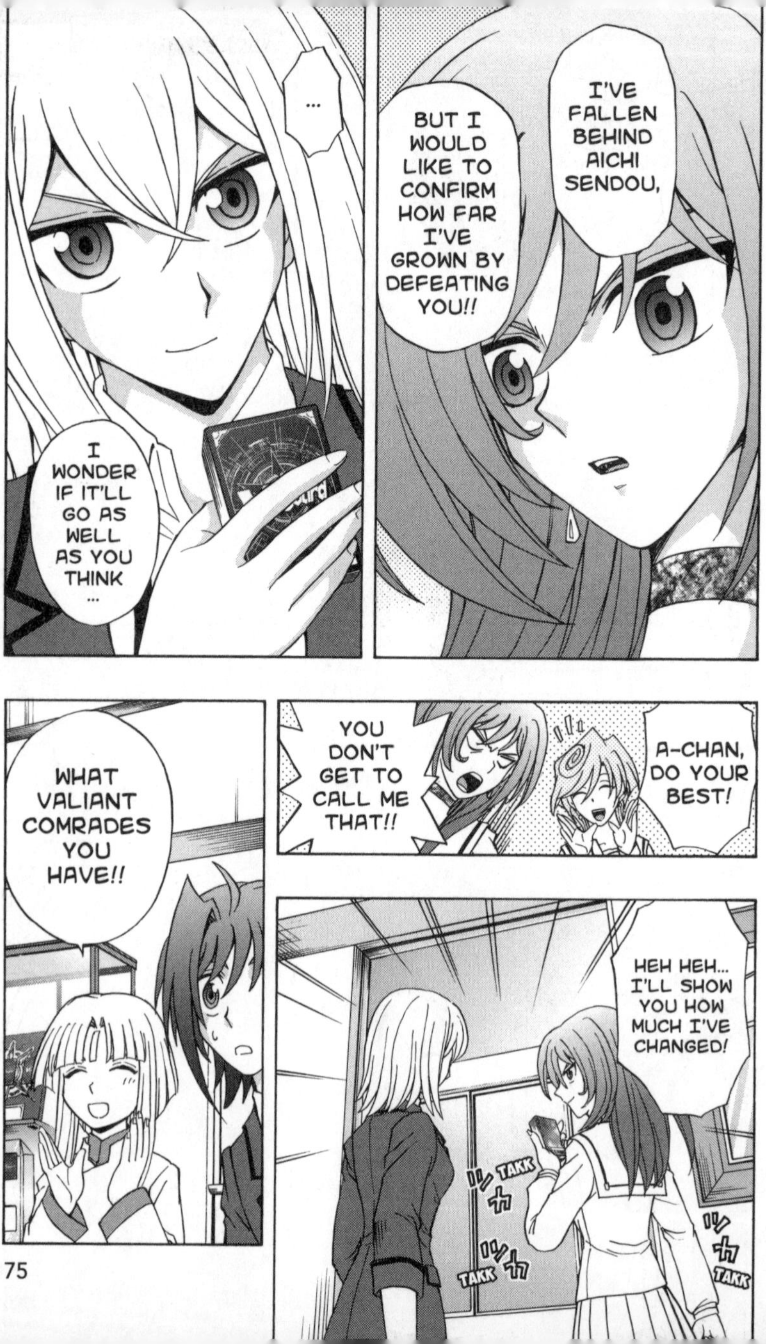
I'VE FALLEN BEHIND AICHI SENDOU,
BUT I WOULD LIKE TO CONFIRM HOW FAR I'VE GROWN BY DEFEATING YOU!!
...
I WONDER IF IT'LL GO AS WELL AS YOU THINK ...
A-CHAN, DO YOUR BEST!
YOU DON'T GET TO CALL ME THAT!!
HEH HEH... I'LL SHOW YOU HOW MUCH I'VE CHANGED!
TAKK
TAKK
TAKK
WHAT VALIANT COMRADES YOU HAVE!!

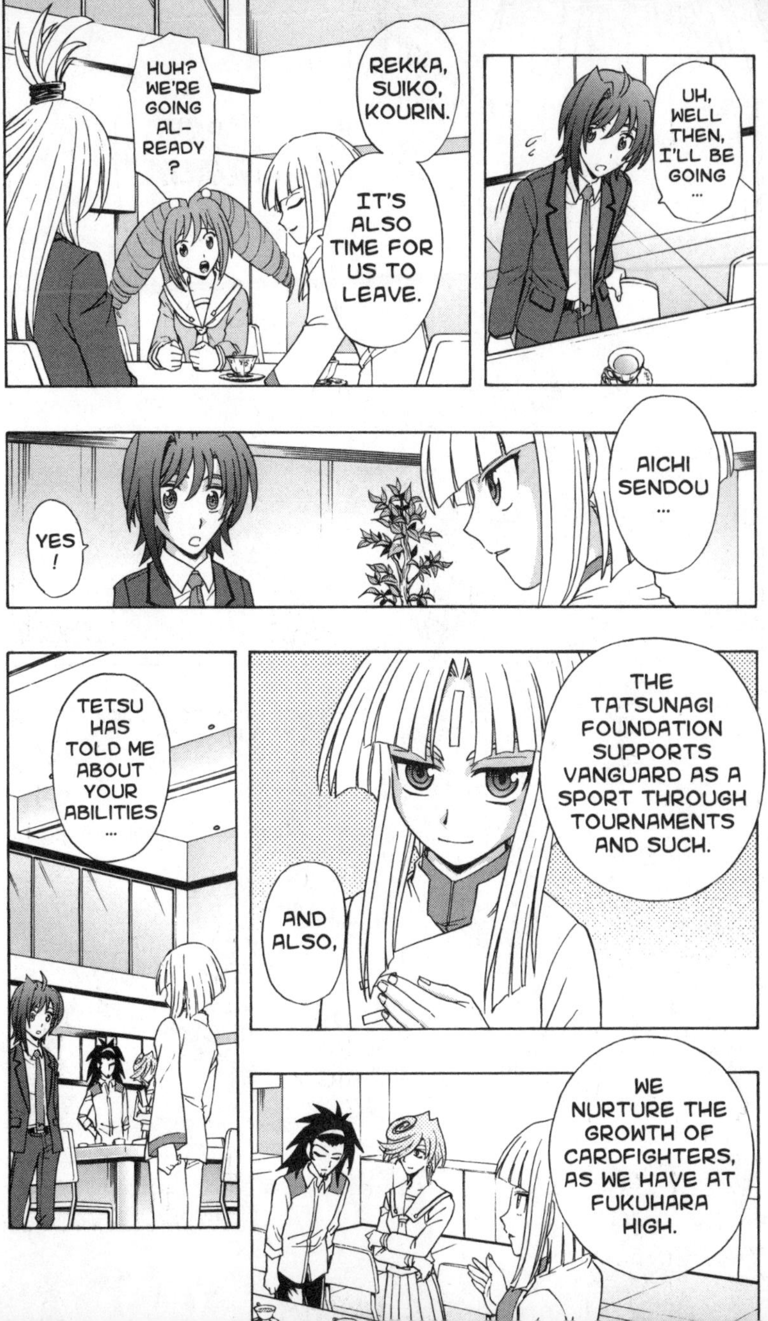
UH, WELL THEN, I'LL BE GOING ...
REKKA, SUIKO, KOURIN.
HUH? WE'RE GOING AL-READY ?
IT'S ALSO TIME FOR US TO LEAVE.
AICHI SENDOU ...
YES !
THE TATSUNAGI FOUNDATION SUPPORTS VANGUARD AS A SPORT THROUGH TOURNAMENTS AND SUCH.
AND ALSO,
WE NURTURE THE GROWTH OF CARDFIGHTERS, AS WE HAVE AT FUKUHARA HIGH.
TETSU HAS TOLD ME ABOUT YOUR ABILITIES ...

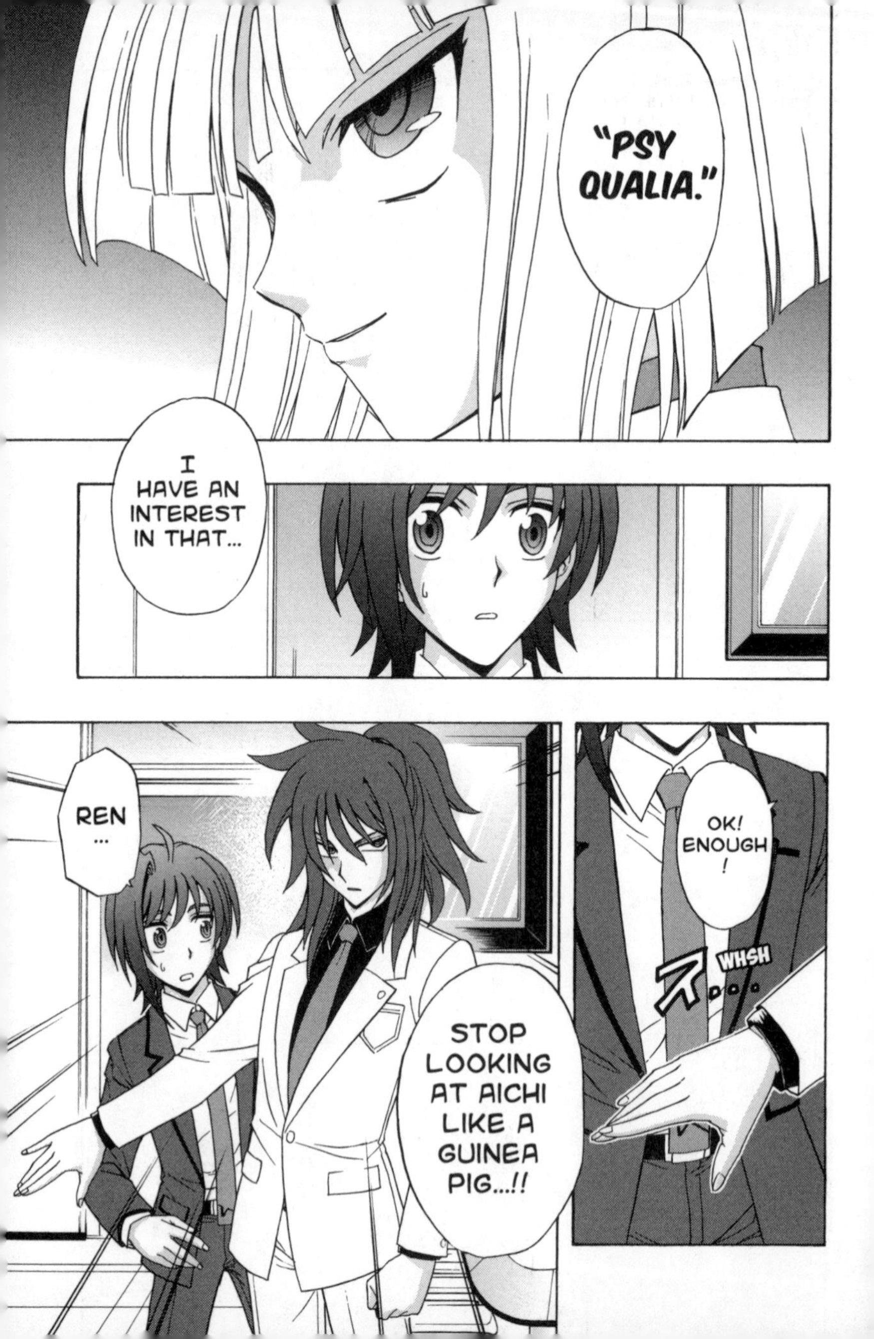
"PSY QUALIA."
I HAVE AN INTEREST IN THAT...
OK! ENOUGH!
WHSH
STOP LOOKING AT AICHI LIKE A GUINEA PIG...!!
REN...

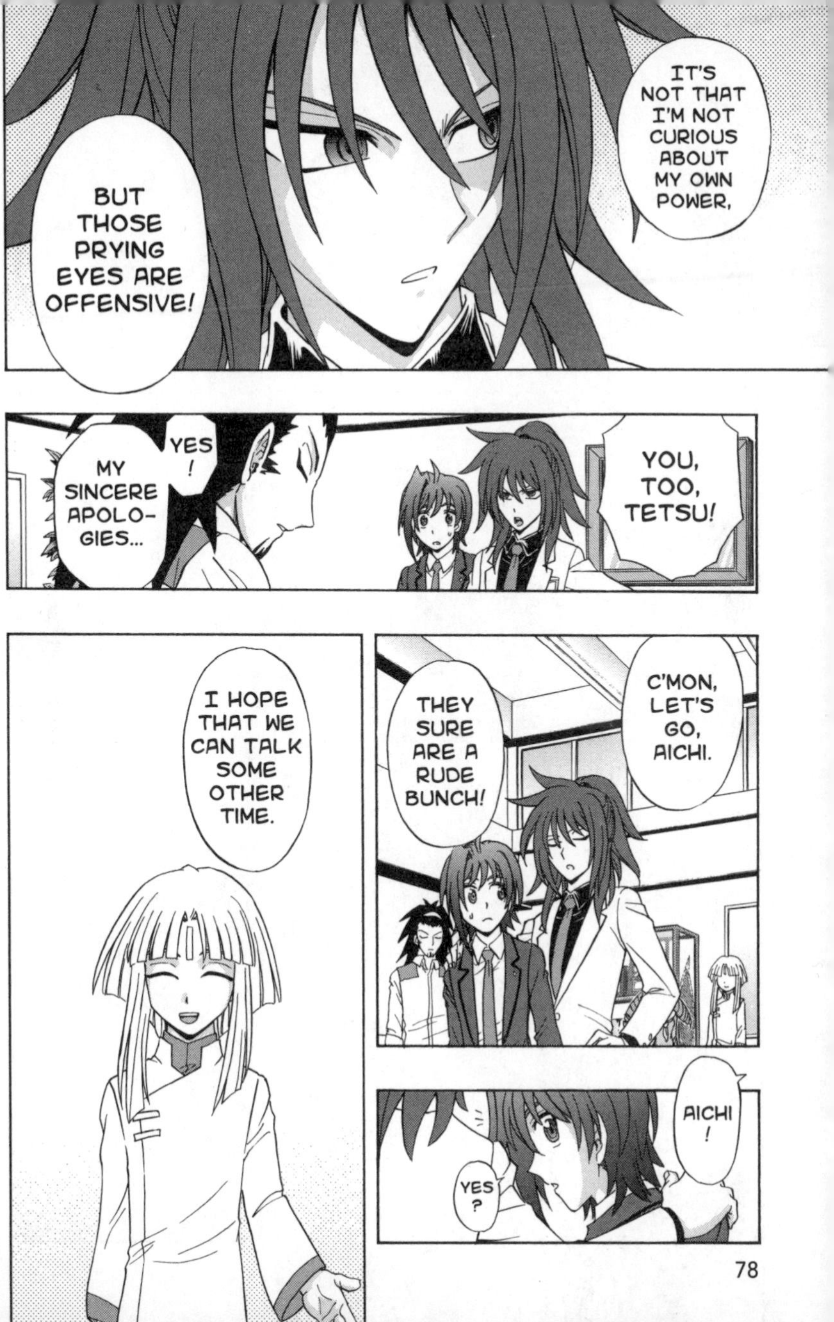
IT'S NOT THAT I'M NOT CURIOUS ABOUT MY OWN POWER,
BUT THOSE PRYING EYES ARE OFFENSIVE!
YOU, TOO, TETSU!
YES!
MY SINCERE APOLOGIES...
C'MON, LET'S GO, AICHI.
THEY SURE ARE A RUDE BUNCH!
AICHI!
YES?
I HOPE THAT WE CAN TALK SOME OTHER TIME.

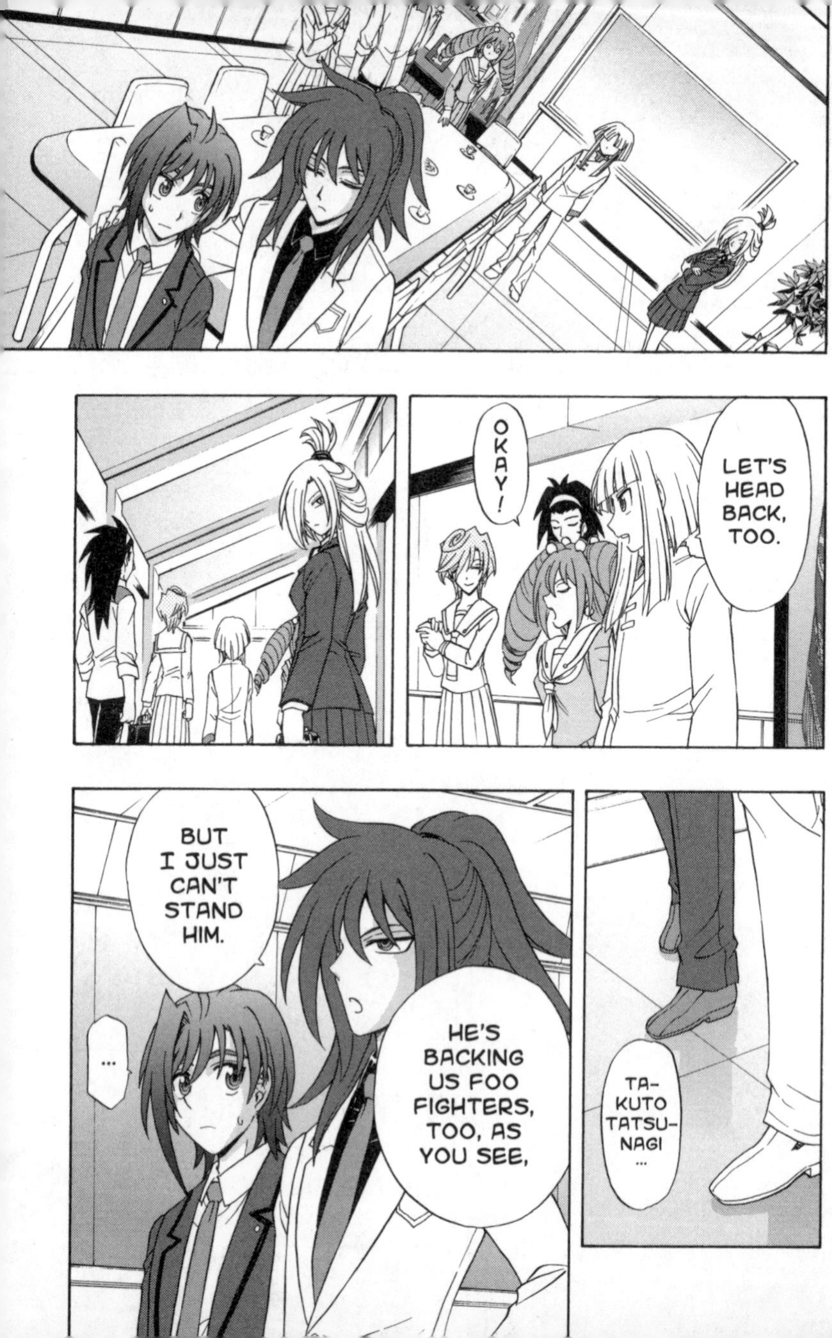
LET'S HEAD BACK, TOO.
OKAY!
TA-KUTO TATSU-NAGI ...
HE'S BACKING US FOO FIGHTERS, TOO, AS YOU SEE,
BUT I JUST CAN'T STAND HIM.
...

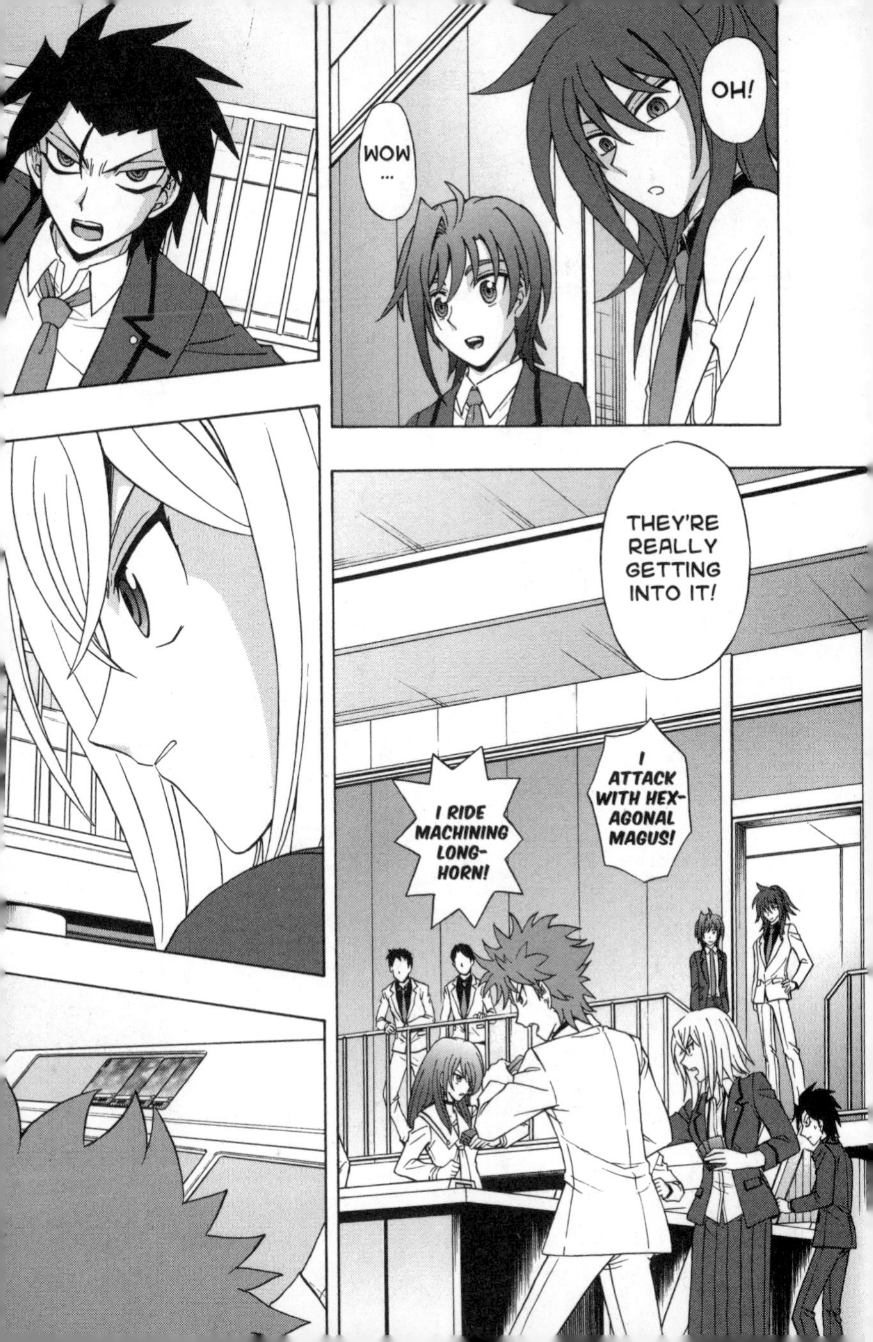
OH!
WOW ...
THEY'RE REALLY GETTING INTO IT!
I ATTACK WITH HEX-AGONAL MAGUS!
I RIDE MACHINING LONG-HORN!

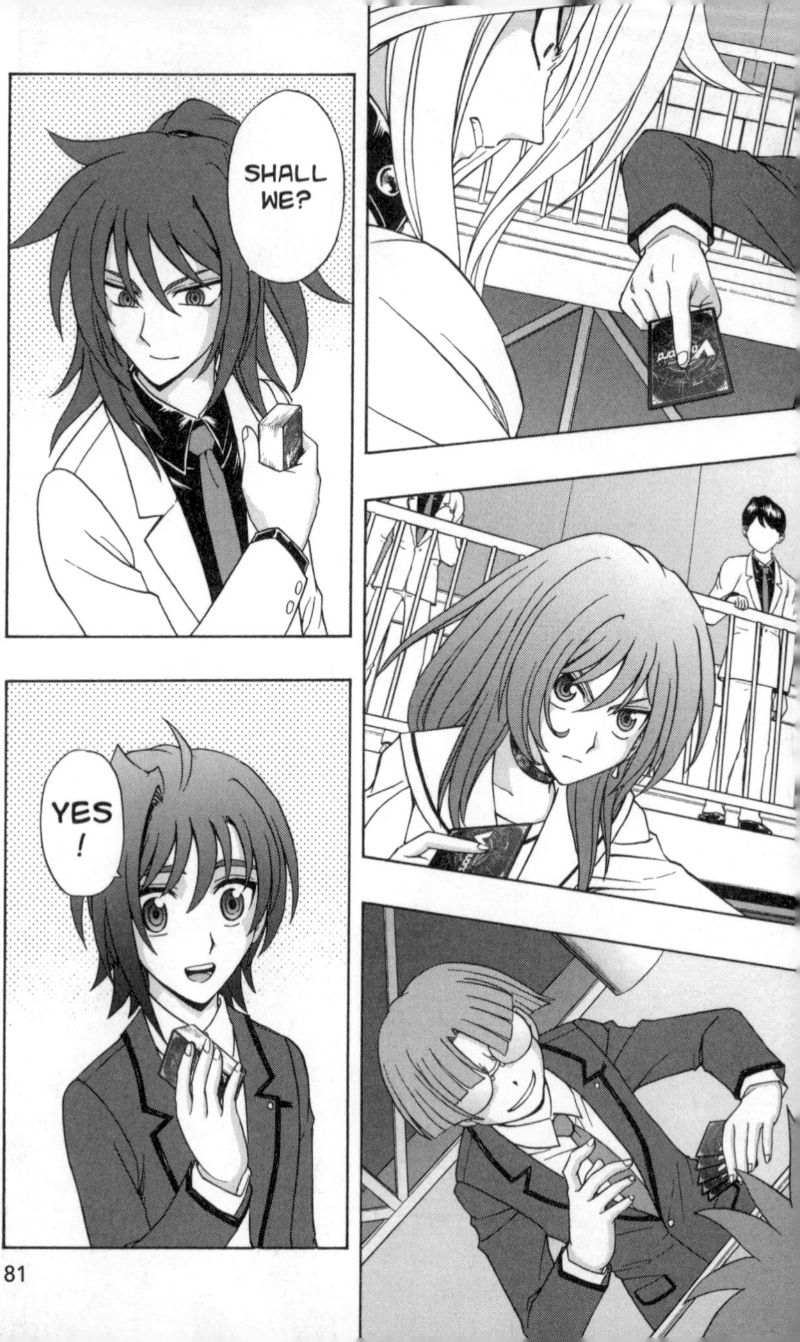
SHALL WE?
YES!

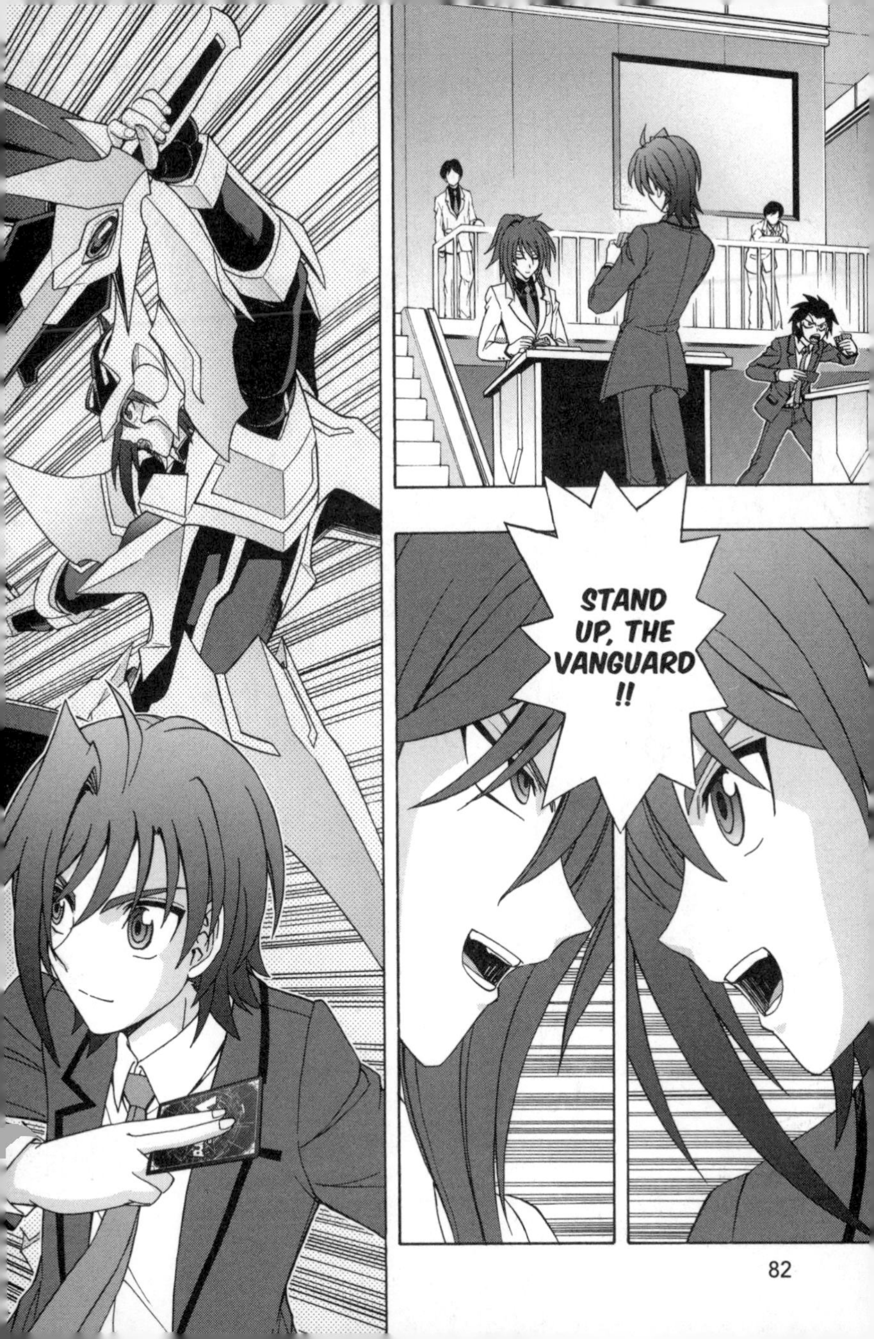
STAND UP, THE VANGUARD!!

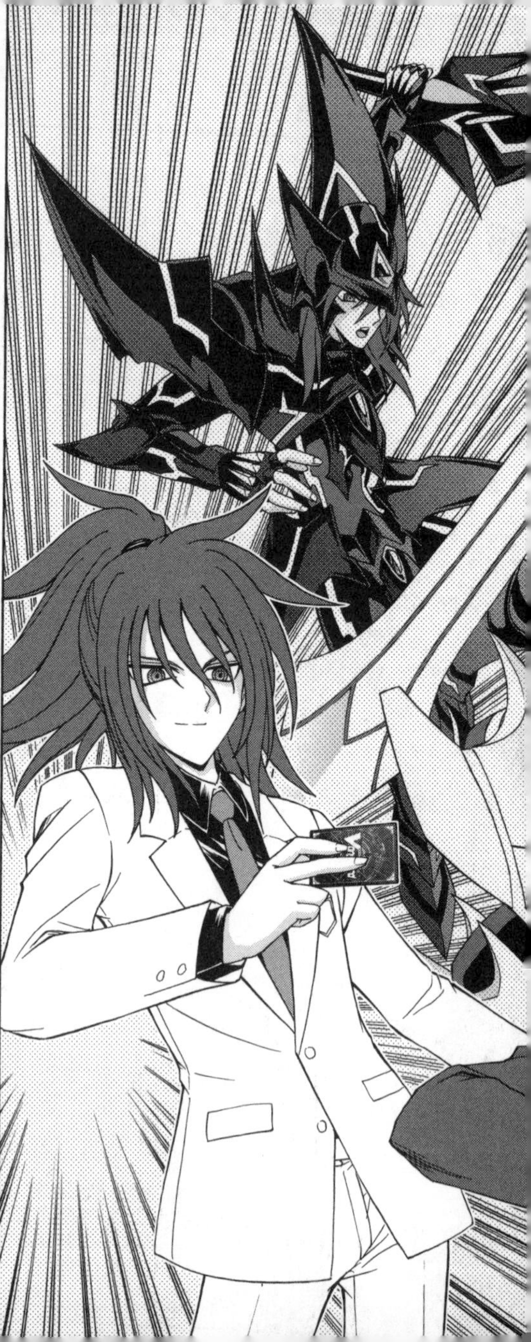

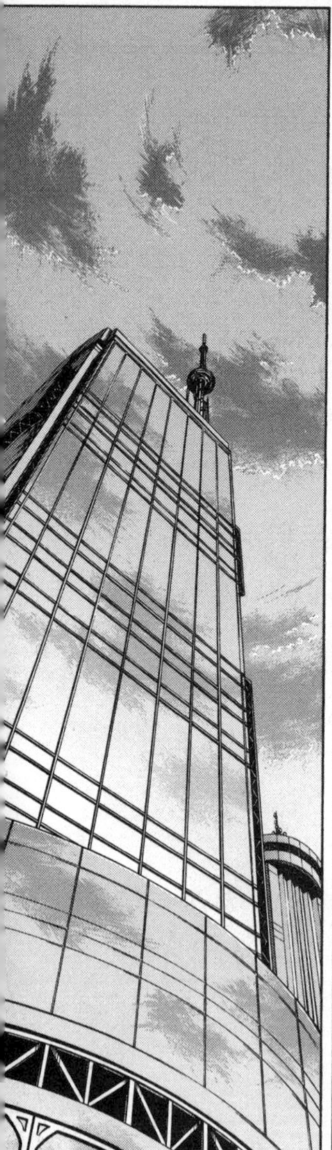

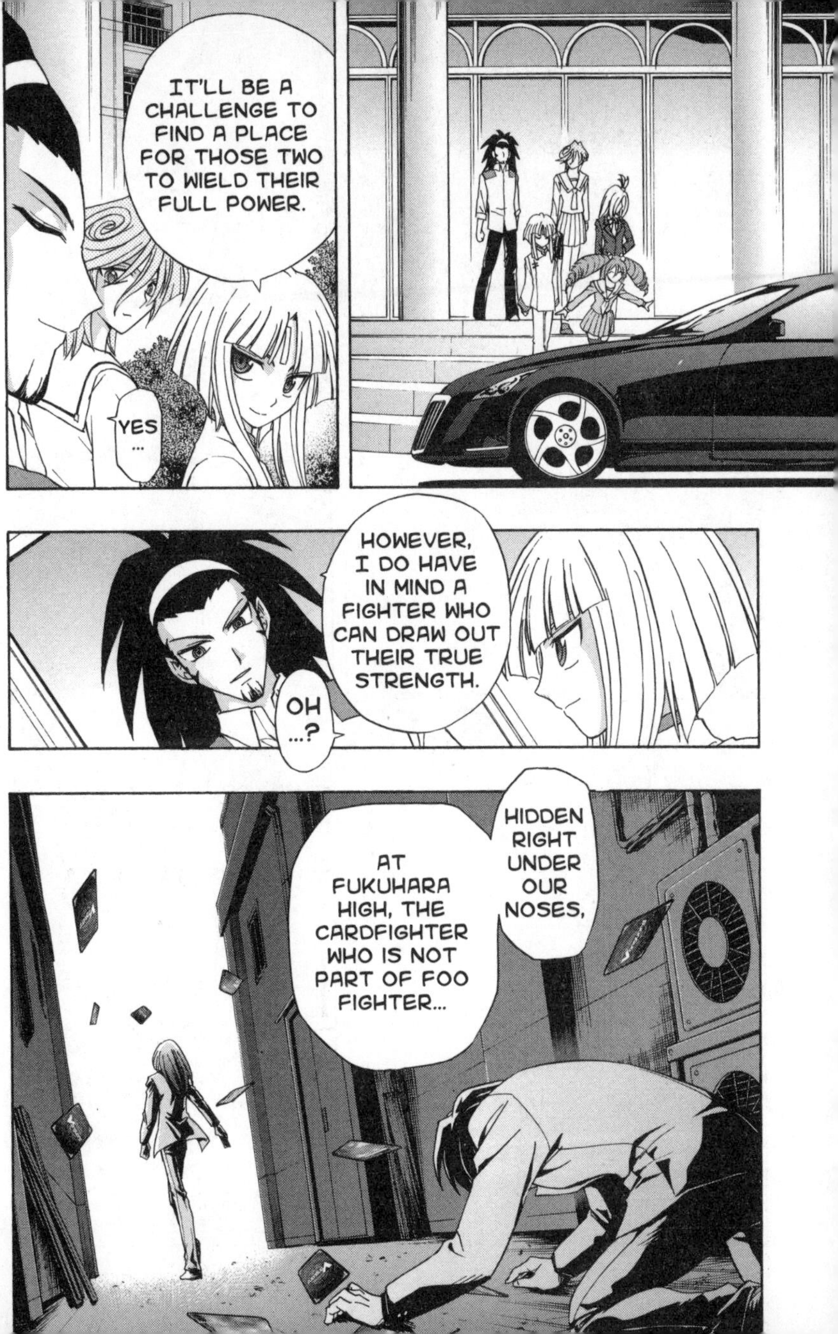
IT'LL BE A CHALLENGE TO FIND A PLACE FOR THOSE TWO TO WIELD THEIR FULL POWER.
YES ...
HOWEVER, I DO HAVE IN MIND A FIGHTER WHO CAN DRAW OUT THEIR TRUE STRENGTH.
OH ...?
HIDDEN RIGHT UNDER OUR NOSES,
AT FUKUHARA HIGH, THE CARDFIGHTER WHO IS NOT PART OF FOO FIGHTER...

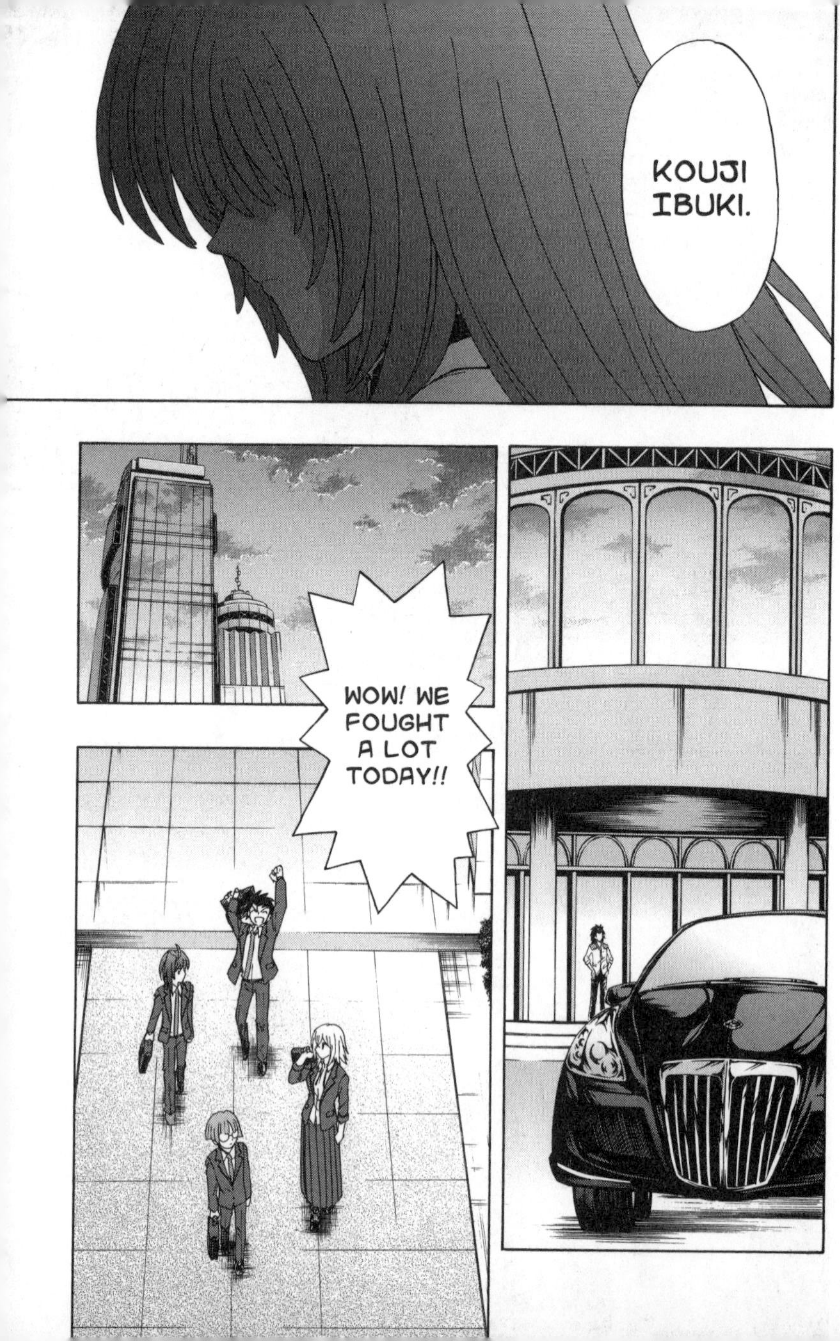
KOUJI IBUKI.
WOW! WE FOUGHT A LOT TODAY!!

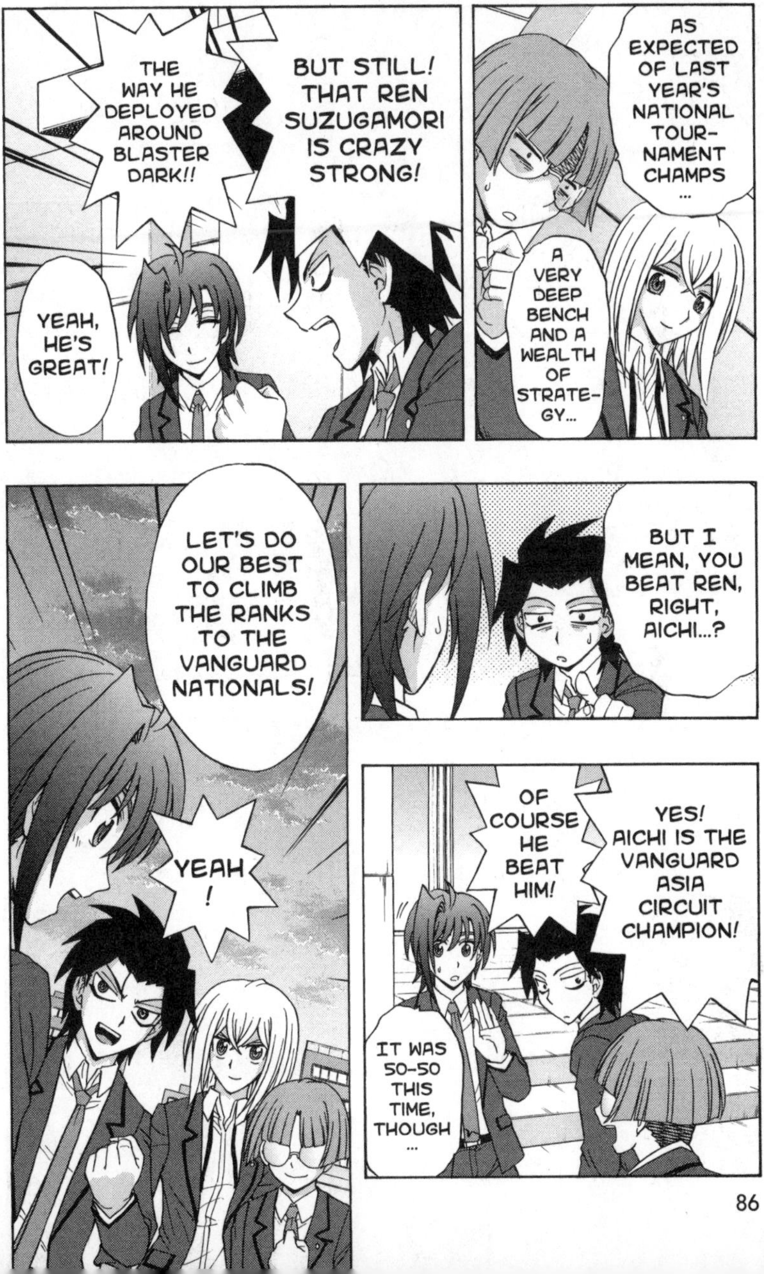
AS EXPECTED OF LAST YEAR'S NATIONAL TOUR-NAMENT CHAMPS ...
A VERY DEEP BENCH AND A WEALTH OF STRATE-GY...
BUT STILL! THAT REN SUZUGAMORI IS CRAZY STRONG!
THE WAY HE DEPLOYED AROUND BLASTER DARK!!
YEAH, HE'S GREAT!
BUT I MEAN, YOU BEAT REN, RIGHT, AICHI...?
YES! AICHI IS THE VANGUARD ASIA CIRCUIT CHAMPION!
OF COURSE HE BEAT HIM!
IT WAS 50-50 THIS TIME, THOUGH ...
LET'S DO OUR BEST TO CLIMB THE RANKS TO THE VANGUARD NATIONALS!
YEAH!

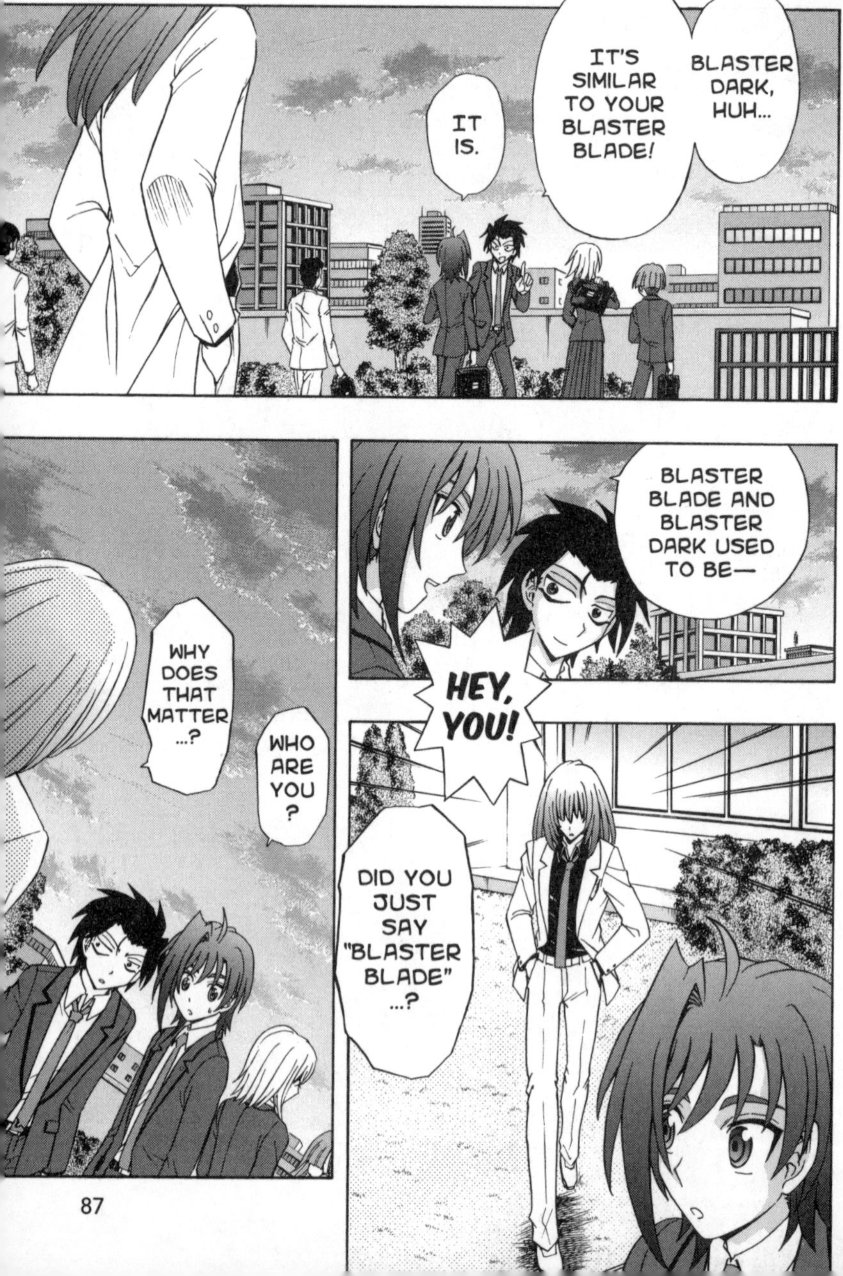
BLASTER DARK, HUH...
IT'S SIMILAR TO YOUR BLASTER BLADE!
IT IS.
BLASTER BLADE AND BLASTER DARK USED TO BE—
HEY, YOU!
DID YOU JUST SAY "BLASTER BLADE" ...?
WHO ARE YOU ?
WHY DOES THAT MATTER ...?

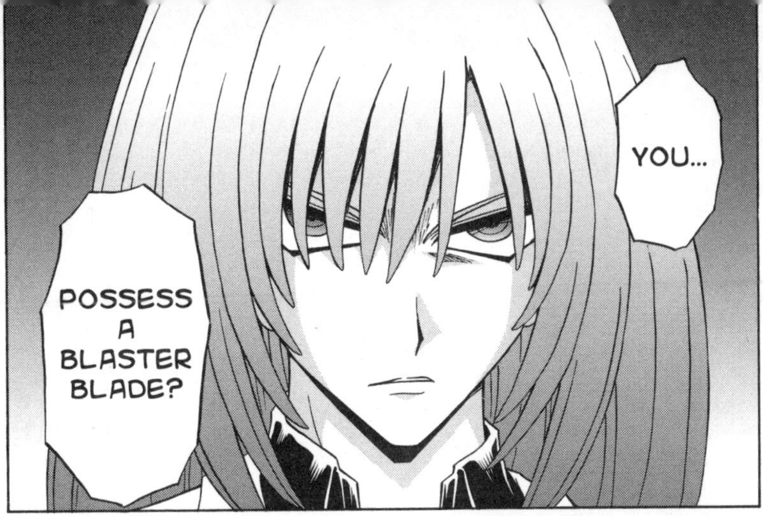
YOU...
POSSESS A BLASTER BLADE?

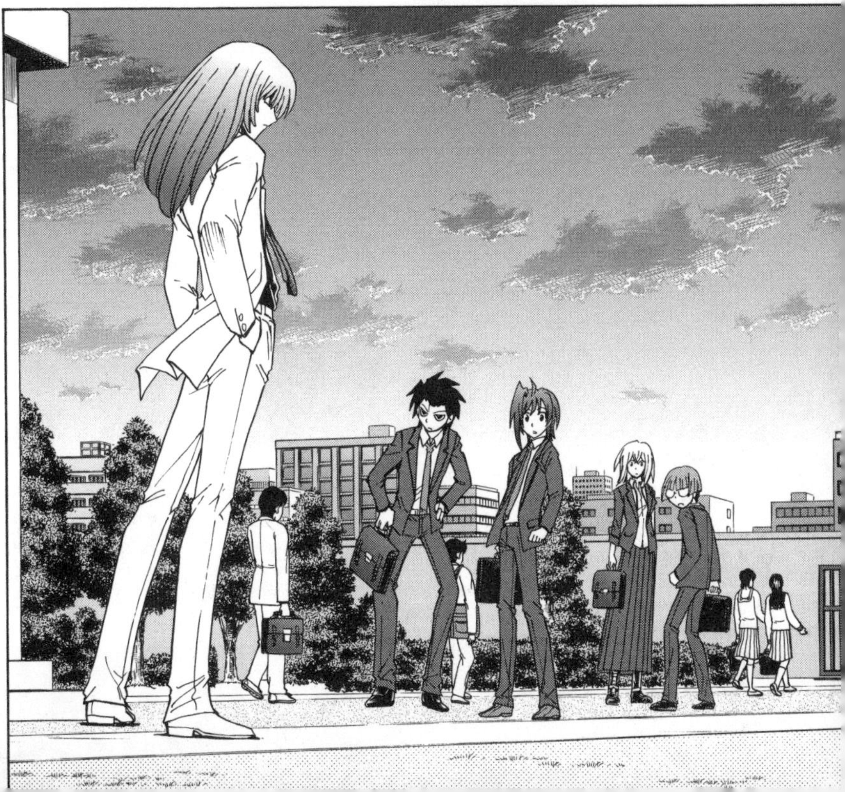

CARDFIGHT!! Vanguard

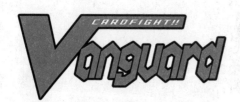

BONUS! CARDFIGHT!! Vanguard

# BONUS! VANGUARD NEVER-BEFORE-SEEN IMAGE BOARDS

Takuto (tentative)
Card Tournament sponsor
Stature similar to Aichi
This is my first attempt; I will redraw later
(Itou)

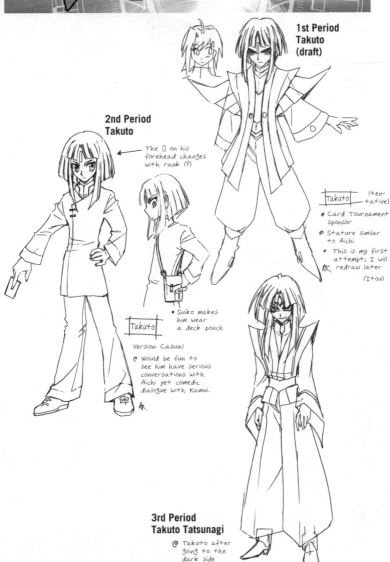

1st Period Takuto (draft)

The ▯ on his forehead changes with rank (?)
Suiko makes him wear a deck pouch
Takuto
Version: Casual
Would be fun to see him have serious conversations with Aichi yet comedic dialogue with Kamui.

2nd Period Takuto

Takuto after going to the dark side

3rd Period Takuto Tatsunagi

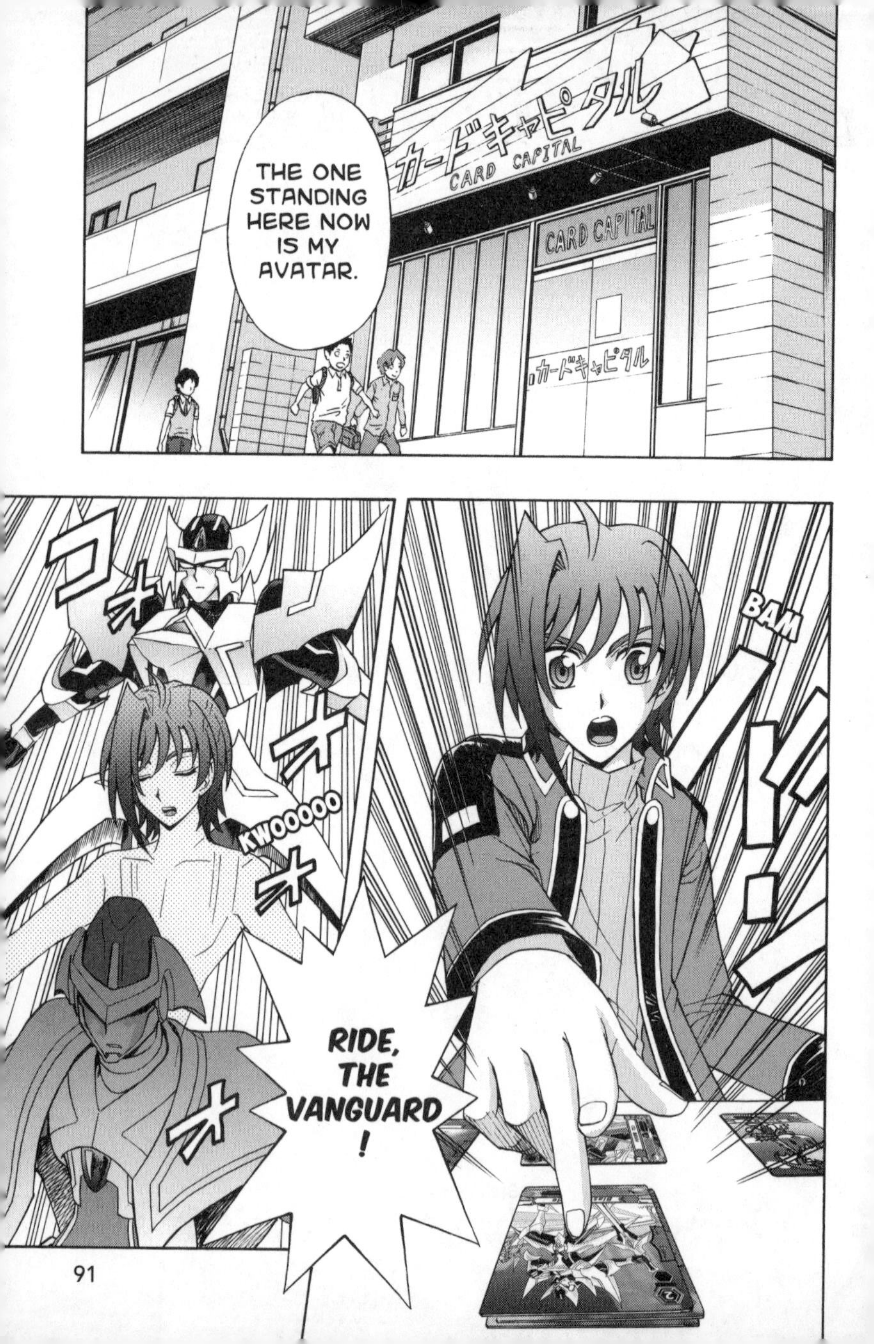
カードキャピタル
CARD CAPITAL
THE ONE STANDING HERE NOW IS MY AVATAR.
CARD CAPITAL
カードキャピタル
BAM
!!
RIDE, THE VANGUARD!
コオオオオ
KWOOOOO

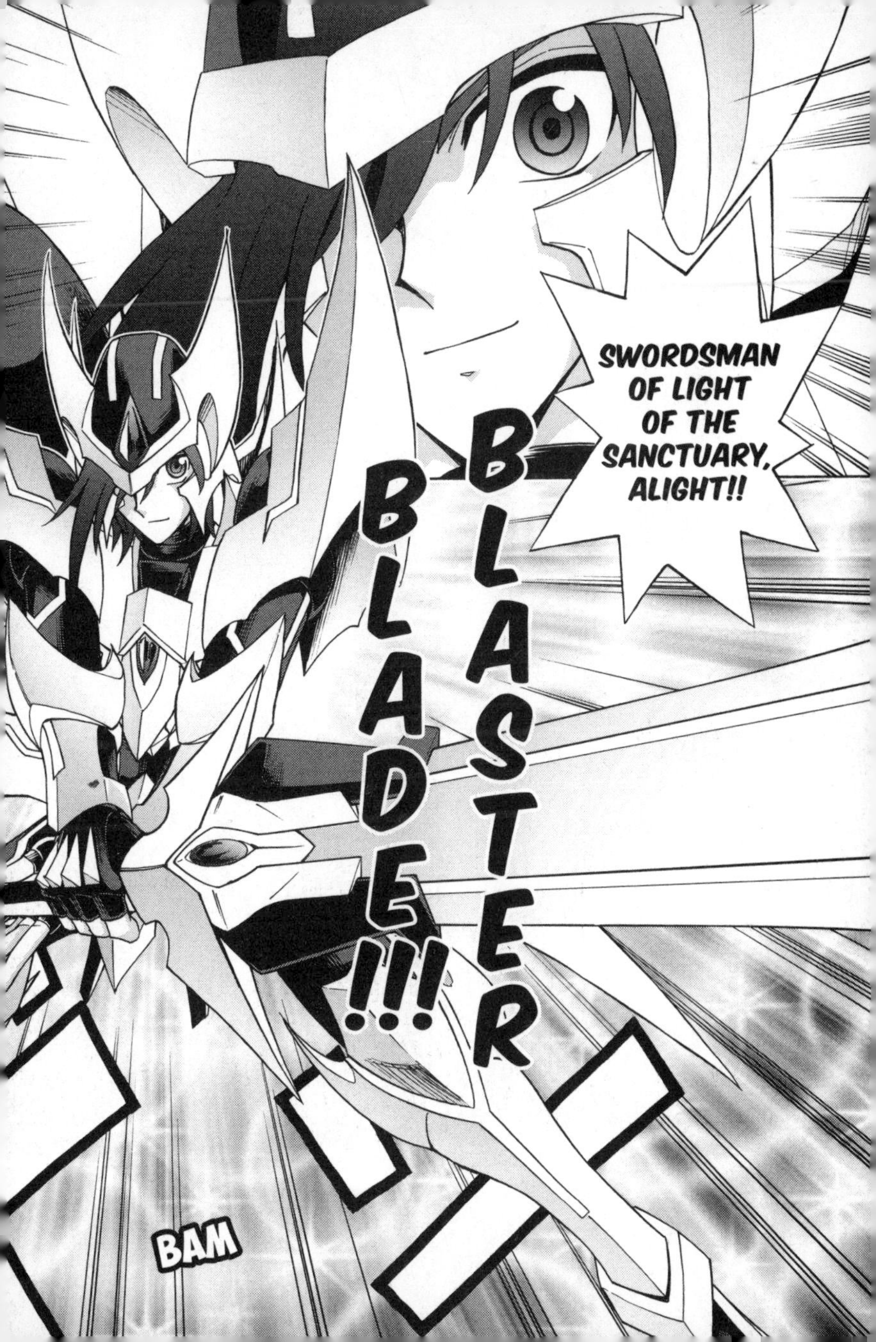
SWORDSMAN OF LIGHT OF THE SANCTUARY, ALIGHT!!
BLASTER BLADE!!!
BAM

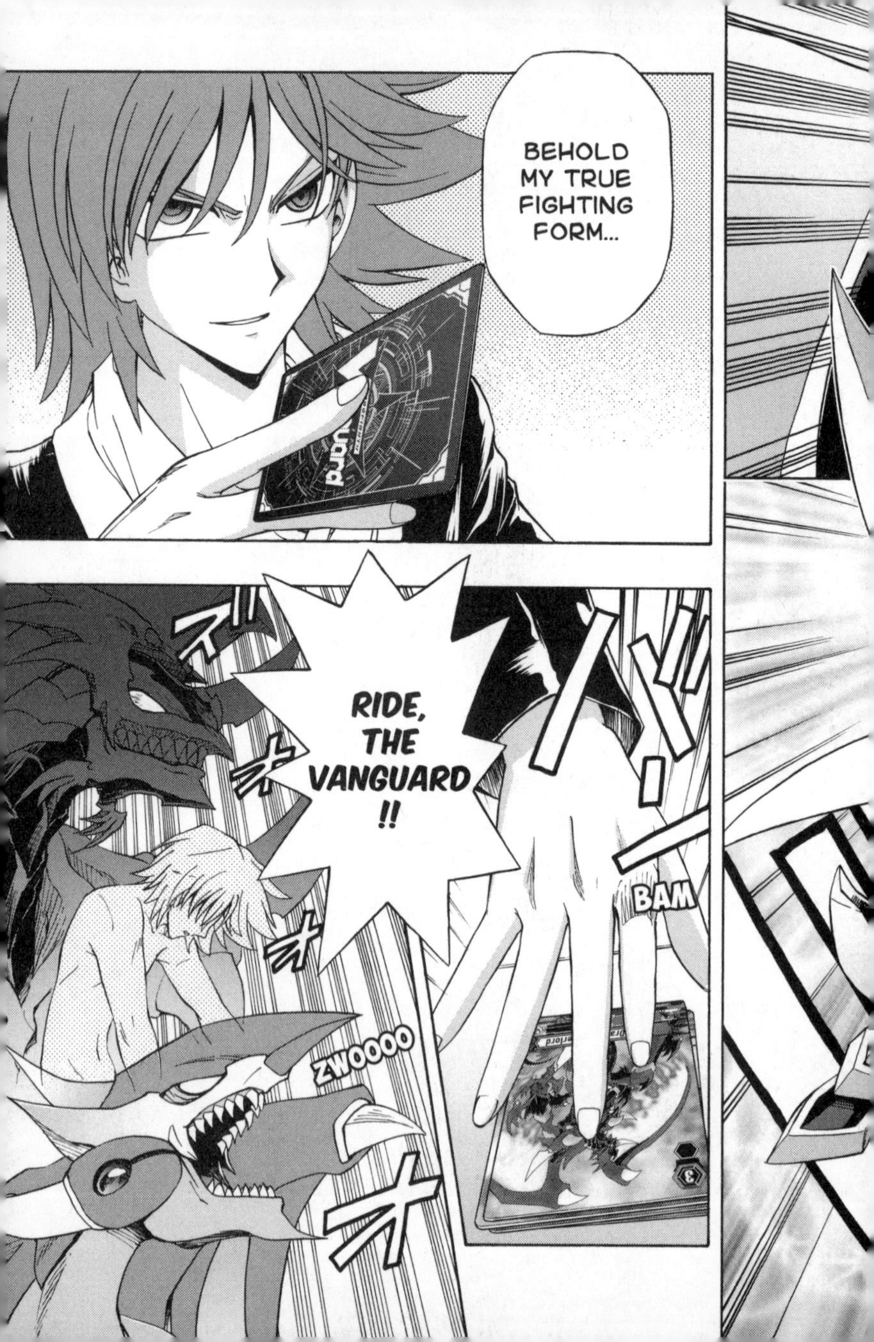
BEHOLD MY TRUE FIGHTING FORM...
RIDE, THE VANGUARD !!
BAM
ZWOOOO

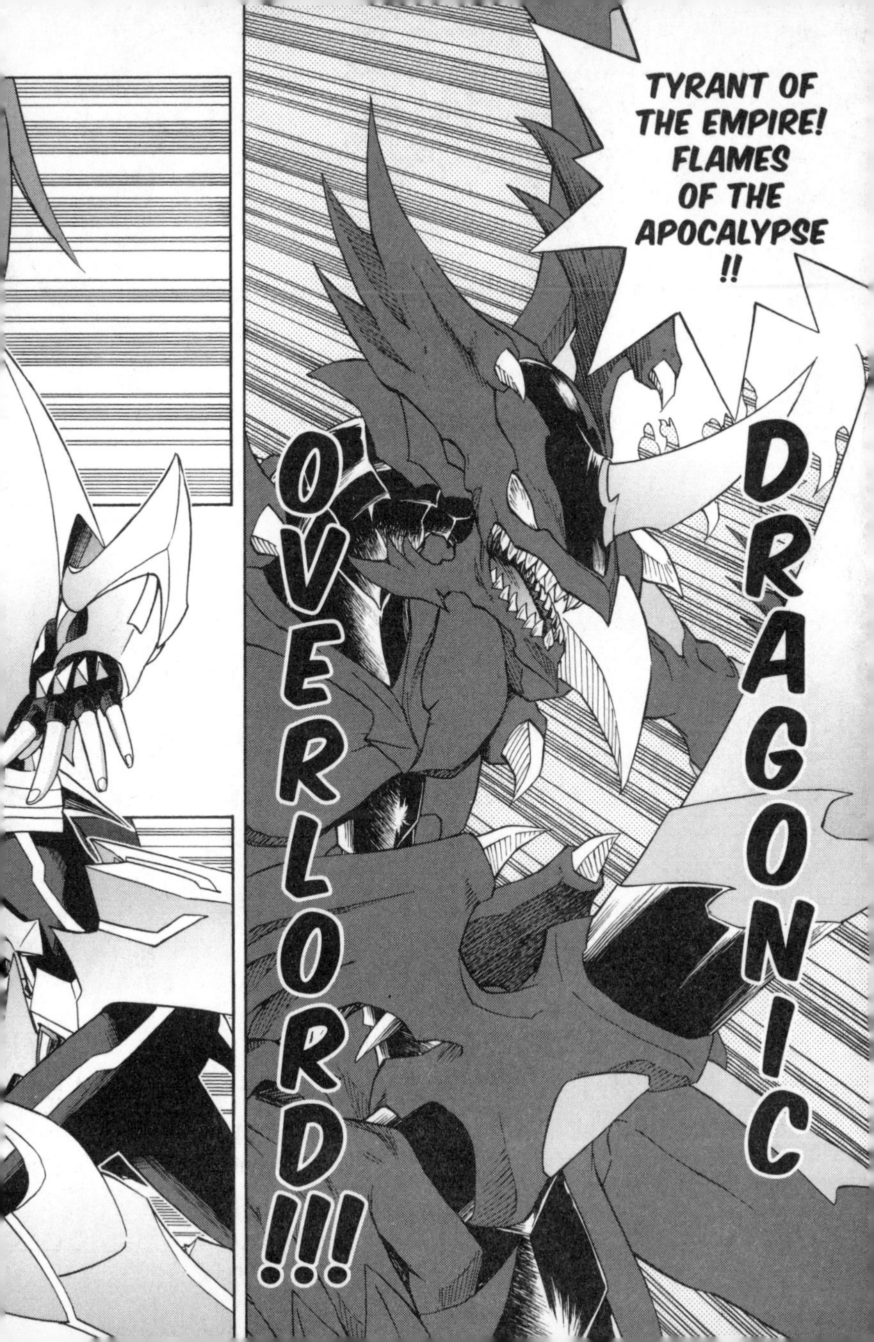
TYRANT OF THE EMPIRE! FLAMES OF THE APOCALYPSE !!
DRAGONIC
OVERLORD!!!

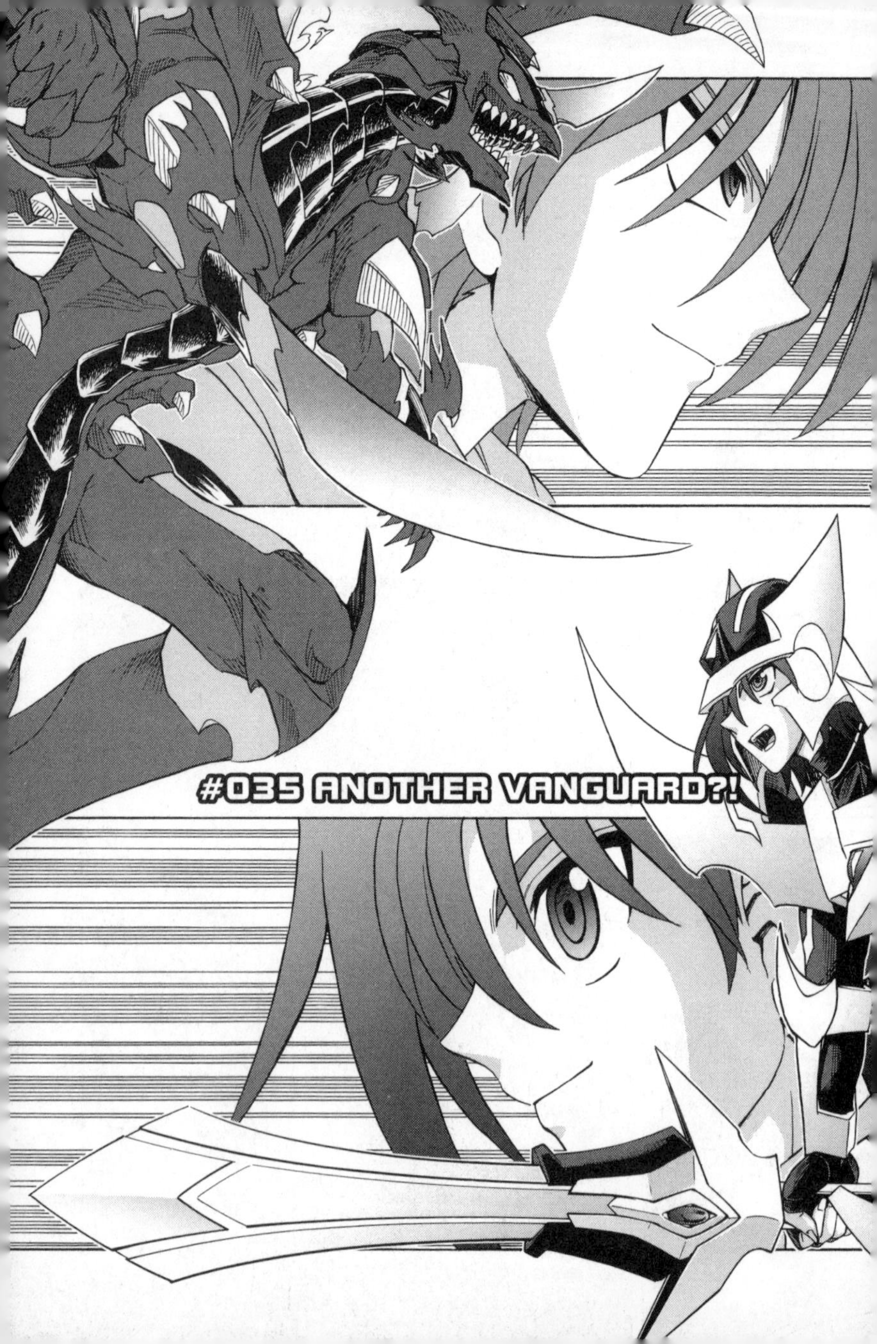
#035 ANOTHER VANGUARD?!

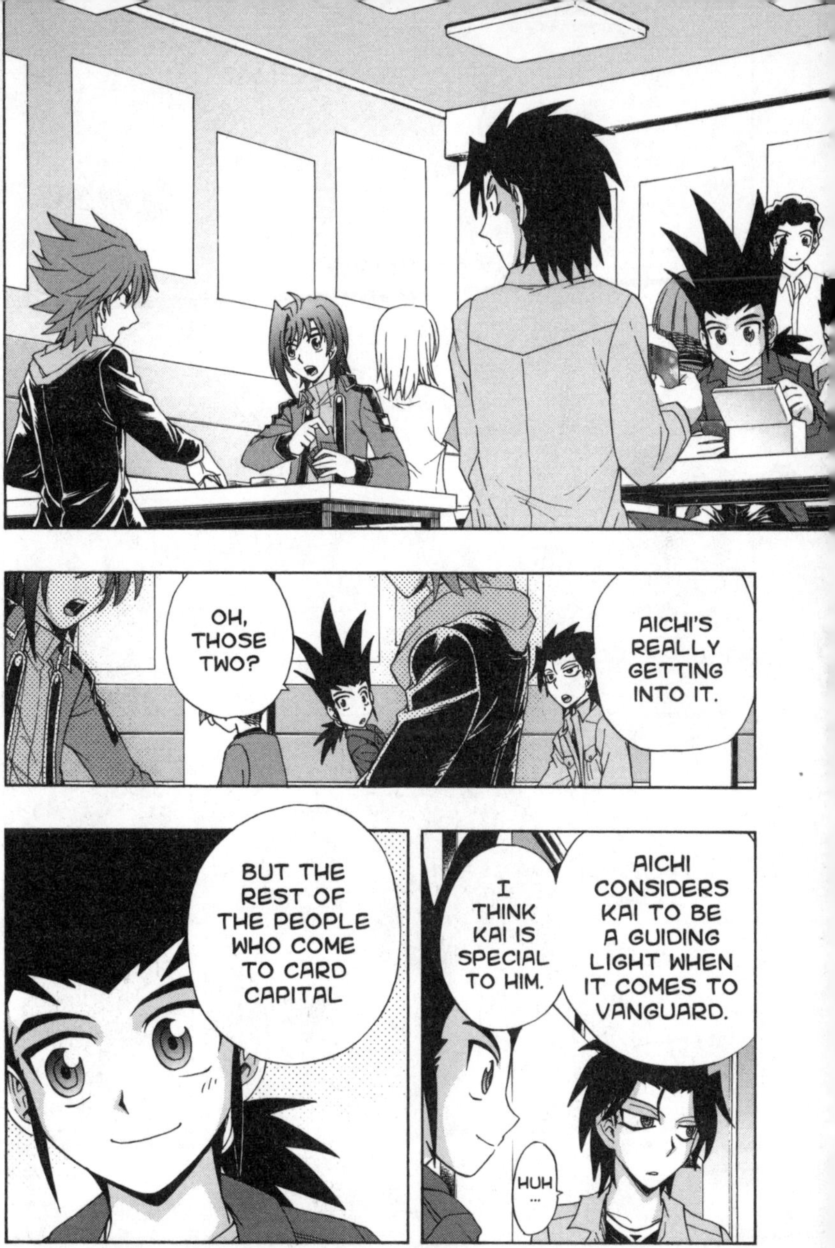
AICHI'S REALLY GETTING INTO IT.
OH, THOSE TWO?
AICHI CONSIDERS KAI TO BE A GUIDING LIGHT WHEN IT COMES TO VANGUARD.
I THINK KAI IS SPECIAL TO HIM.
HUH ...
BUT THE REST OF THE PEOPLE WHO COME TO CARD CAPITAL

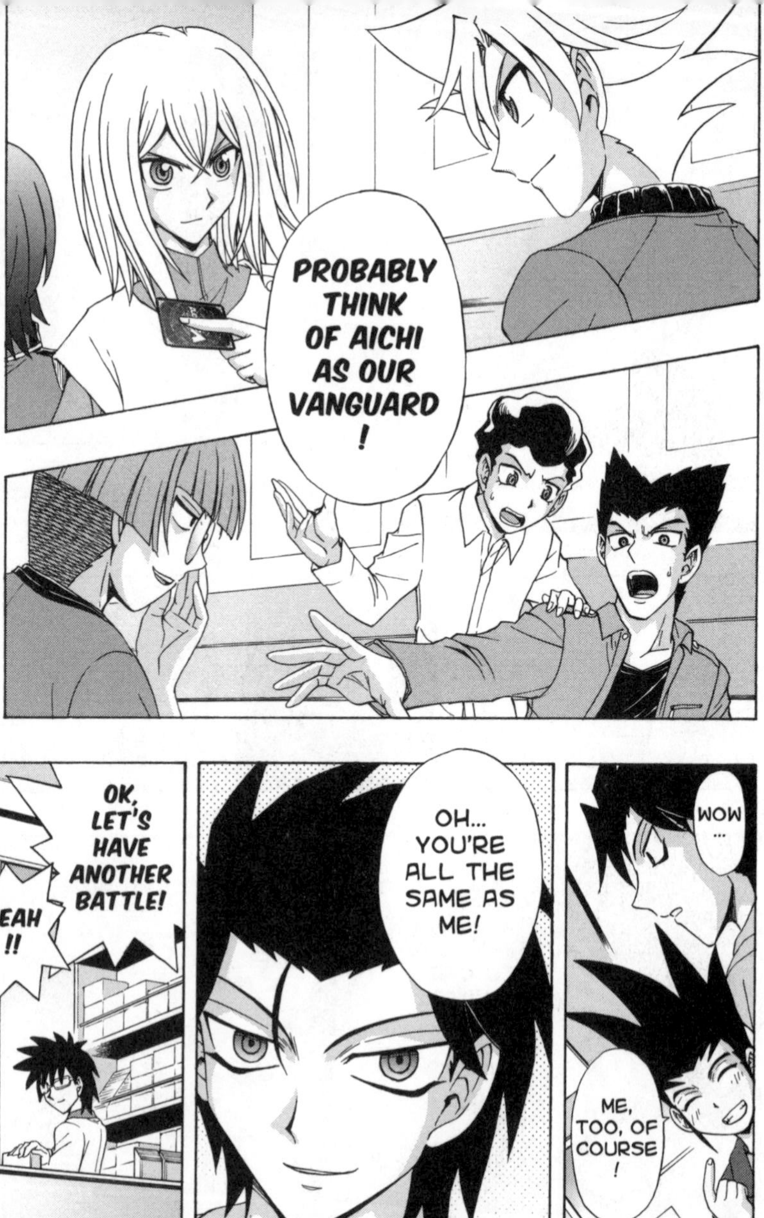
PROBABLY THINK OF AICHI AS OUR VANGUARD!
WOW...
ME, TOO, OF COURSE!
OH... YOU'RE ALL THE SAME AS ME!
OK, LET'S HAVE ANOTHER BATTLE!
YEAH!!

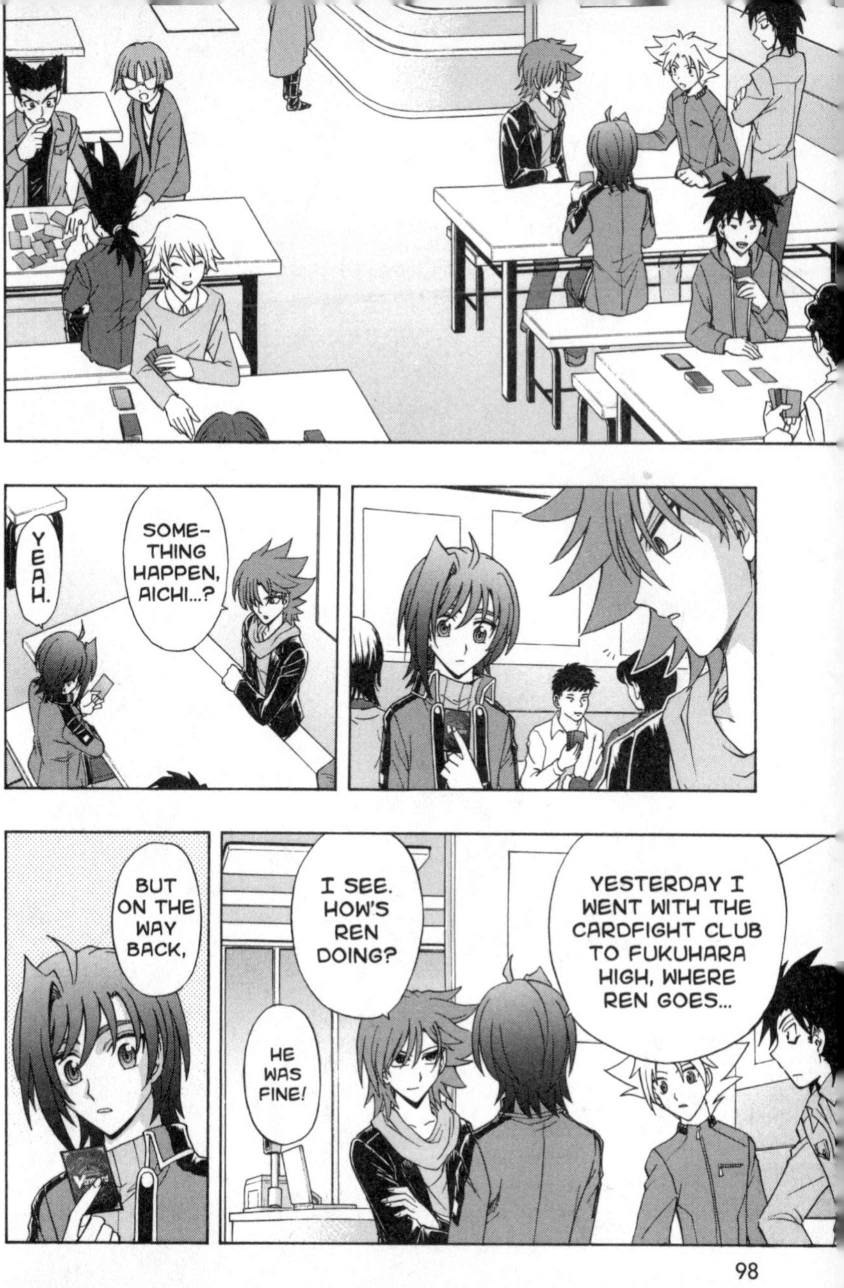
SOME-THING HAPPEN, AICHI...?
YEAH.
YESTERDAY I WENT WITH THE CARDFIGHT CLUB TO FUKUHARA HIGH, WHERE REN GOES...
I SEE. HOW'S REN DOING?
HE WAS FINE!
BUT ON THE WAY BACK,

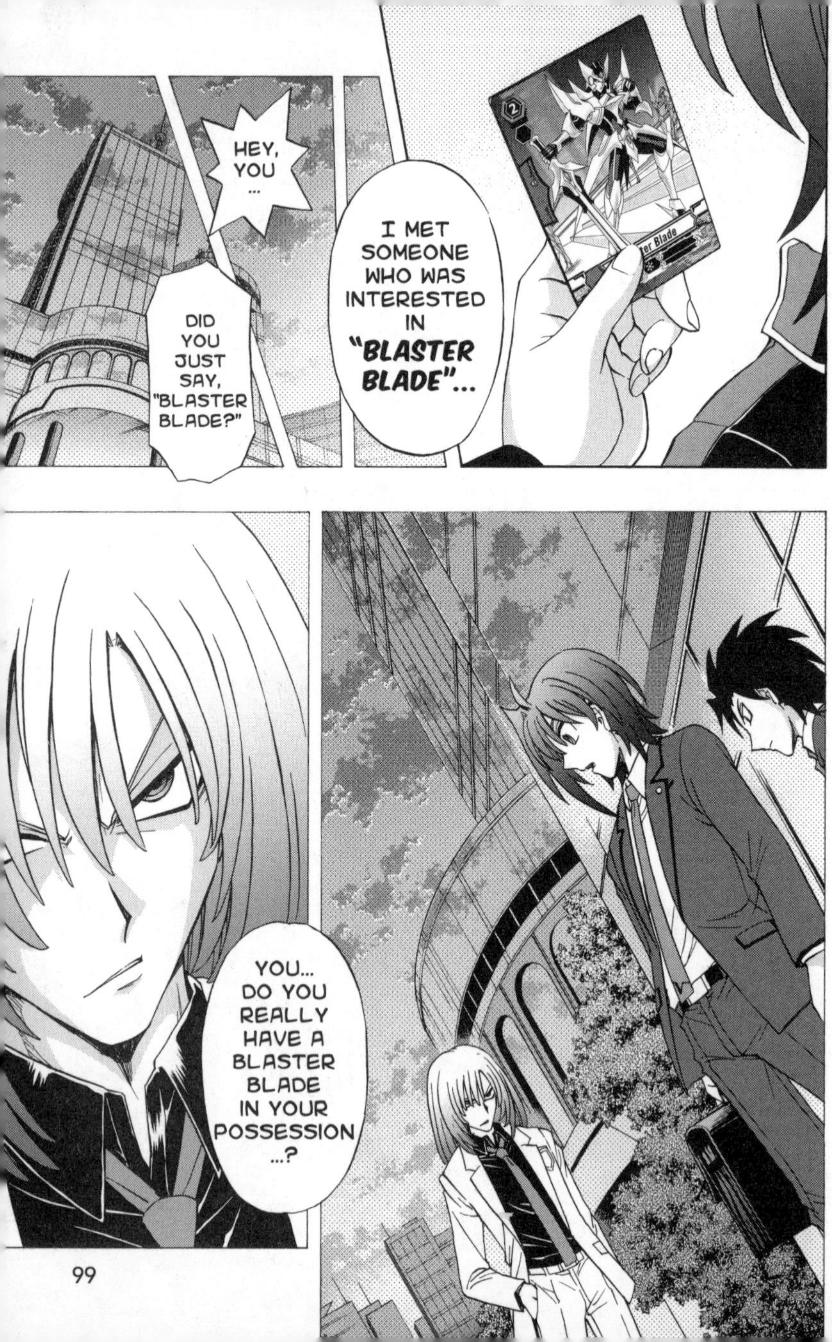
I MET SOMEONE WHO WAS INTERESTED IN "BLASTER BLADE"...
HEY, YOU ...
DID YOU JUST SAY, "BLASTER BLADE?"
YOU... DO YOU REALLY HAVE A BLASTER BLADE IN YOUR POSSESSION ...?

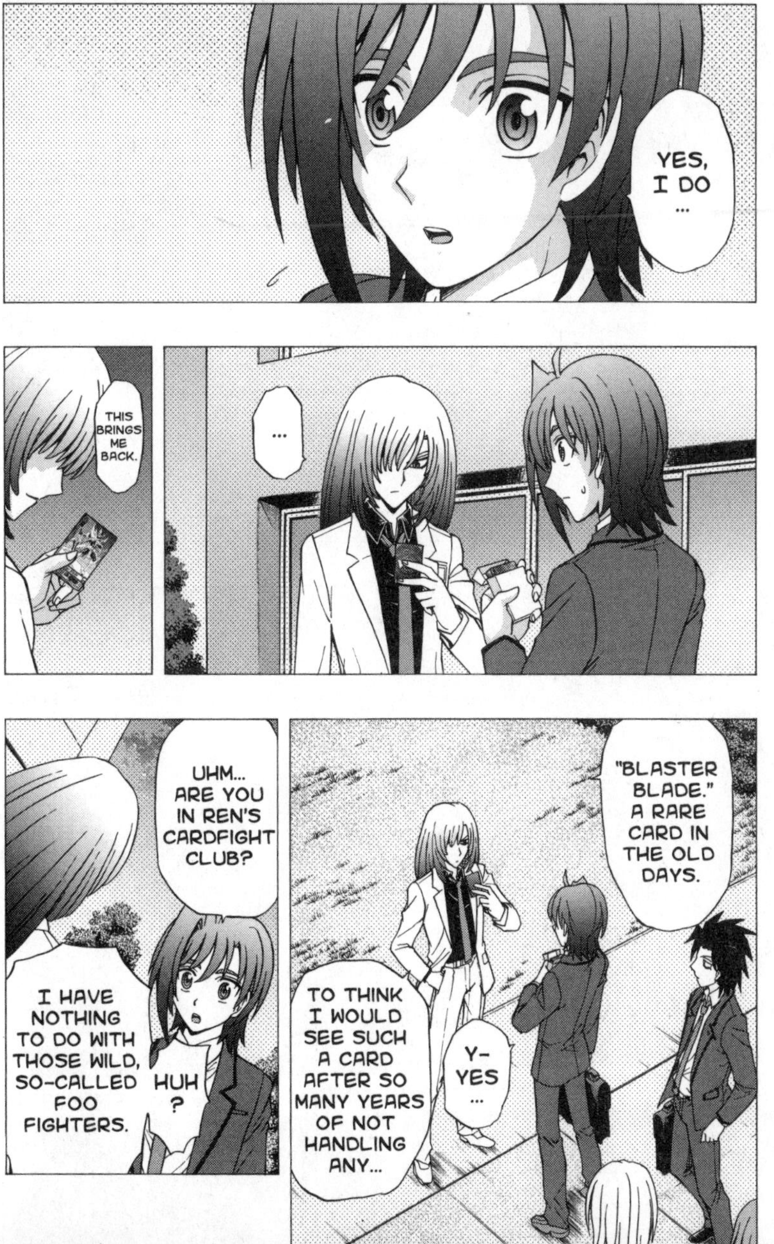

YES, I DO ...
...
THIS BRINGS ME BACK.
"BLASTER BLADE." A RARE CARD IN THE OLD DAYS.
TO THINK I WOULD SEE SUCH A CARD AFTER SO MANY YEARS OF NOT HANDLING ANY...
Y-YES ...
UHM... ARE YOU IN REN'S CARDFIGHT CLUB?
HUH?
I HAVE NOTHING TO DO WITH THOSE WILD, SO-CALLED FOO FIGHTERS.

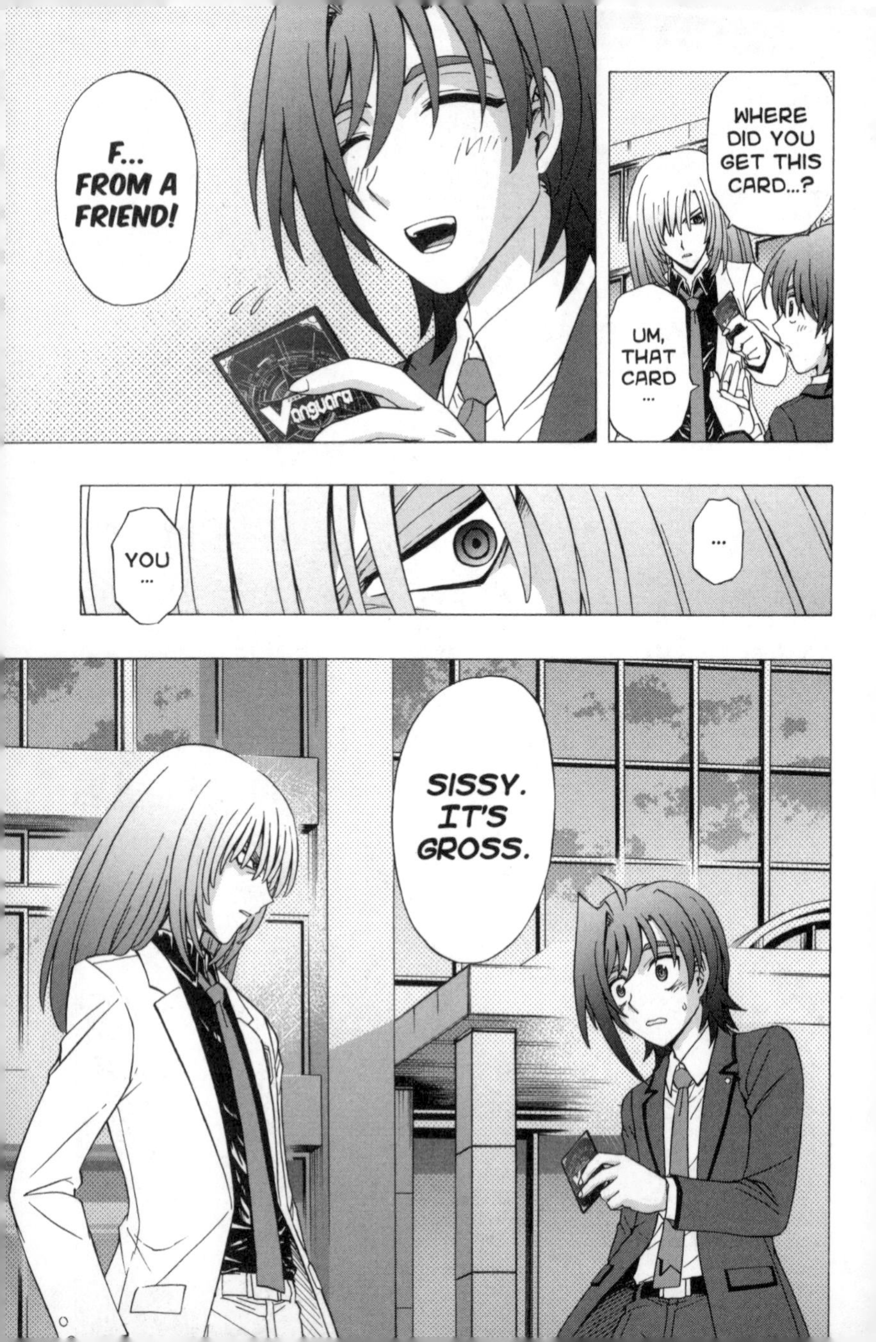
WHERE DID YOU GET THIS CARD...?
UM, THAT CARD ...
F... FROM A FRIEND!
Vanguard
...
YOU ...
SISSY. IT'S GROSS.

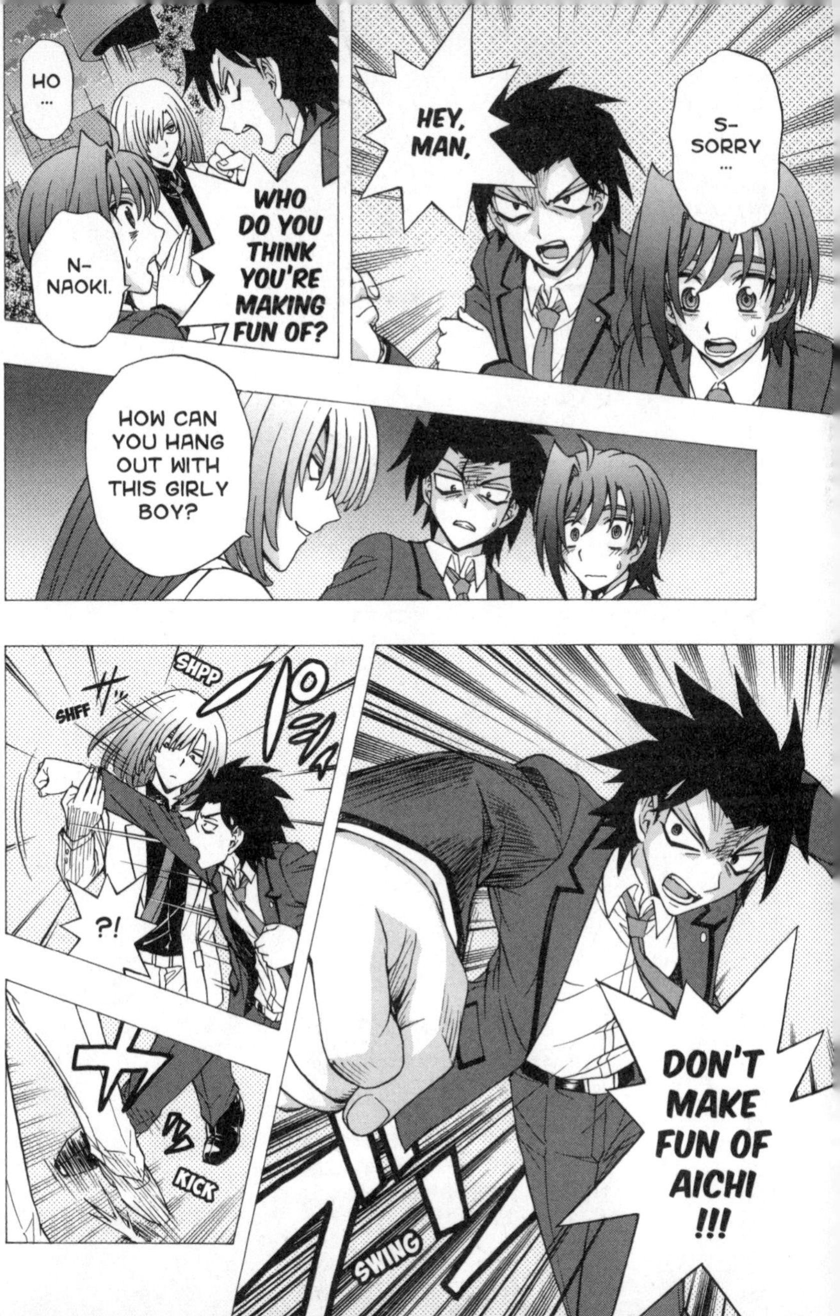
S-SORRY ...
HEY, MAN,
HO ...
WHO DO YOU THINK YOU'RE MAKING FUN OF?
N-NAOKI.
HOW CAN YOU HANG OUT WITH THIS GIRLY BOY?
DON'T MAKE FUN OF AICHI !!!
SWING
SHPP
SHFF
?!
KICK

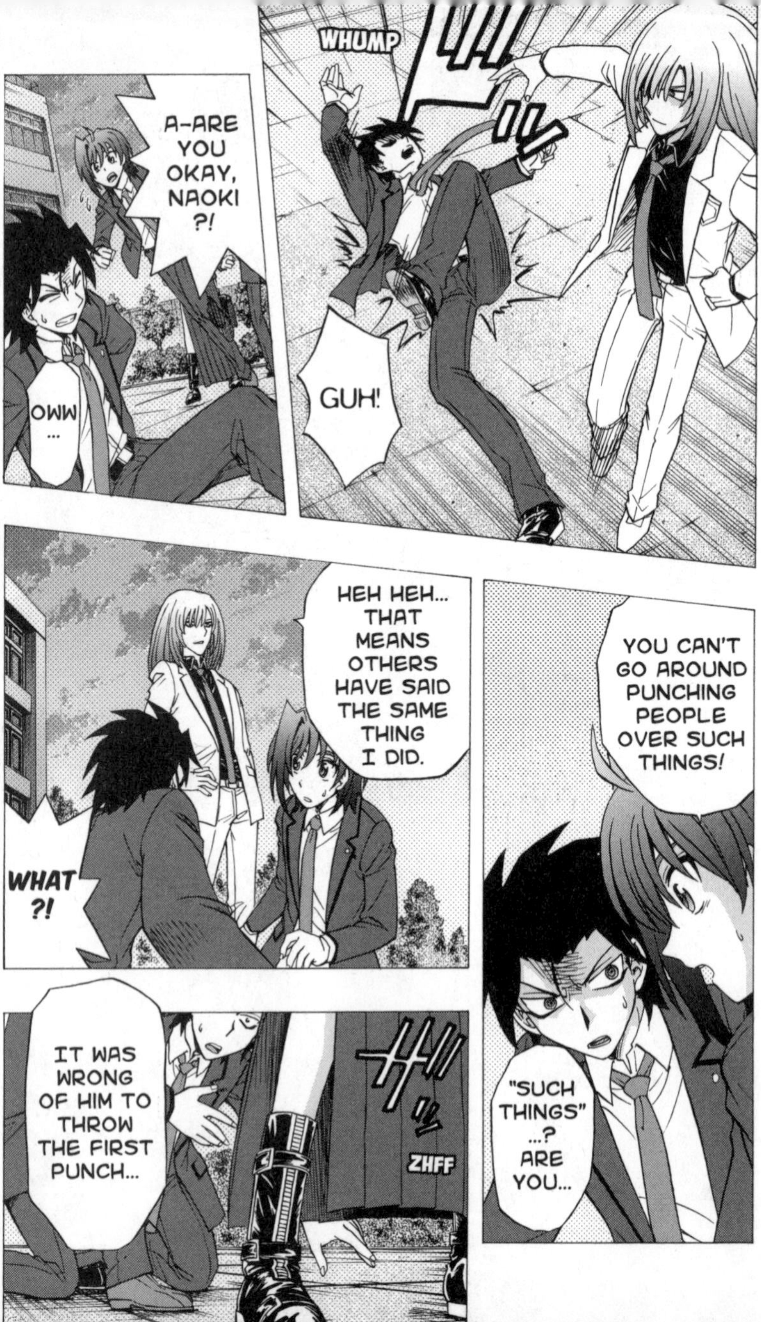
WHUMP
GUH!
A-ARE YOU OKAY, NAOKI?!
OWW...
YOU CAN'T GO AROUND PUNCHING PEOPLE OVER SUCH THINGS!
"SUCH THINGS"...? ARE YOU...
HEH HEH... THAT MEANS OTHERS HAVE SAID THE SAME THING I DID.
WHAT?!
IT WAS WRONG OF HIM TO THROW THE FIRST PUNCH...
ZHFF

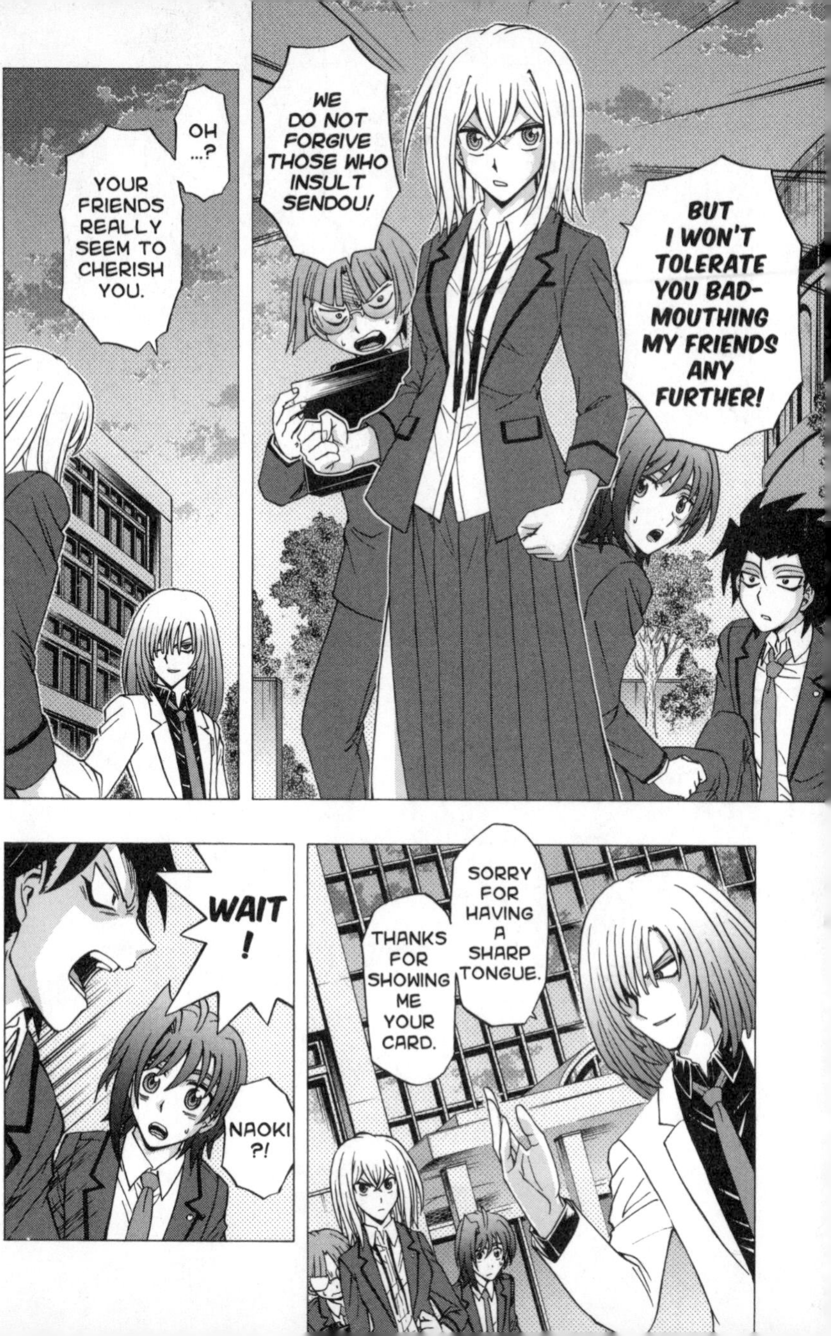
BUT I WON'T TOLERATE YOU BAD-MOUTHING MY FRIENDS ANY FURTHER!
WE DO NOT FORGIVE THOSE WHO INSULT SENDOU!
OH ...?
YOUR FRIENDS REALLY SEEM TO CHERISH YOU.
SORRY FOR HAVING A SHARP TONGUE.
THANKS FOR SHOWING ME YOUR CARD.
WAIT!
NAOKI ?!

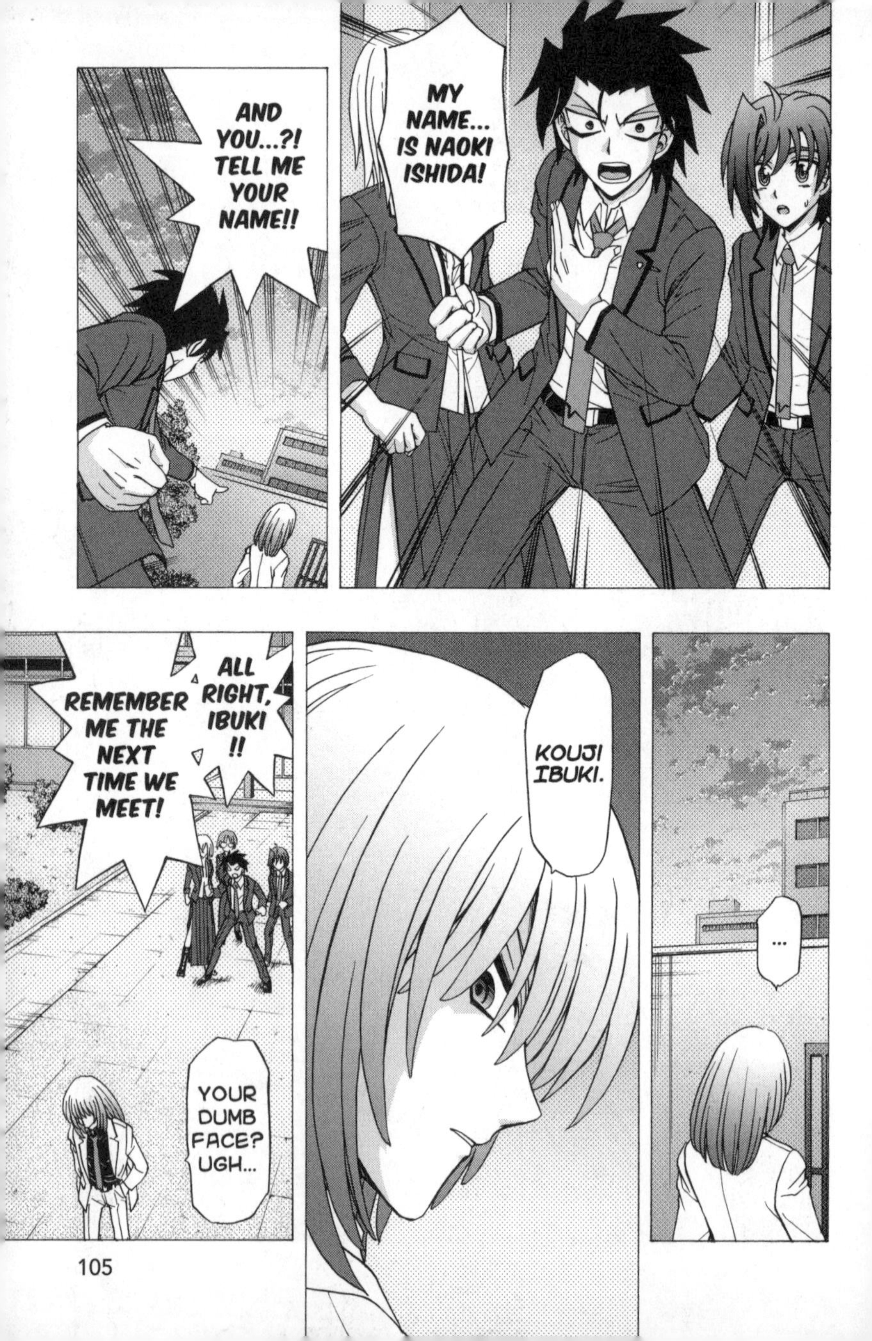
MY NAME... IS NAOKI ISHIDA!
AND YOU...?! TELL ME YOUR NAME!!
...
KOUJI IBUKI.
ALL RIGHT, IBUKI !!
REMEMBER ME THE NEXT TIME WE MEET!
YOUR DUMB FACE? UGH...

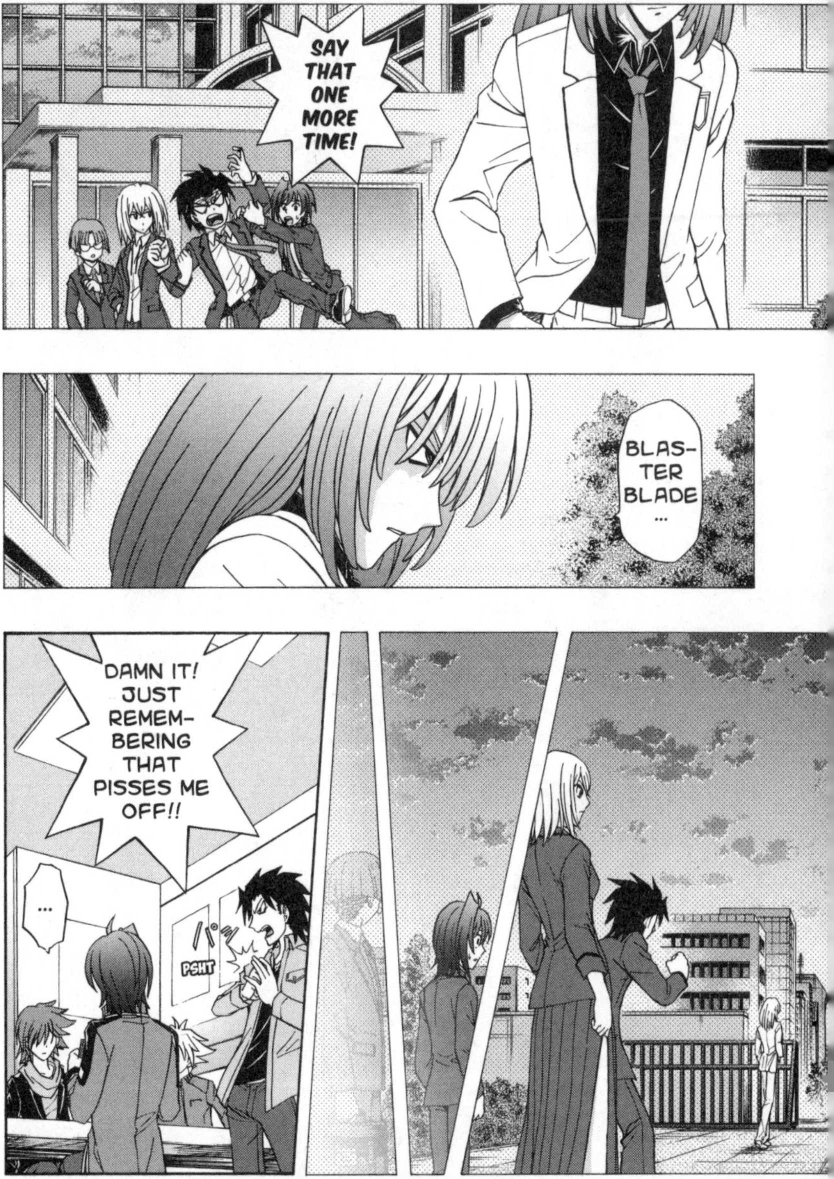

SAY THAT ONE MORE TIME!
BLASTER BLADE ...
DAMN IT! JUST REMEMBERING THAT PISSES ME OFF!!
PSHT
...

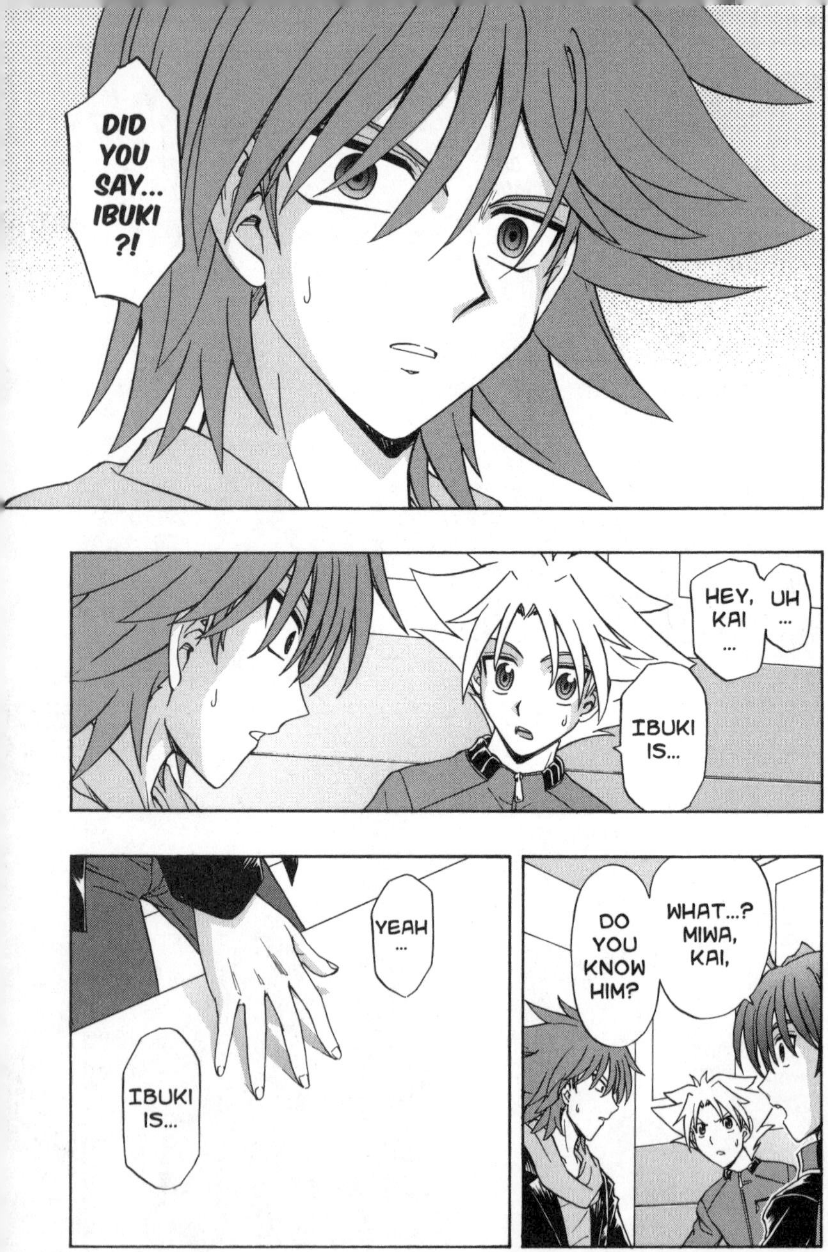
DID YOU SAY... IBUKI ?!
UH ...
HEY, KAI ...
IBUKI IS...
WHAT...? MIWA, KAI,
DO YOU KNOW HIM?
YEAH ...
IBUKI IS...

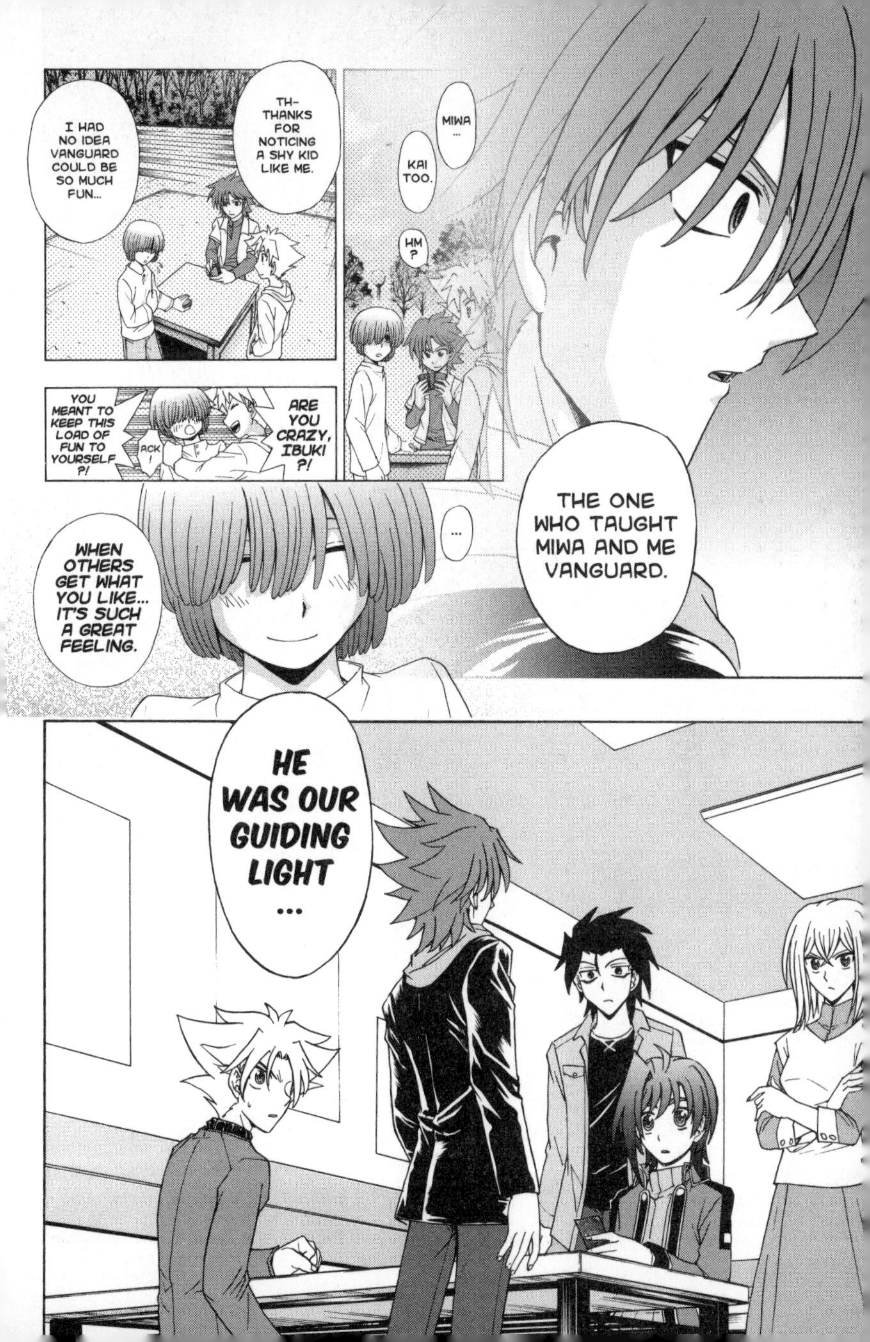
MIWA ...
KAI TOO.
HM ?
THE ONE WHO TAUGHT MIWA AND ME VANGUARD.
TH-THANKS FOR NOTICING A SHY KID LIKE ME.
I HAD NO IDEA VANGUARD COULD BE SO MUCH FUN...
ARE YOU CRAZY, IBUKI ?!
ACK !
YOU MEANT TO KEEP THIS LOAD OF FUN TO YOURSELF ?!
...
WHEN OTHERS GET WHAT YOU LIKE... IT'S SUCH A GREAT FEELING.
HE WAS OUR GUIDING LIGHT ...

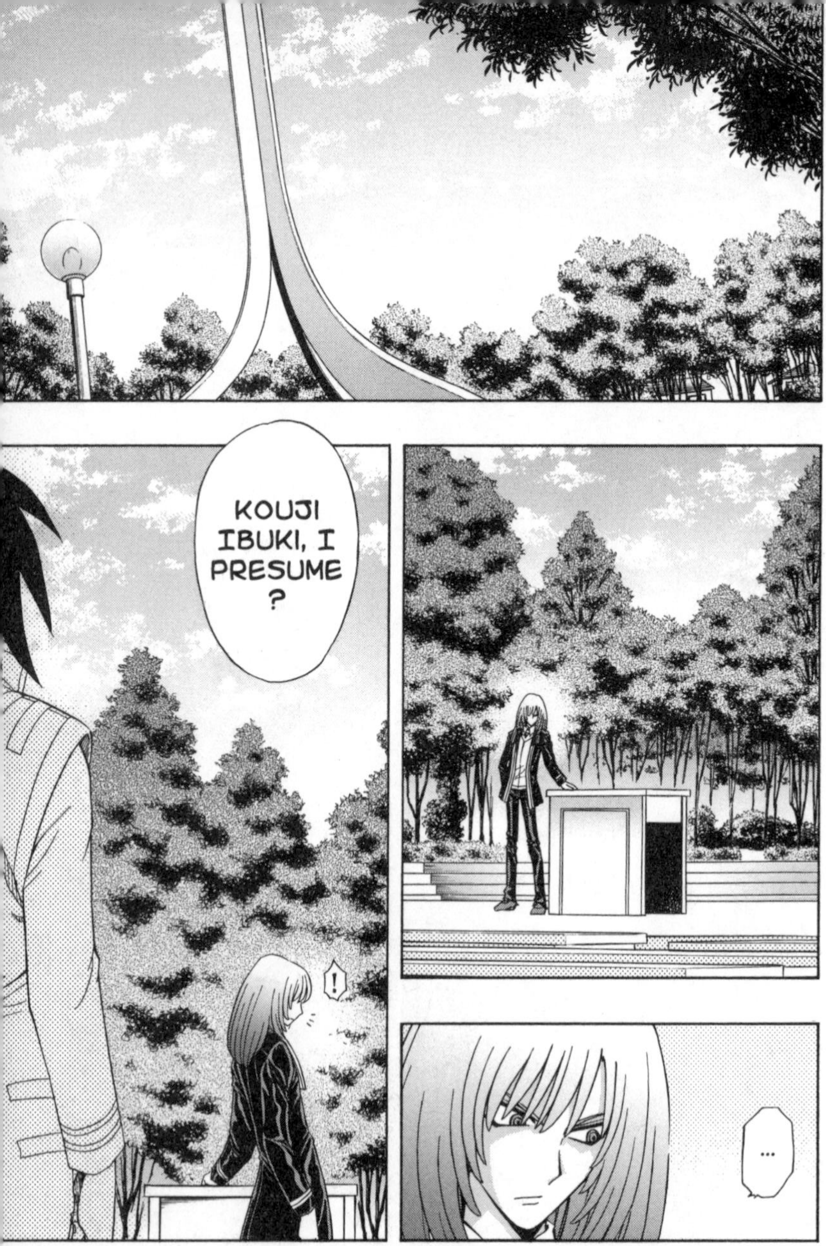
...
KOUJI IBUKI, I PRESUME?
!

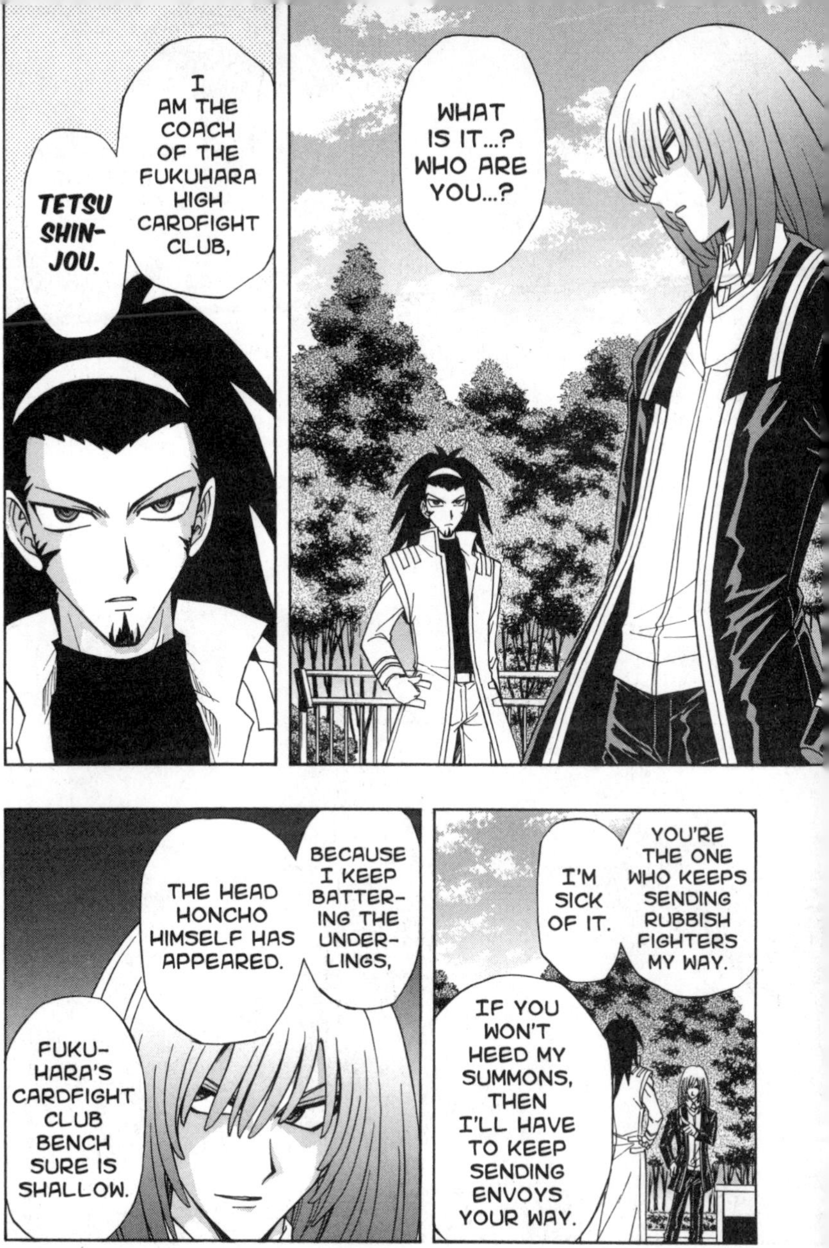
WHAT IS IT...? WHO ARE YOU...?
I AM THE COACH OF THE FUKUHARA HIGH CARDFIGHT CLUB,
TETSU SHIN-JOU.
YOU'RE THE ONE WHO KEEPS SENDING RUBBISH FIGHTERS MY WAY.
I'M SICK OF IT.
IF YOU WON'T HEED MY SUMMONS, THEN I'LL HAVE TO KEEP SENDING ENVOYS YOUR WAY.
BECAUSE I KEEP BATTER-ING THE UNDER-LINGS,
THE HEAD HONCHO HIMSELF HAS APPEARED.
FUKU-HARA'S CARDFIGHT CLUB BENCH SURE IS SHALLOW.

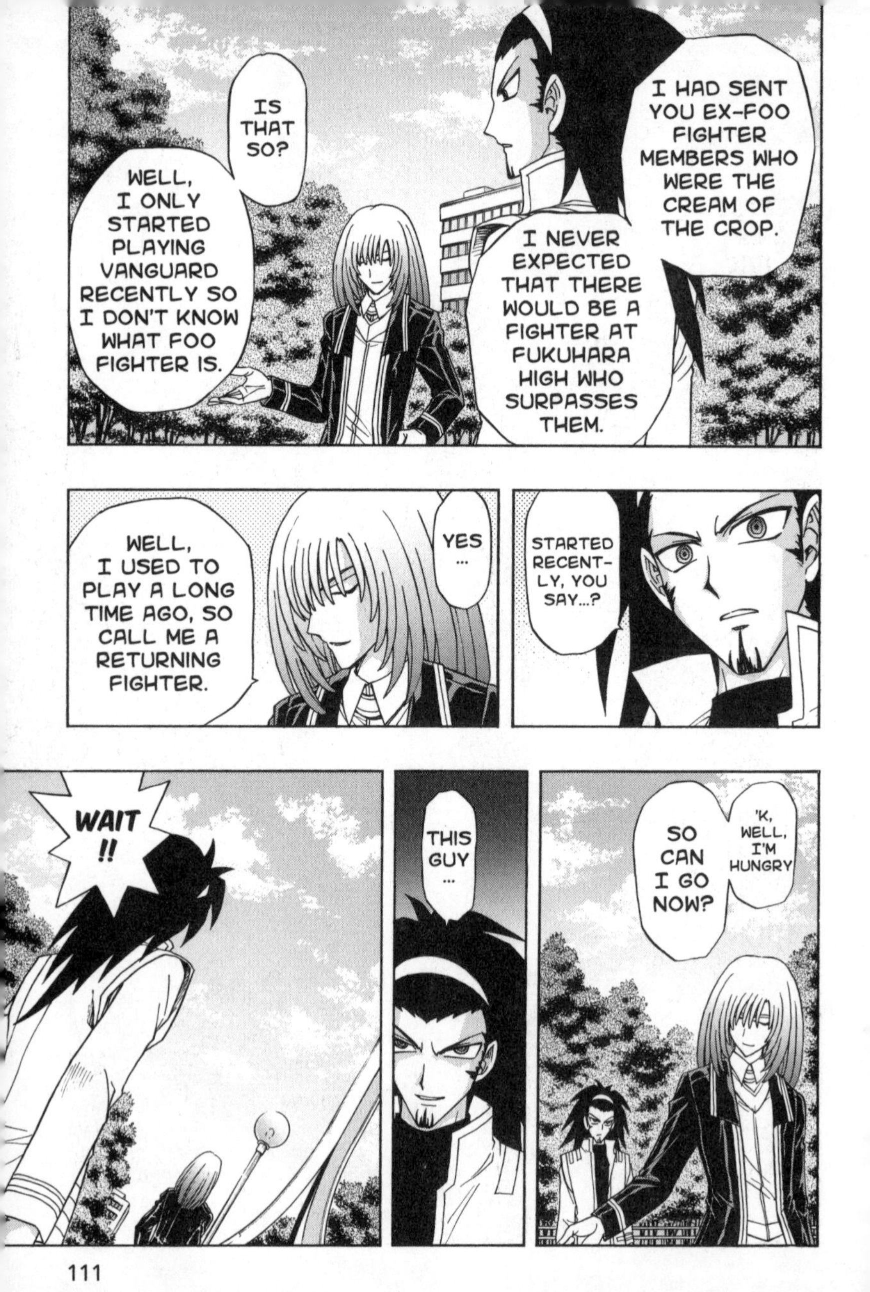
I HAD SENT YOU EX-FOO FIGHTER MEMBERS WHO WERE THE CREAM OF THE CROP.
I NEVER EXPECTED THAT THERE WOULD BE A FIGHTER AT FUKUHARA HIGH WHO SURPASSES THEM.
IS THAT SO?
WELL, I ONLY STARTED PLAYING VANGUARD RECENTLY SO I DON'T KNOW WHAT FOO FIGHTER IS.
STARTED RECENT-LY, YOU SAY...?
YES ...
WELL, I USED TO PLAY A LONG TIME AGO, SO CALL ME A RETURNING FIGHTER.
'K, WELL, I'M HUNGRY
SO CAN I GO NOW?
THIS GUY ...
WAIT !!

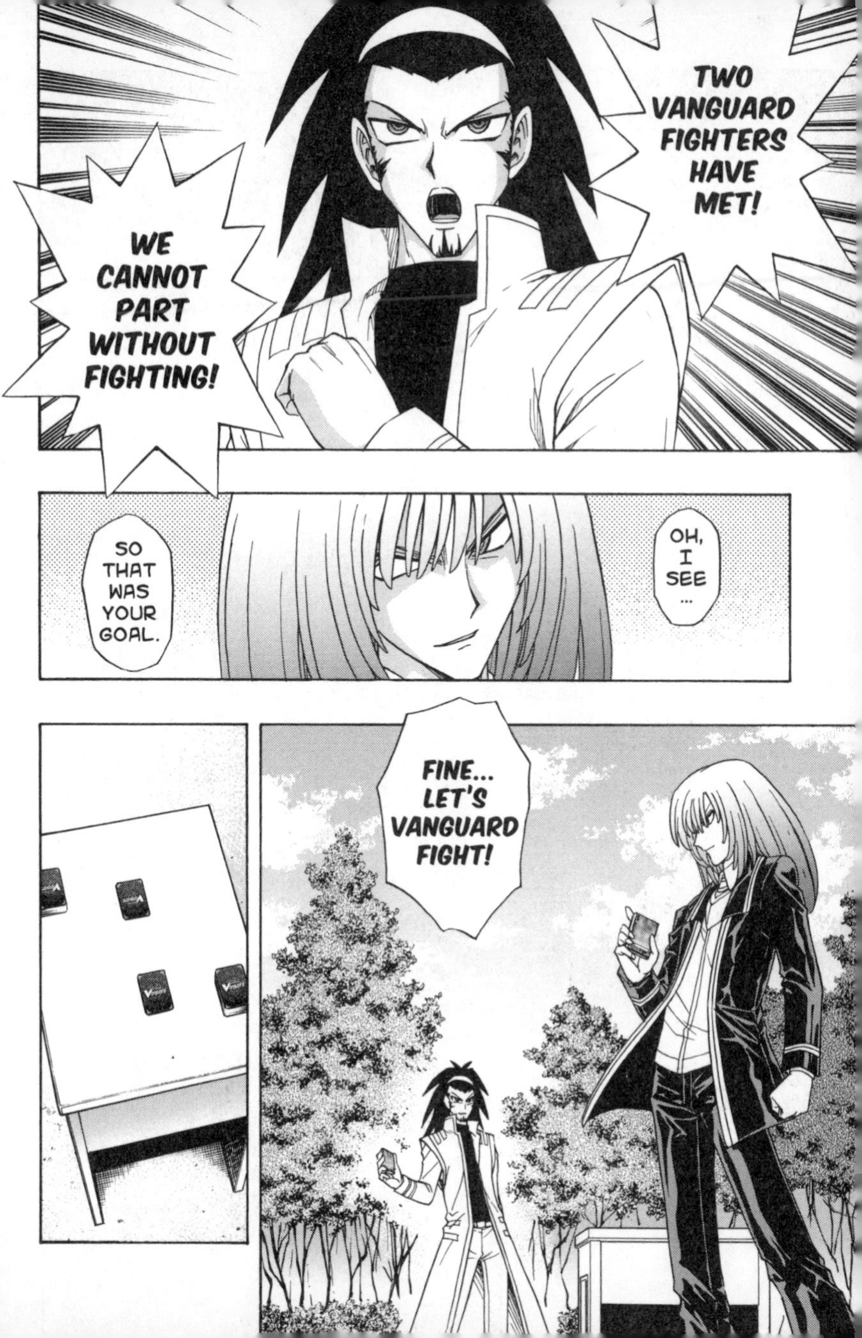
TWO VANGUARD FIGHTERS HAVE MET!
WE CANNOT PART WITHOUT FIGHTING!
OH, I SEE...
SO THAT WAS YOUR GOAL.
FINE... LET'S VANGUARD FIGHT!

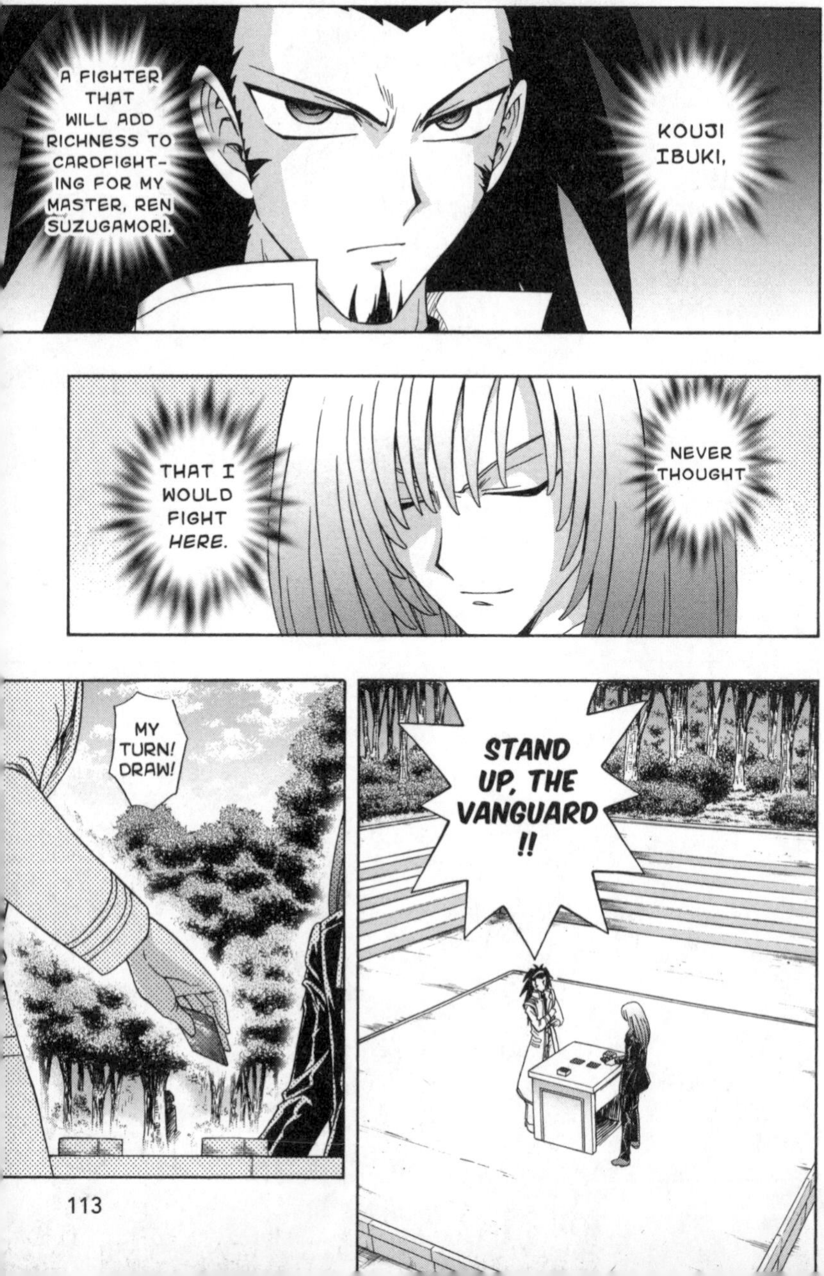
KOUJI IBUKI,
A FIGHTER THAT WILL ADD RICHNESS TO CARDFIGHTING FOR MY MASTER, REN SUZUGAMORI.
NEVER THOUGHT
THAT I WOULD FIGHT HERE.
STAND UP, THE VANGUARD !!
MY TURN! DRAW!

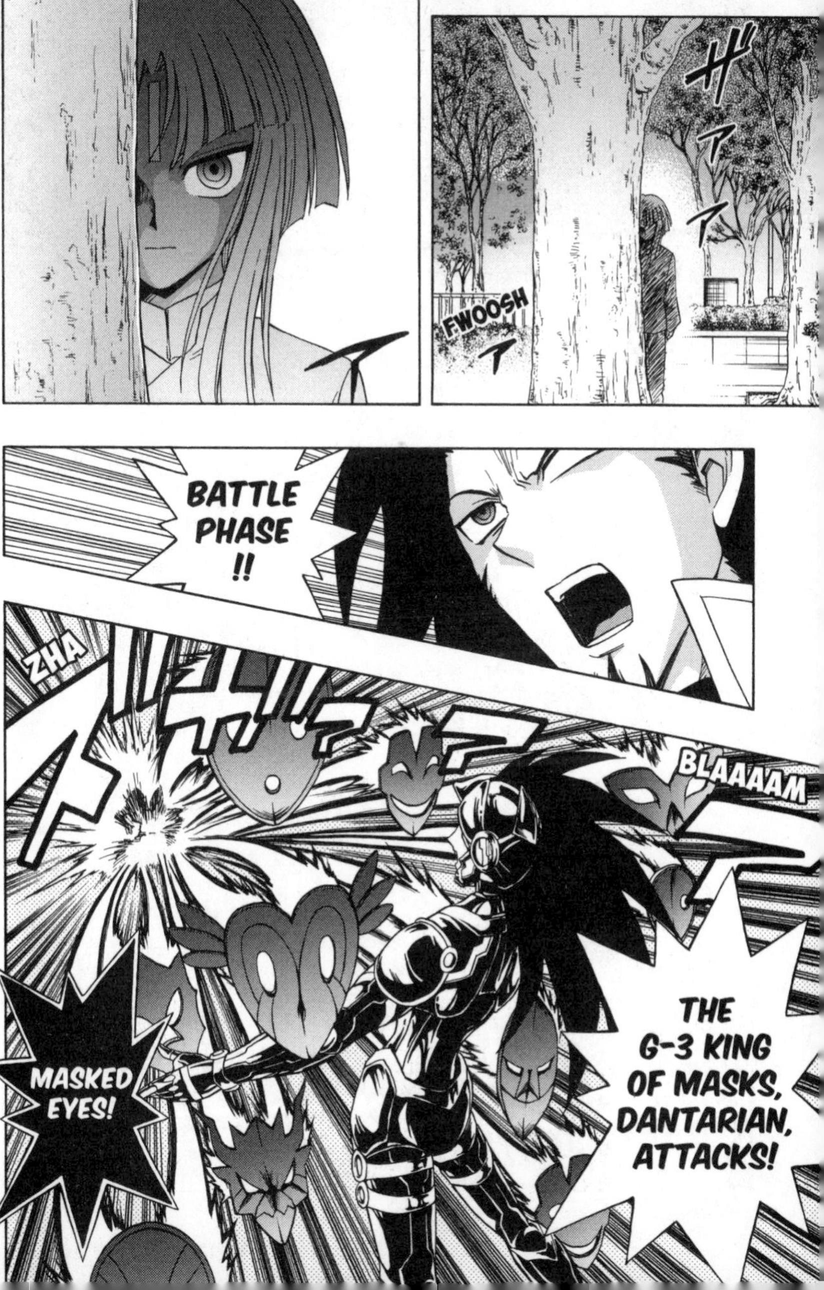
FWOOSH
BATTLE PHASE !!
ZHA
BLAAAAM
THE G-3 KING OF MASKS, DANTARIAN, ATTACKS!
MASKED EYES!

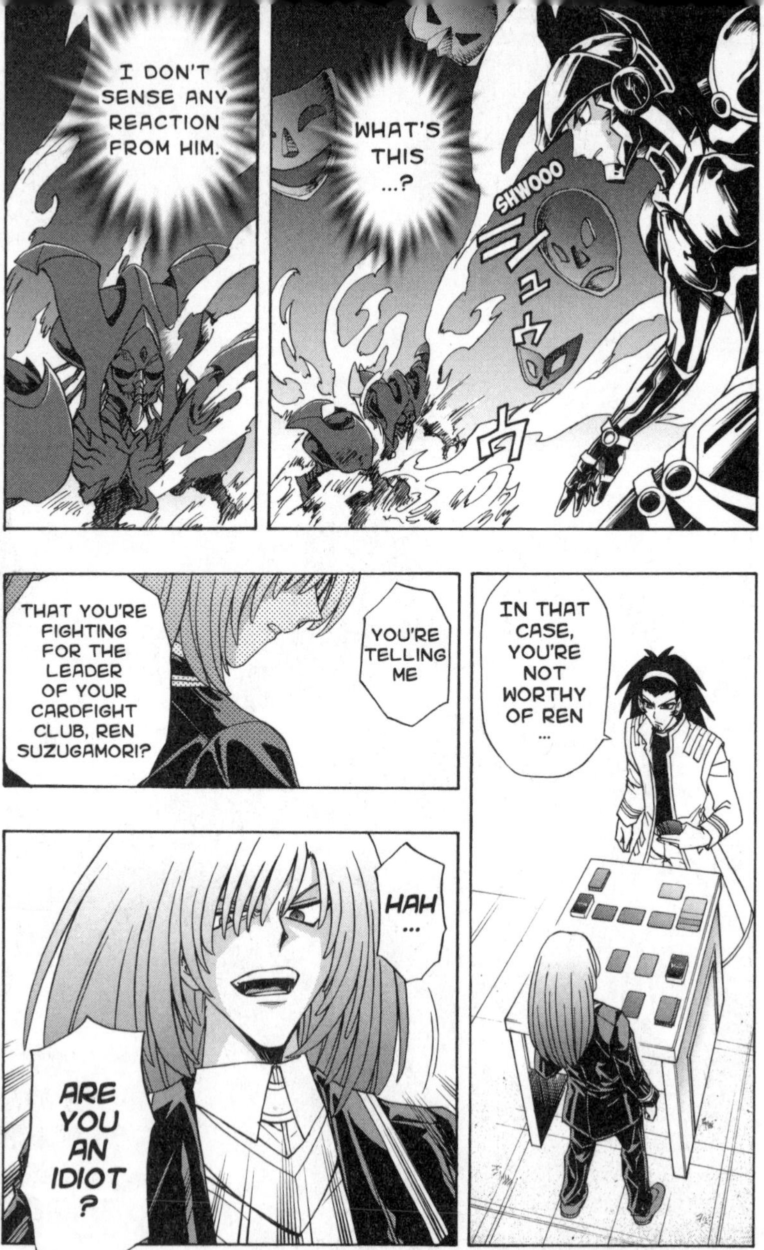
WHAT'S THIS ...?
SHWOOO
I DON'T SENSE ANY REACTION FROM HIM.
IN THAT CASE, YOU'RE NOT WORTHY OF REN ...
YOU'RE TELLING ME
THAT YOU'RE FIGHTING FOR THE LEADER OF YOUR CARDFIGHT CLUB, REN SUZUGAMORI?
HAH ...
ARE YOU AN IDIOT ?

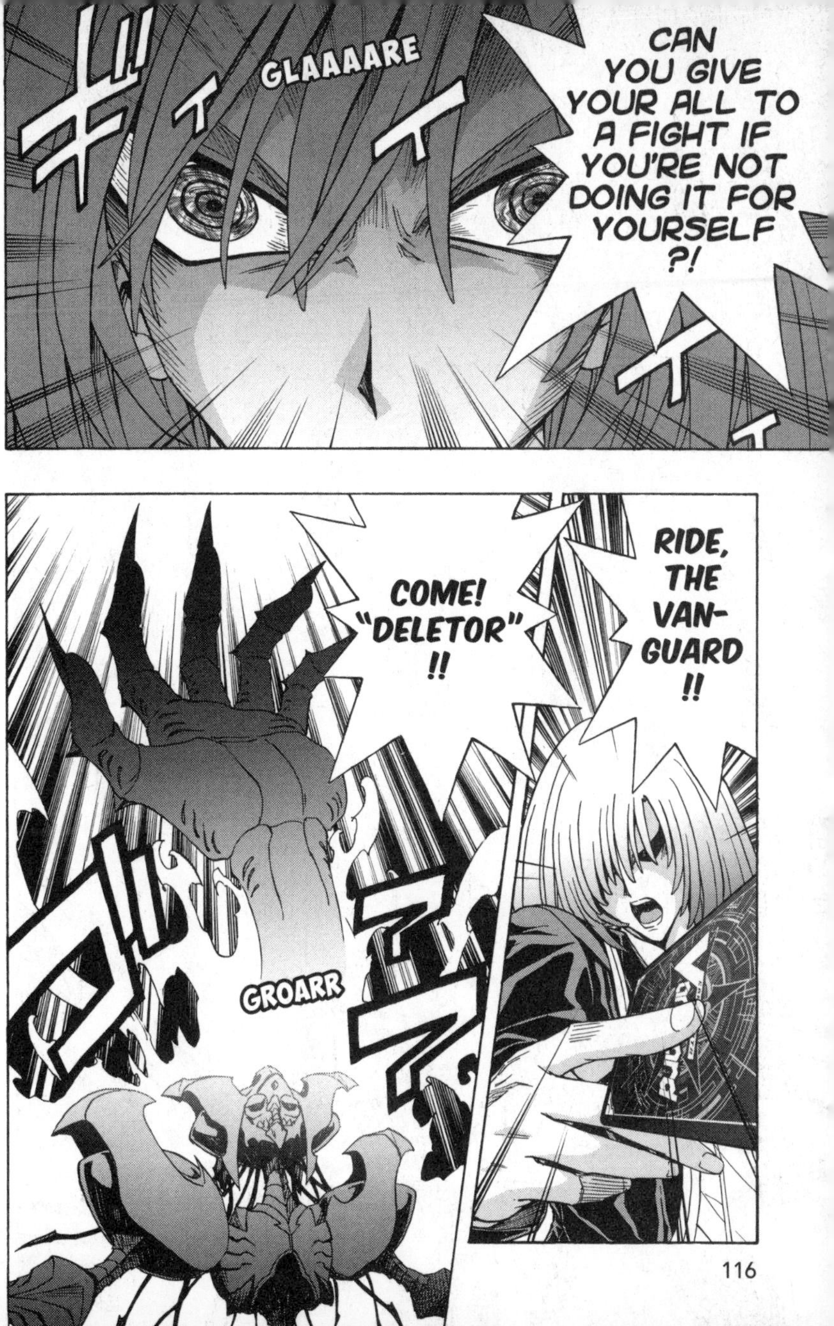
CAN YOU GIVE YOUR ALL TO A FIGHT IF YOU'RE NOT DOING IT FOR YOURSELF ?!
GLAAAARE
RIDE, THE VAN-GUARD !!
COME! "DELETOR" !!
GROARR

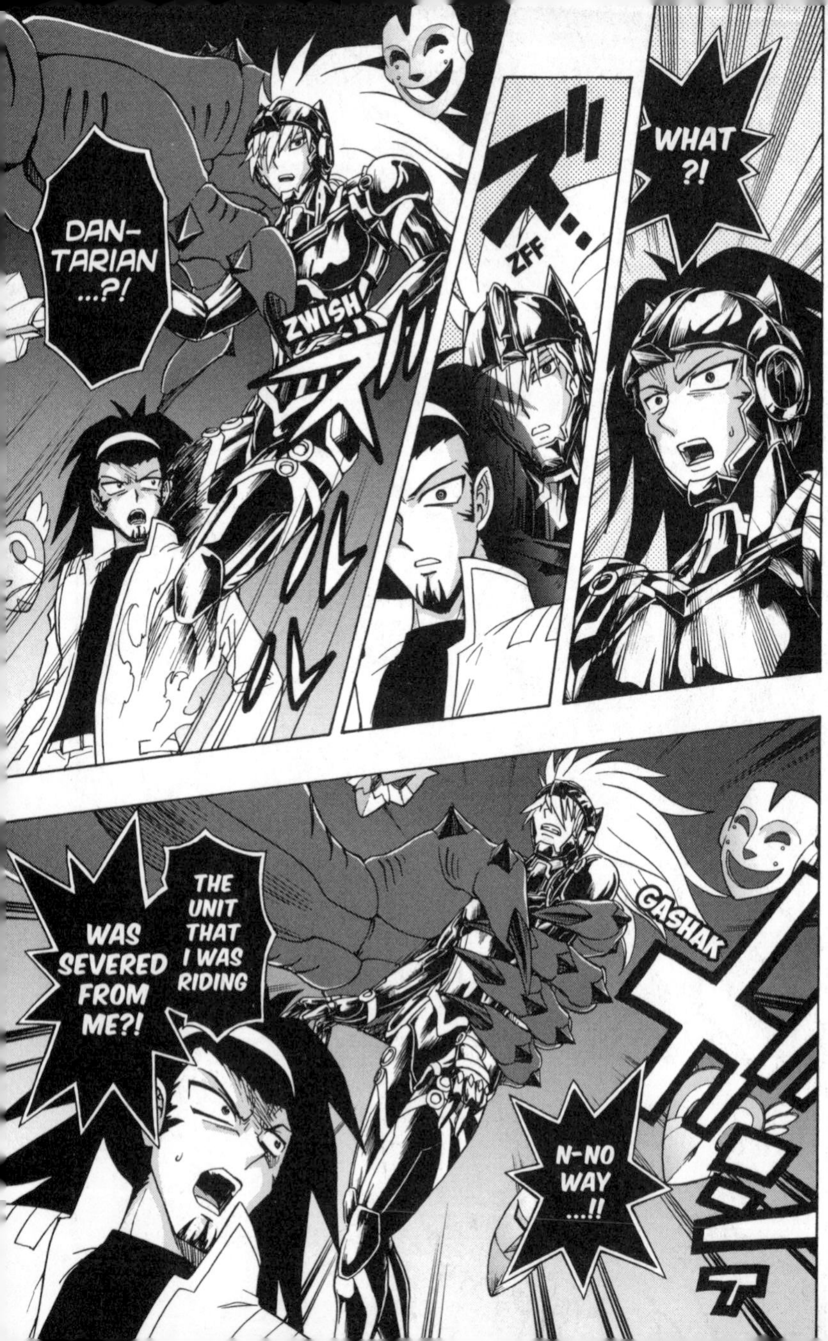
WHAT ?!
ZFF
DAN-TARIAN ...?!
ZWISH
GASHAK
N-NO WAY ...!!
THE UNIT THAT I WAS RIDING
WAS SEVERED FROM ME?!

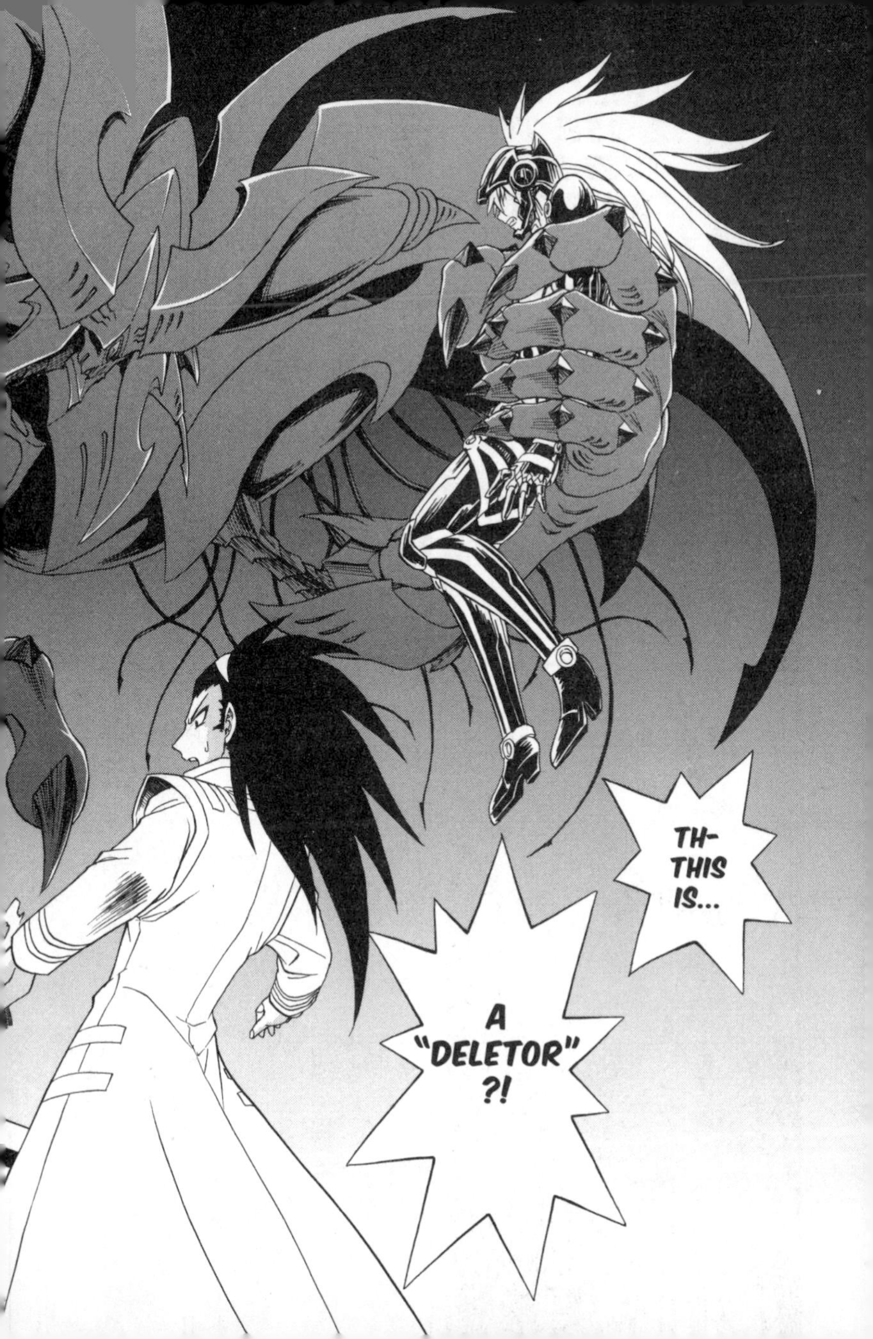
TH- THIS IS...
A "DELETOR" ?!

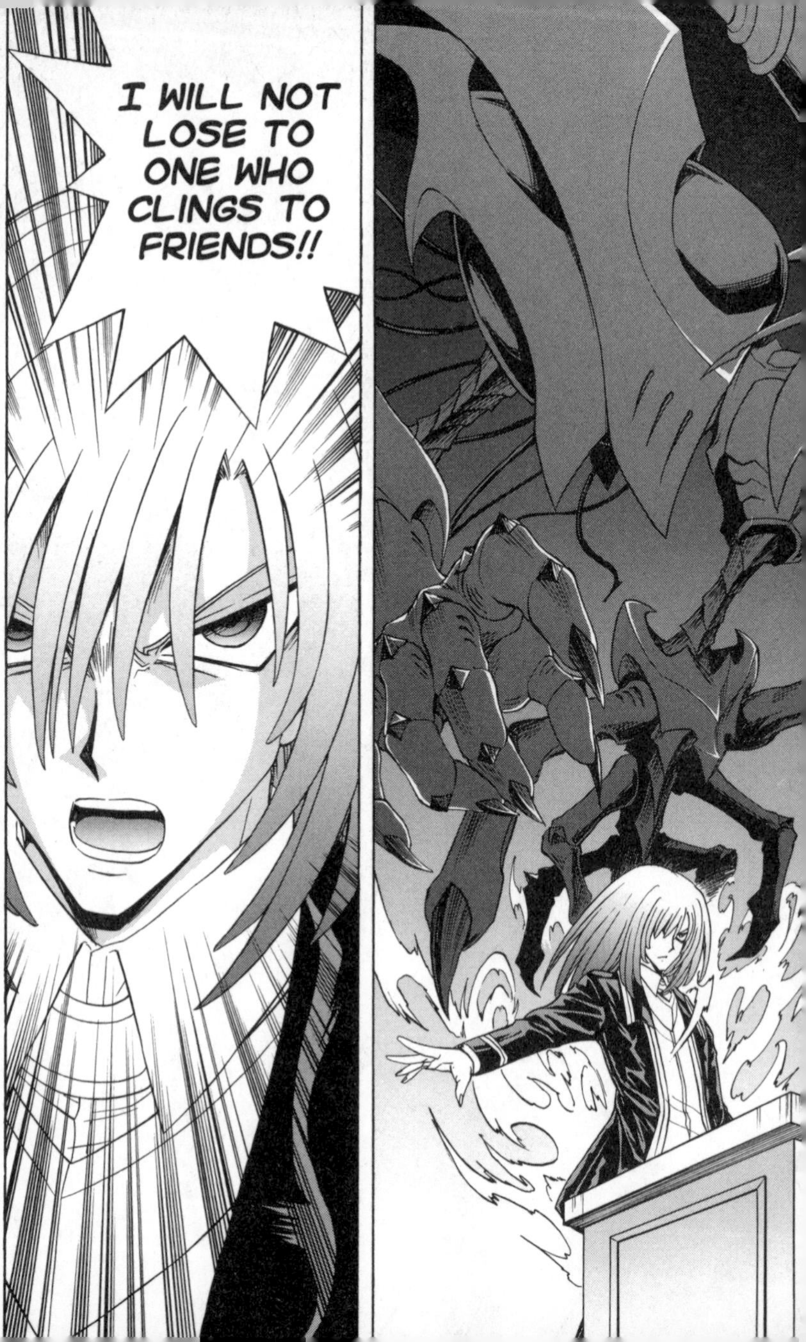
I WILL NOT LOSE TO ONE WHO CLINGS TO FRIENDS!!

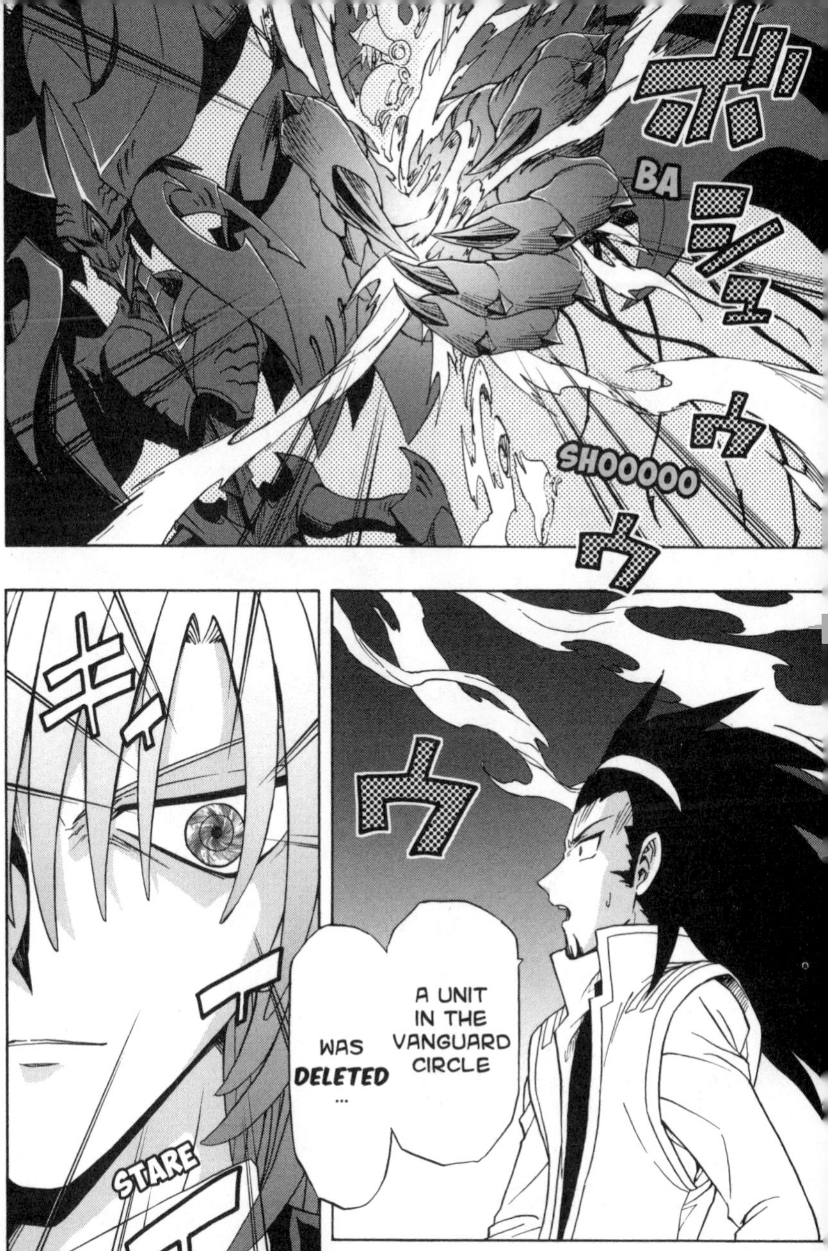
BA
SHOOOOO
A UNIT IN THE VANGUARD CIRCLE WAS DELETED...
STARE

CARDFIGHT!!
Vanguard

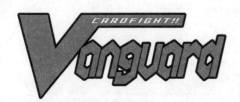

BONUS! CARDFIGHT!! Vanguard

## VANGUARD LAB
## RIDE THE ORIGINAL DESIGNS!

**Blaster Blade**
**#035**

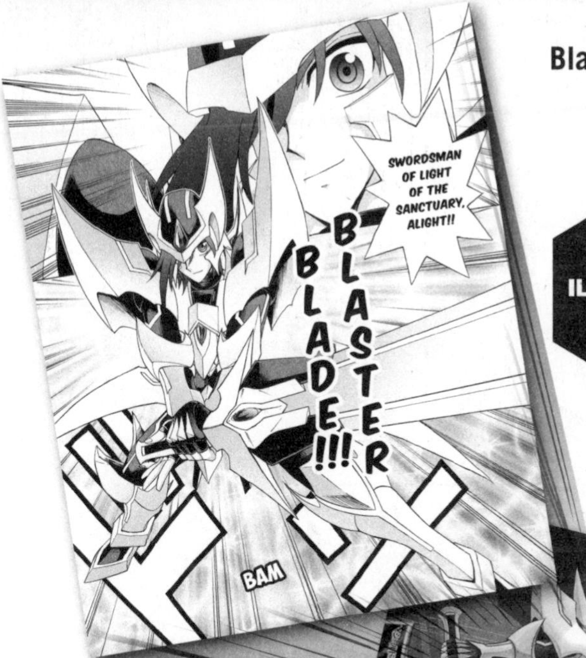
SWORDSMAN OF LIGHT OF THE SANCTUARY, ALIGHT!!
BLASTER BLADE!!!
BAM

COMIC ILLUSTRATION

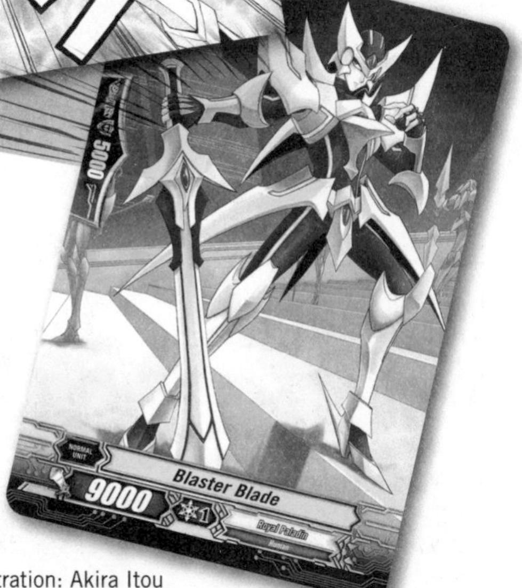
5000
NORMAL UNIT
Blaster Blade
9000
Royal Paladin

CARD ILLUSTRATION

Illustration: Akira Itou

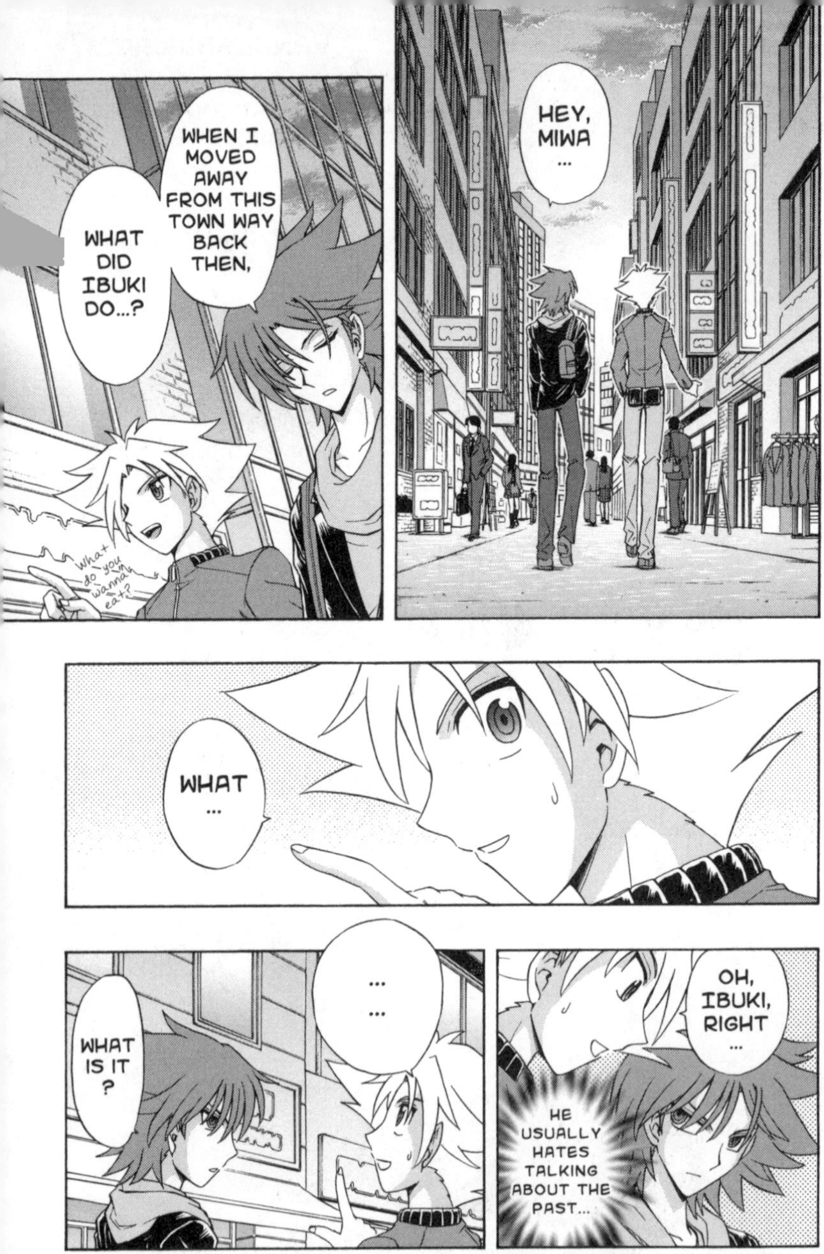
HEY, MIWA ...
WHEN I MOVED AWAY FROM THIS TOWN WAY BACK THEN,
WHAT DID IBUKI DO...?
what do you wanna eat?
WHAT ...
OH, IBUKI, RIGHT ...
HE USUALLY HATES TALKING ABOUT THE PAST...
... ...
WHAT IS IT ?

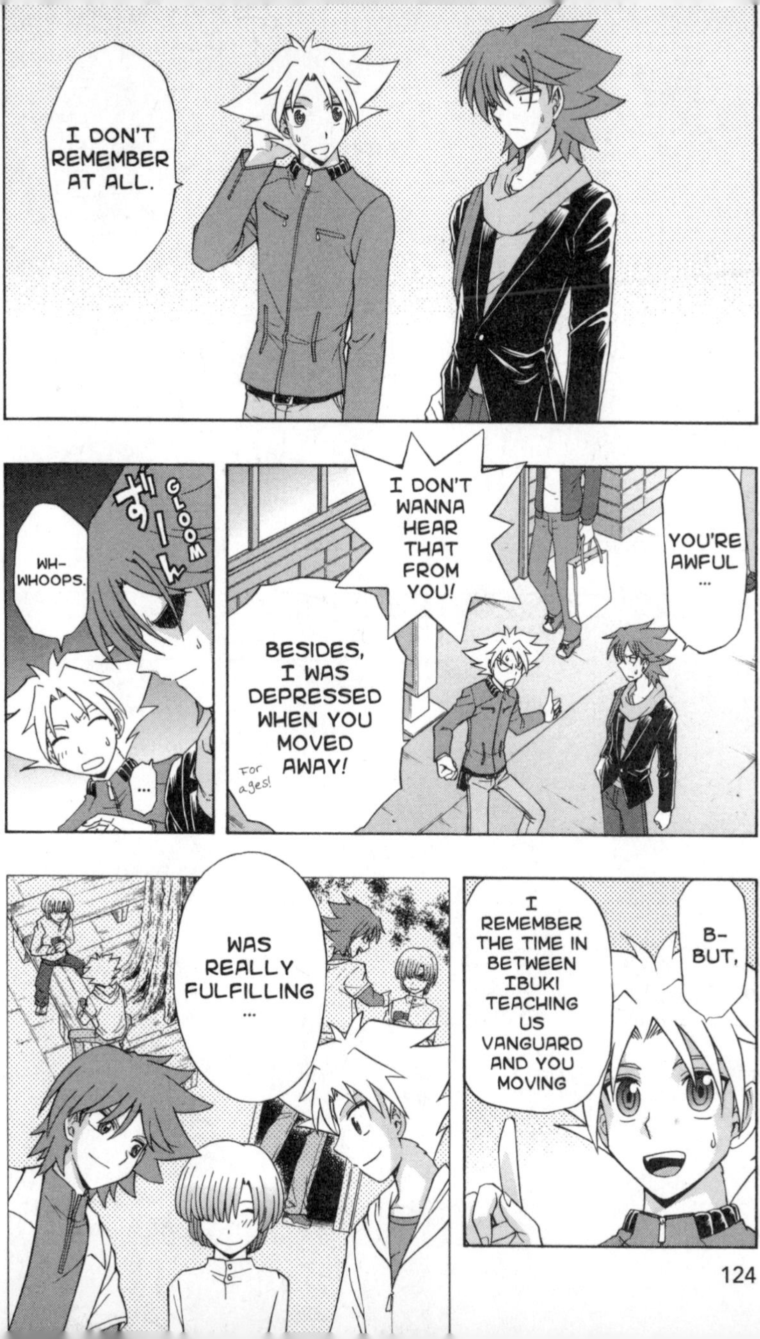
I DON'T REMEMBER AT ALL.
YOU'RE AWFUL ...
I DON'T WANNA HEAR THAT FROM YOU!
BESIDES, I WAS DEPRESSED WHEN YOU MOVED AWAY!
For ages!
ずーん
GLOOM
WH- WHOOPS.
...
B- BUT,
I REMEMBER THE TIME IN BETWEEN IBUKI TEACHING US VANGUARD AND YOU MOVING
WAS REALLY FULFILLING ...

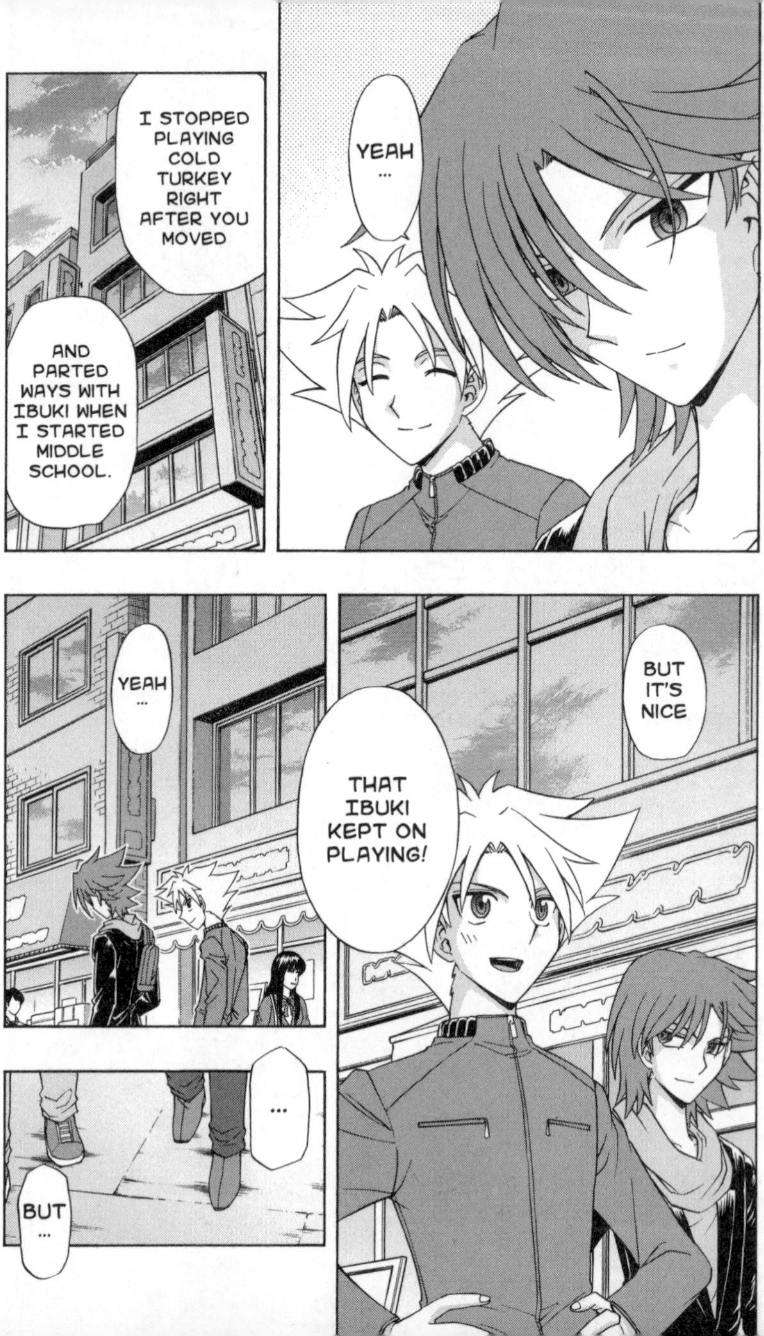
YEAH ...
I STOPPED PLAYING COLD TURKEY RIGHT AFTER YOU MOVED
AND PARTED WAYS WITH IBUKI WHEN I STARTED MIDDLE SCHOOL.
BUT IT'S NICE
THAT IBUKI KEPT ON PLAYING!
YEAH ...
...
BUT ...

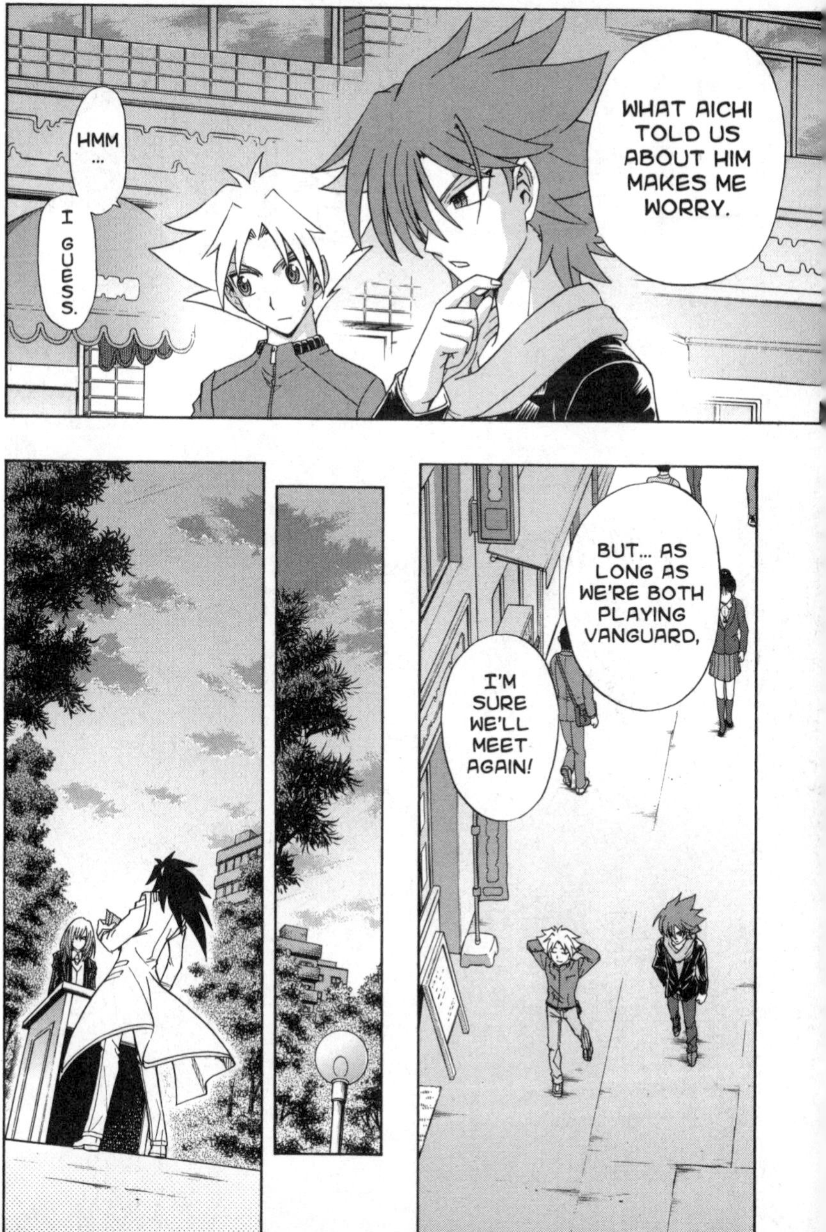
WHAT AICHI TOLD US ABOUT HIM MAKES ME WORRY.
HMM ...
I GUESS.
BUT... AS LONG AS WE'RE BOTH PLAYING VANGUARD,
I'M SURE WE'LL MEET AGAIN!

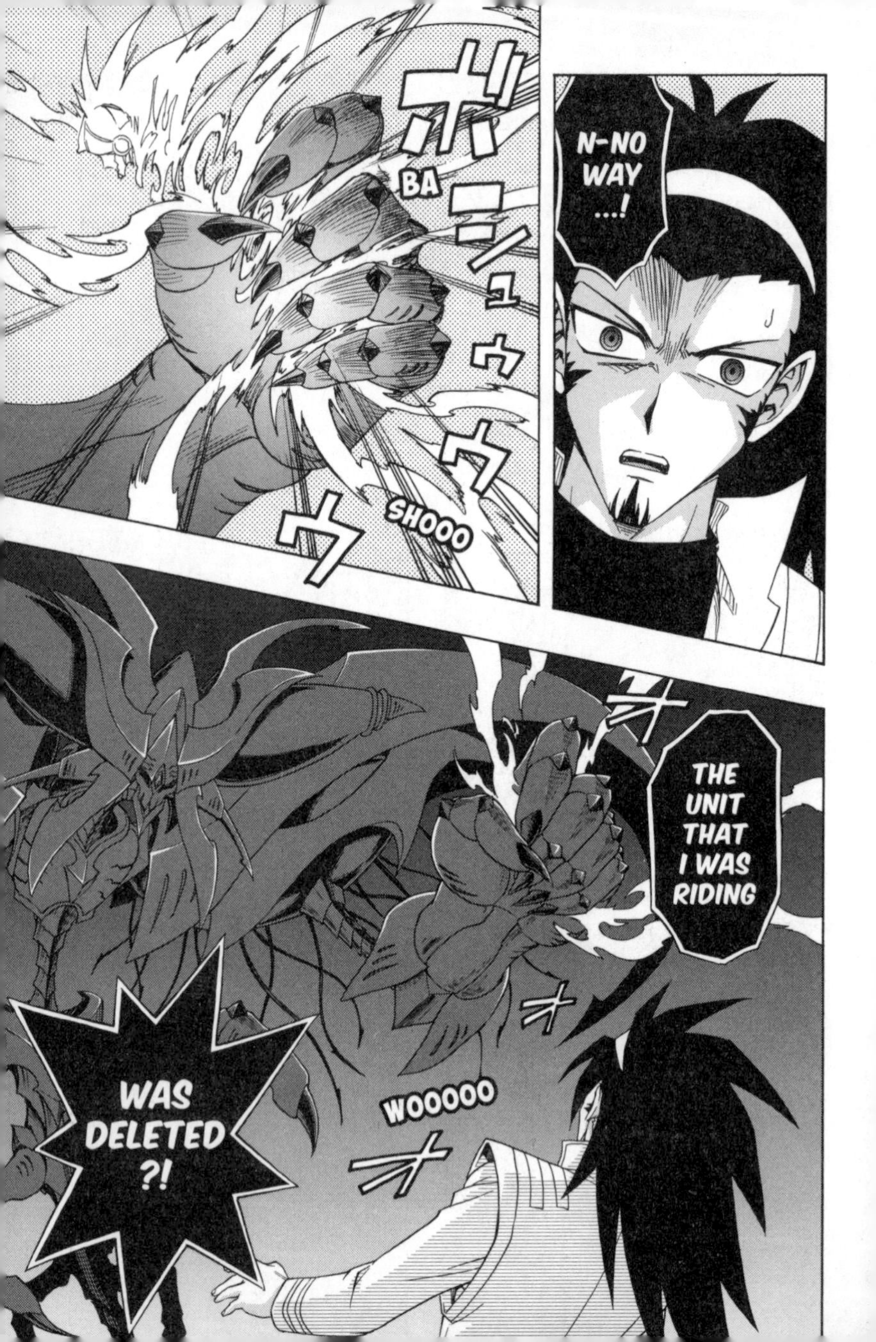
N-NO WAY ...!
BA
SHOOO
THE UNIT THAT I WAS RIDING
WOOOOO
WAS DELETED ?!

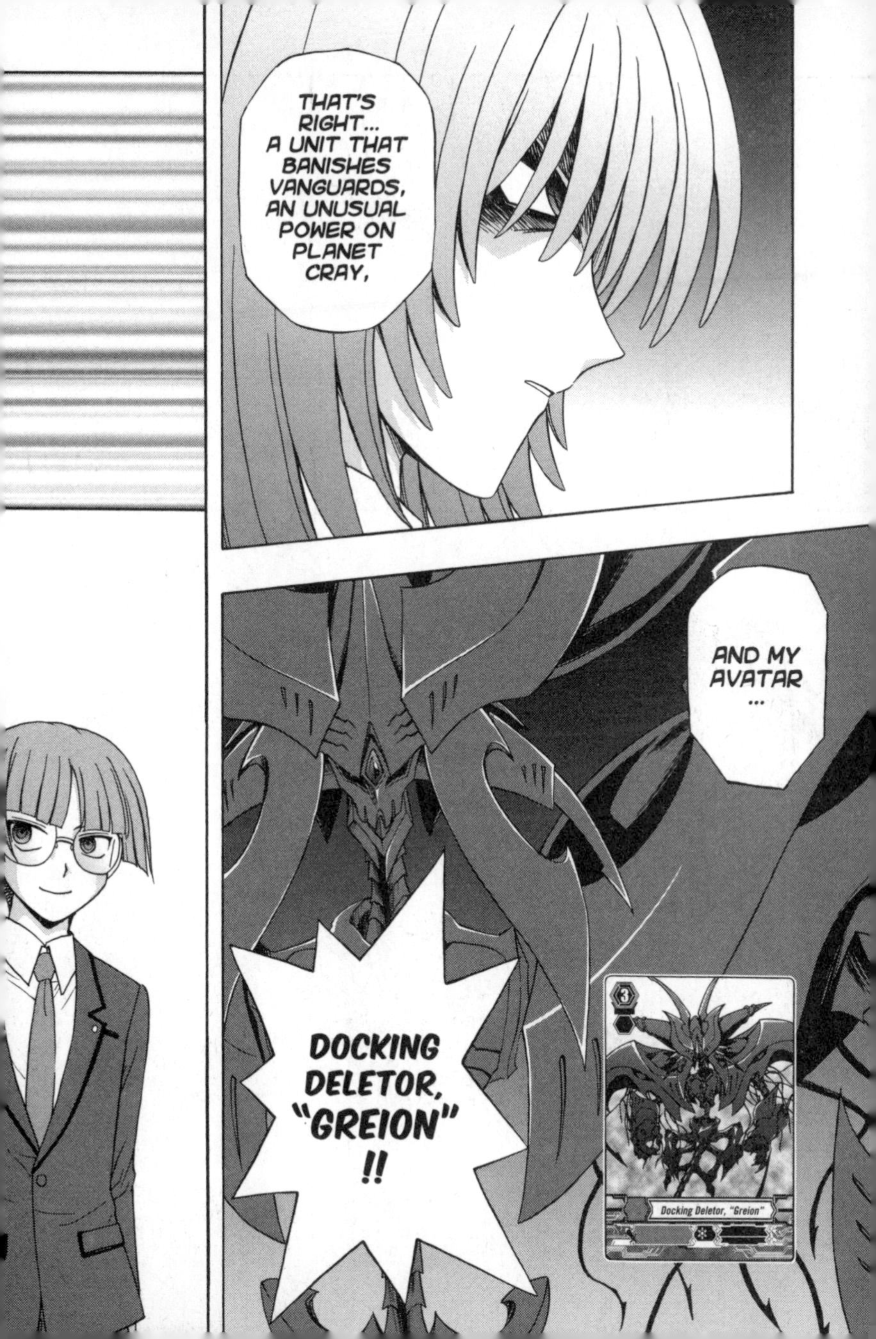
THAT'S RIGHT... A UNIT THAT BANISHES VANGUARDS, AN UNUSUAL POWER ON PLANET CRAY,
AND MY AVATAR ...
DOCKING DELETOR, "GREION" !!
3
Docking Deletor, "Greion"

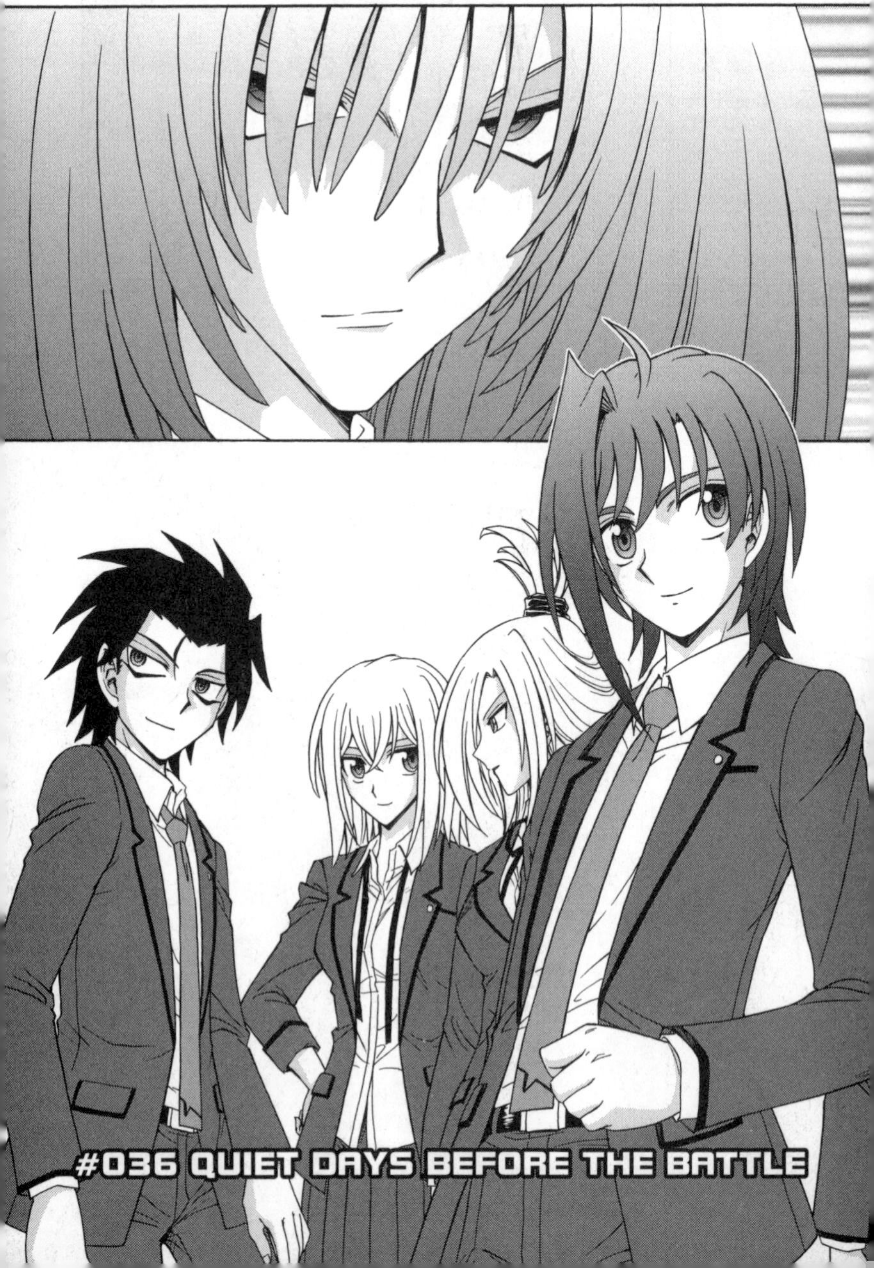
#036 QUIET DAYS BEFORE THE BATTLE

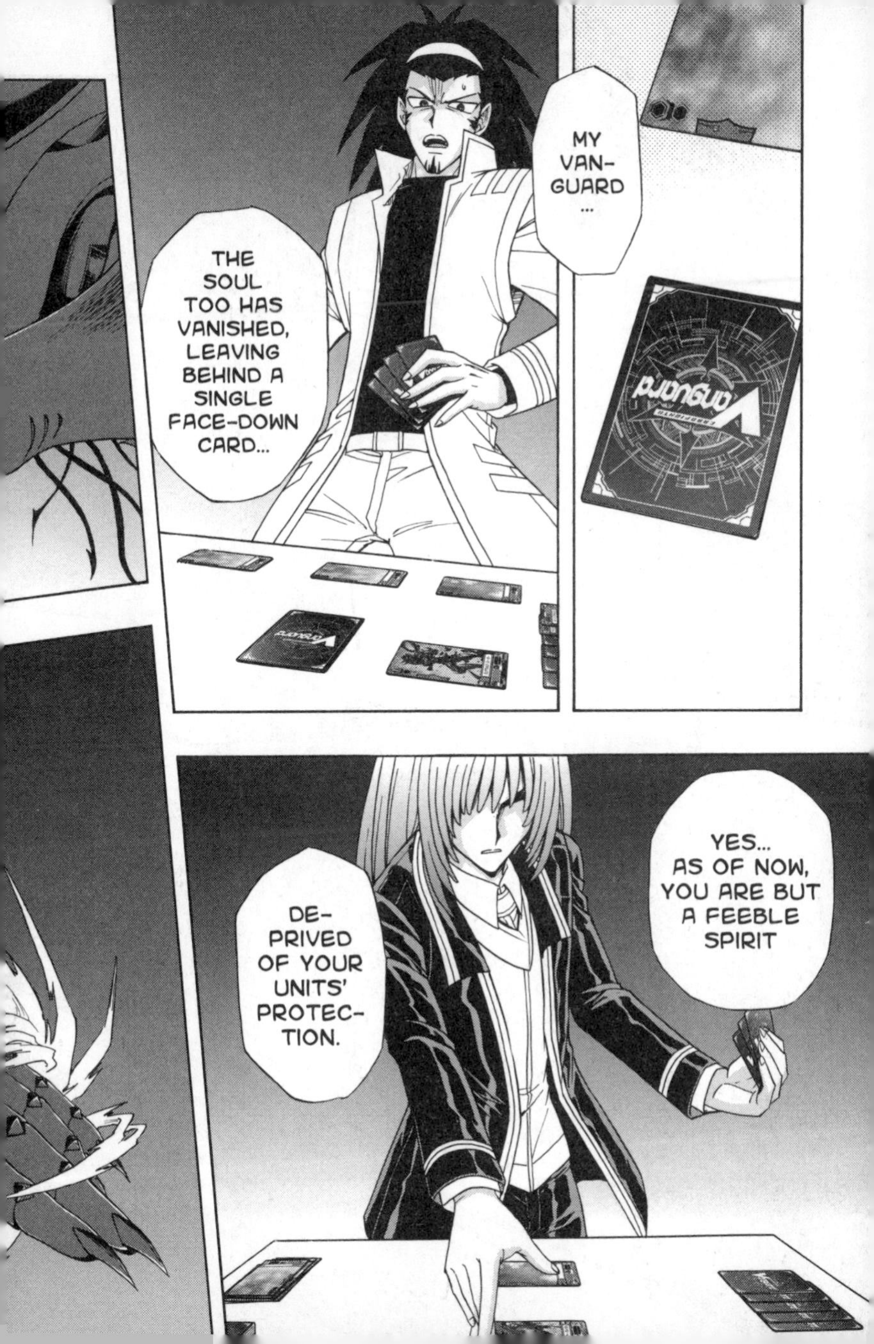
MY VAN-GUARD ...
THE SOUL TOO HAS VANISHED, LEAVING BEHIND A SINGLE FACE-DOWN CARD...
YES... AS OF NOW, YOU ARE BUT A FEEBLE SPIRIT
DE-PRIVED OF YOUR UNITS' PROTECTION.

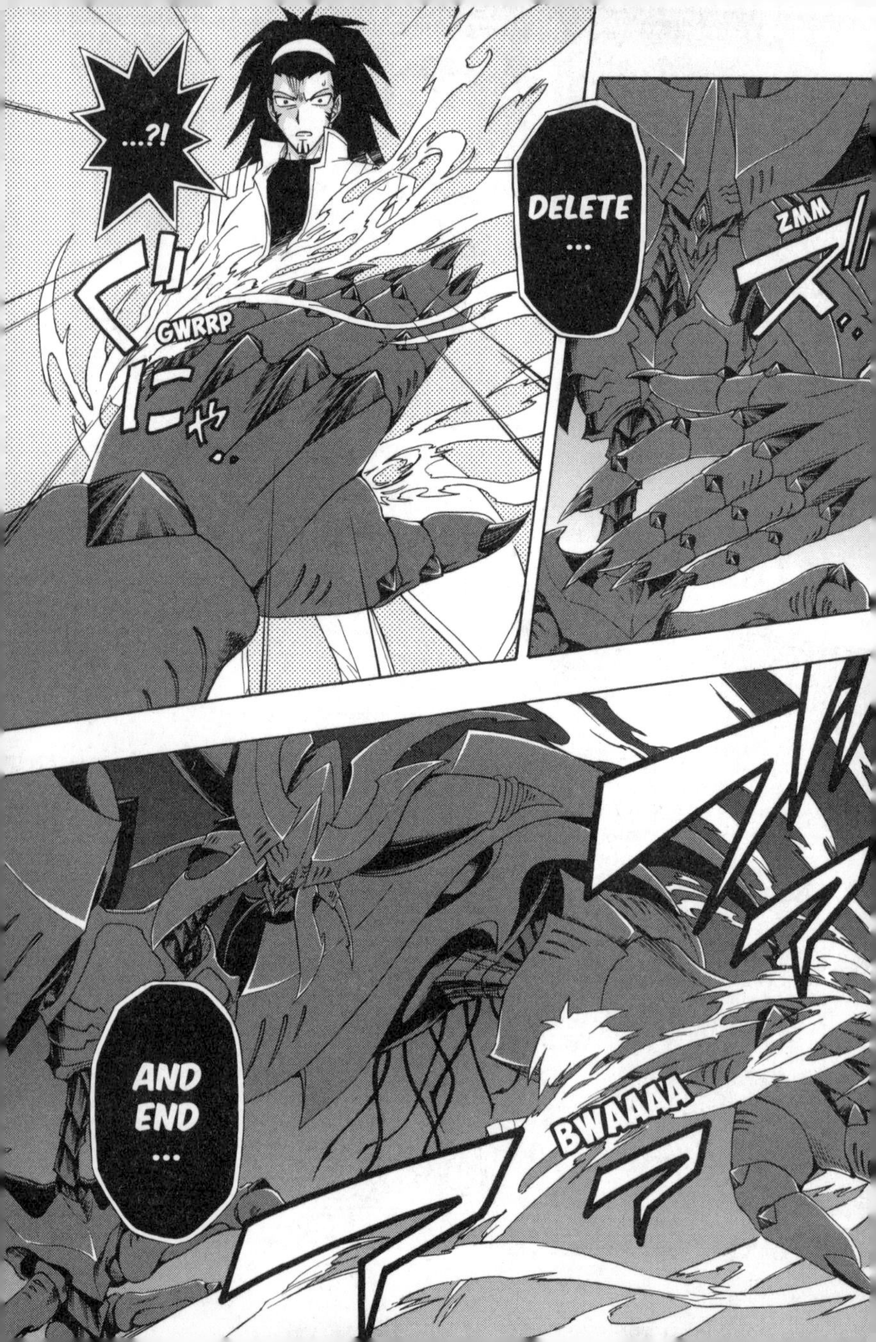
DELETE ...
ZMM
...?!
GWRRP
BWAAAA
AND END ...

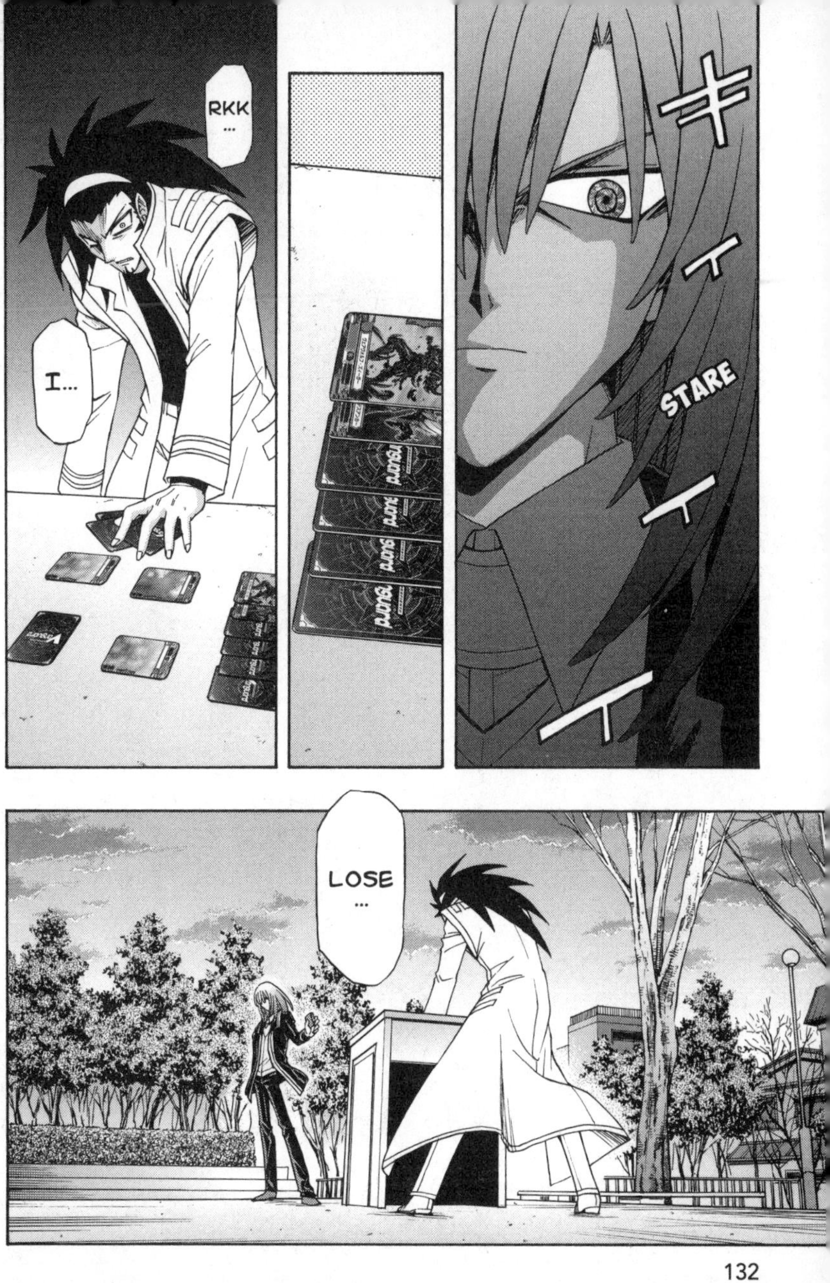

キイイイ
STARE
RKK ...
I...
LOSE ...

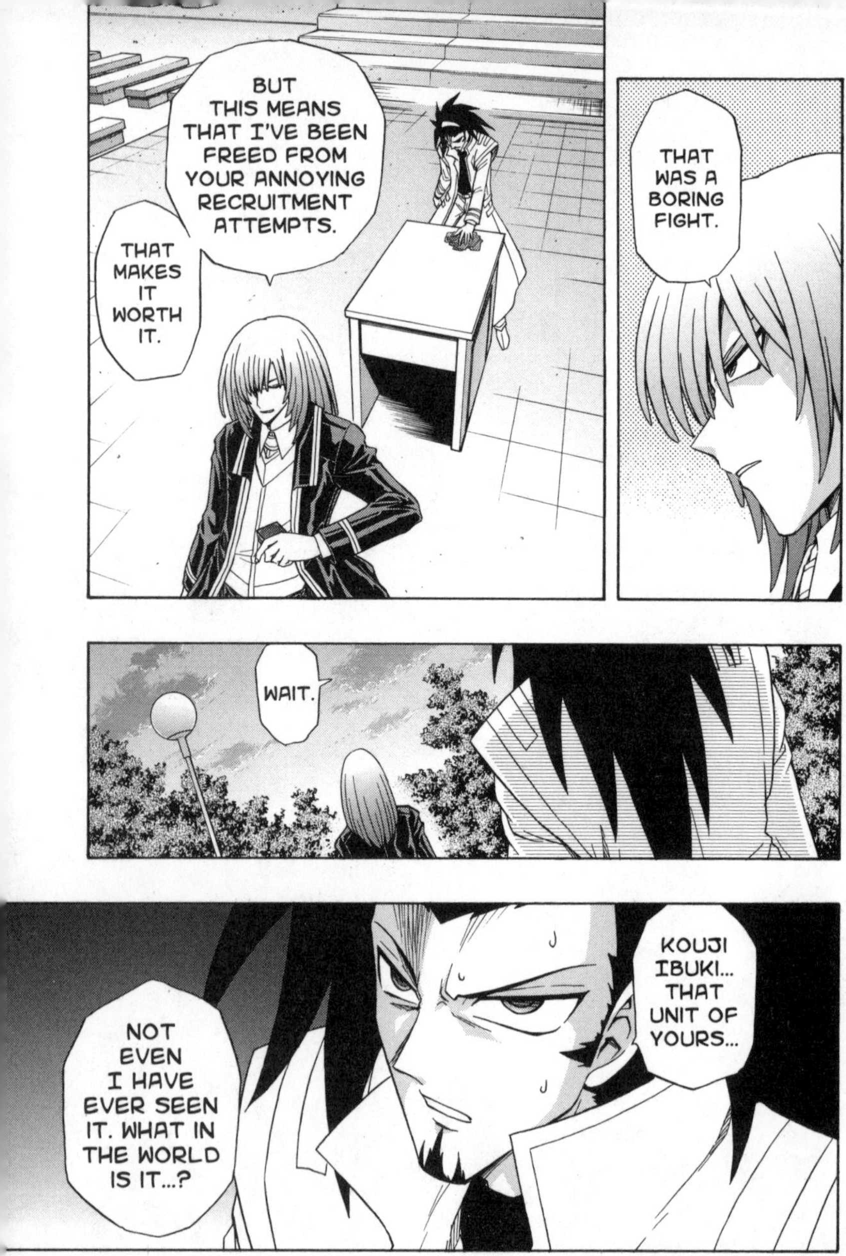
THAT WAS A BORING FIGHT.
BUT THIS MEANS THAT I'VE BEEN FREED FROM YOUR ANNOYING RECRUITMENT ATTEMPTS.
THAT MAKES IT WORTH IT.
WAIT.
KOUJI IBUKI... THAT UNIT OF YOURS...
NOT EVEN I HAVE EVER SEEN IT. WHAT IN THE WORLD IS IT...?

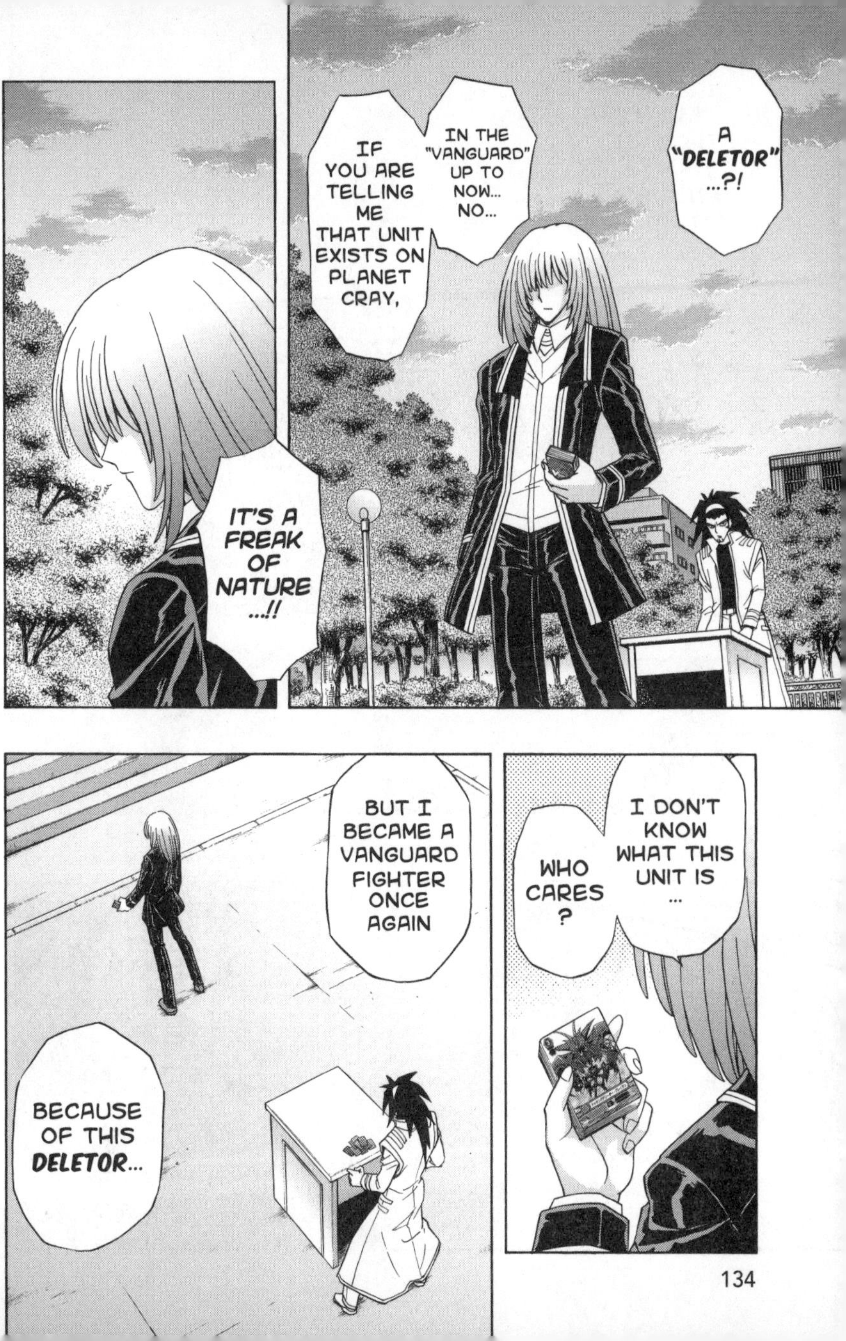
A "**DELETOR**" ...?!
IN THE "VANGUARD" UP TO NOW... NO...
IF YOU ARE TELLING ME THAT UNIT EXISTS ON PLANET CRAY,
IT'S A FREAK OF NATURE ...!!
I DON'T KNOW WHAT THIS UNIT IS ...
WHO CARES ?
BUT I BECAME A VANGUARD FIGHTER ONCE AGAIN
BECAUSE OF THIS **DELETOR**...

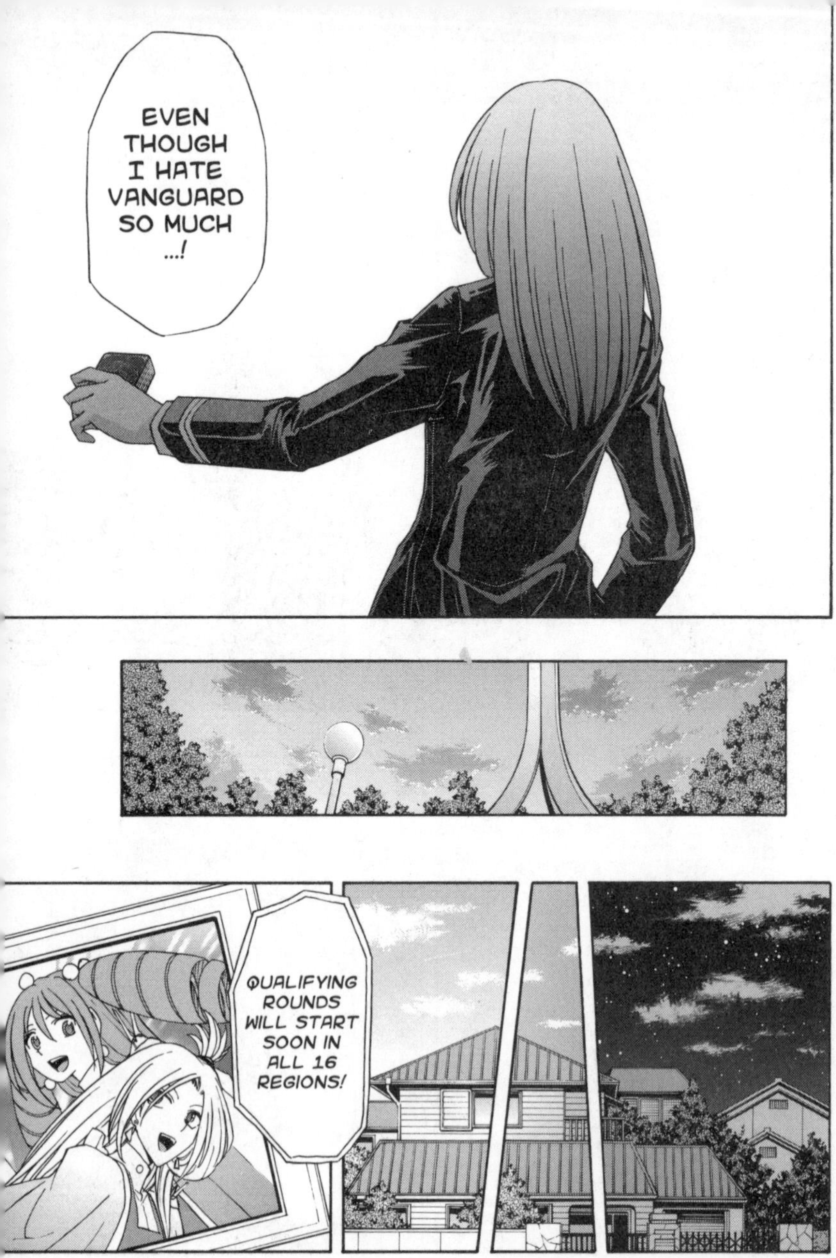
EVEN THOUGH I HATE VANGUARD SO MUCH ...!
QUALIFYING ROUNDS WILL START SOON IN ALL 16 REGIONS!

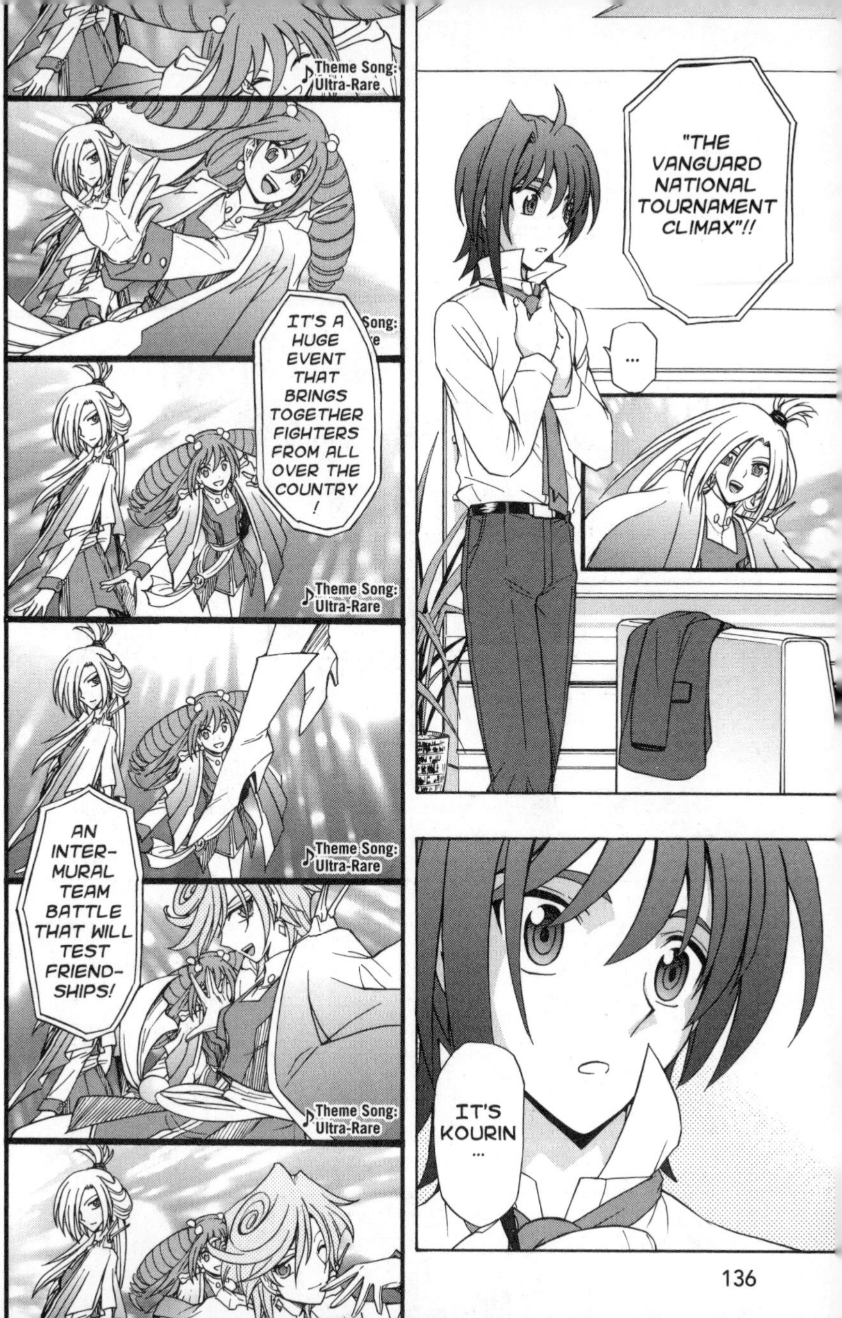
"THE VANGUARD NATIONAL TOURNAMENT CLIMAX"!!
...
IT'S KOURIN ...
♪Theme Song: Ultra-Rare
IT'S A HUGE EVENT THAT BRINGS TOGETHER FIGHTERS FROM ALL OVER THE COUNTRY!
♪Theme Song: Ultra-Rare
AN INTER-MURAL TEAM BATTLE THAT WILL TEST FRIEND-SHIPS!
♪Theme Song: Ultra-Rare
♪Theme Song: Ultra-Rare

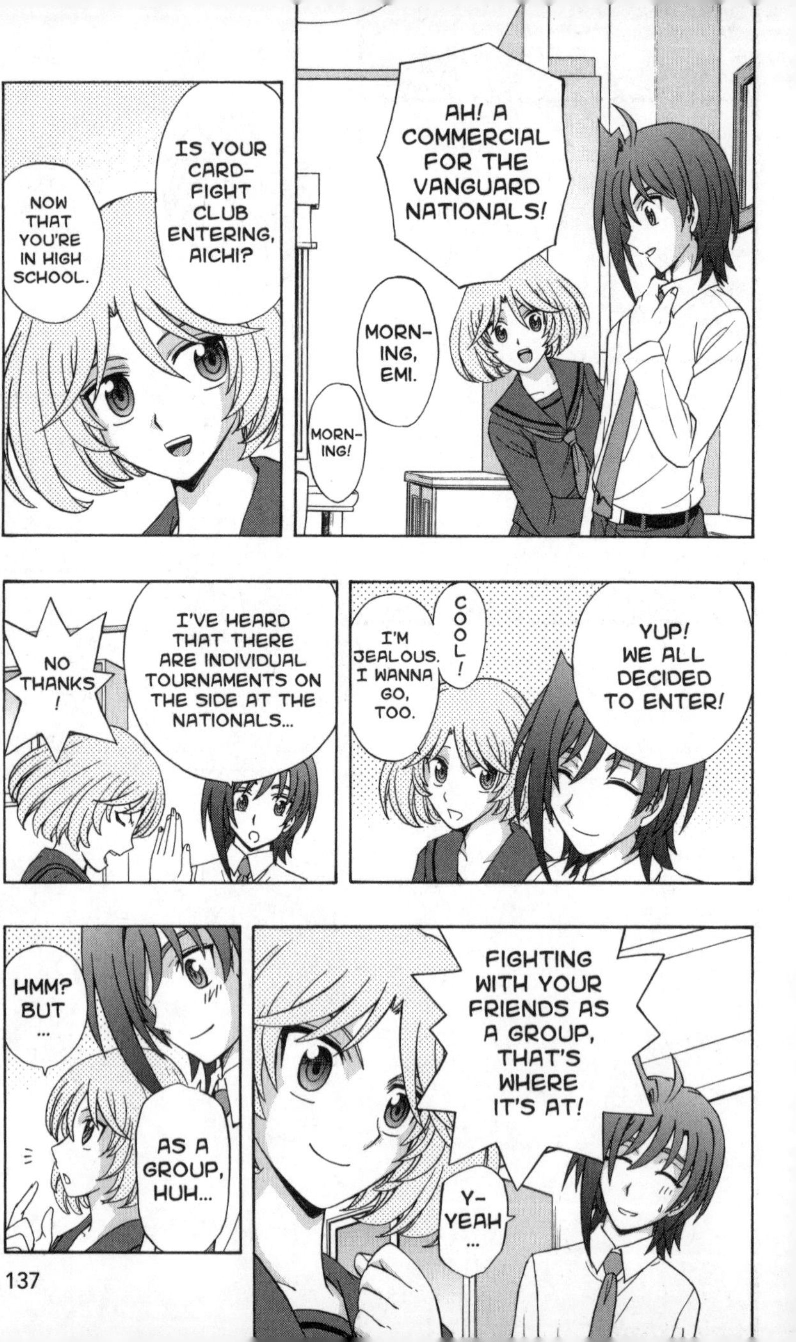
AH! A COMMERCIAL FOR THE VANGUARD NATIONALS!
MORNING, EMI.
MORNING!
IS YOUR CARD-FIGHT CLUB ENTERING, AICHI?
NOW THAT YOU'RE IN HIGH SCHOOL.
YUP! WE ALL DECIDED TO ENTER!
COOL!
I'M JEALOUS. I WANNA GO, TOO.
I'VE HEARD THAT THERE ARE INDIVIDUAL TOURNAMENTS ON THE SIDE AT THE NATIONALS...
NO THANKS!
FIGHTING WITH YOUR FRIENDS AS A GROUP, THAT'S WHERE IT'S AT!
Y-YEAH...
HMM? BUT...
AS A GROUP, HUH...

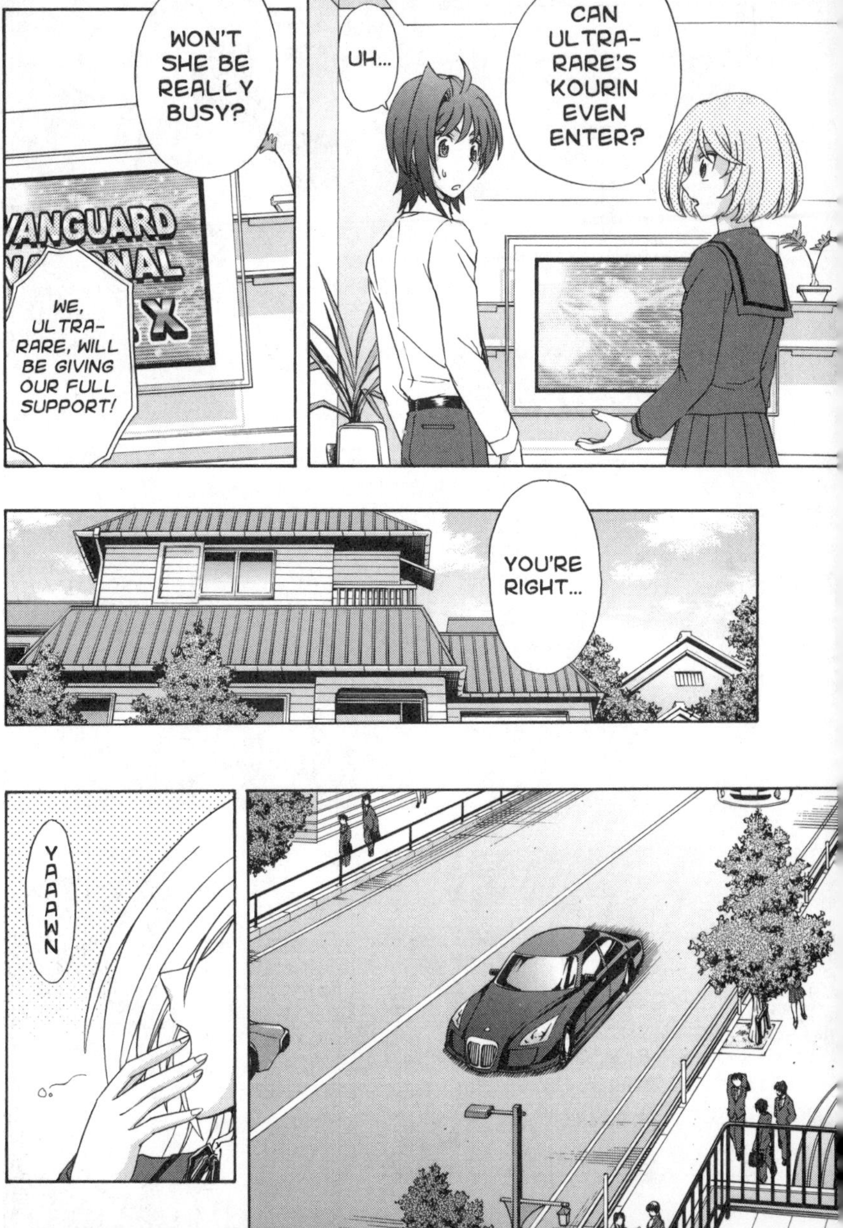
CAN ULTRA-RARE'S KOURIN EVEN ENTER?
UH...
WON'T SHE BE REALLY BUSY?
VANGUARD
WE, ULTRA-RARE, WILL BE GIVING OUR FULL SUPPORT!
YOU'RE RIGHT...
YAAAWN

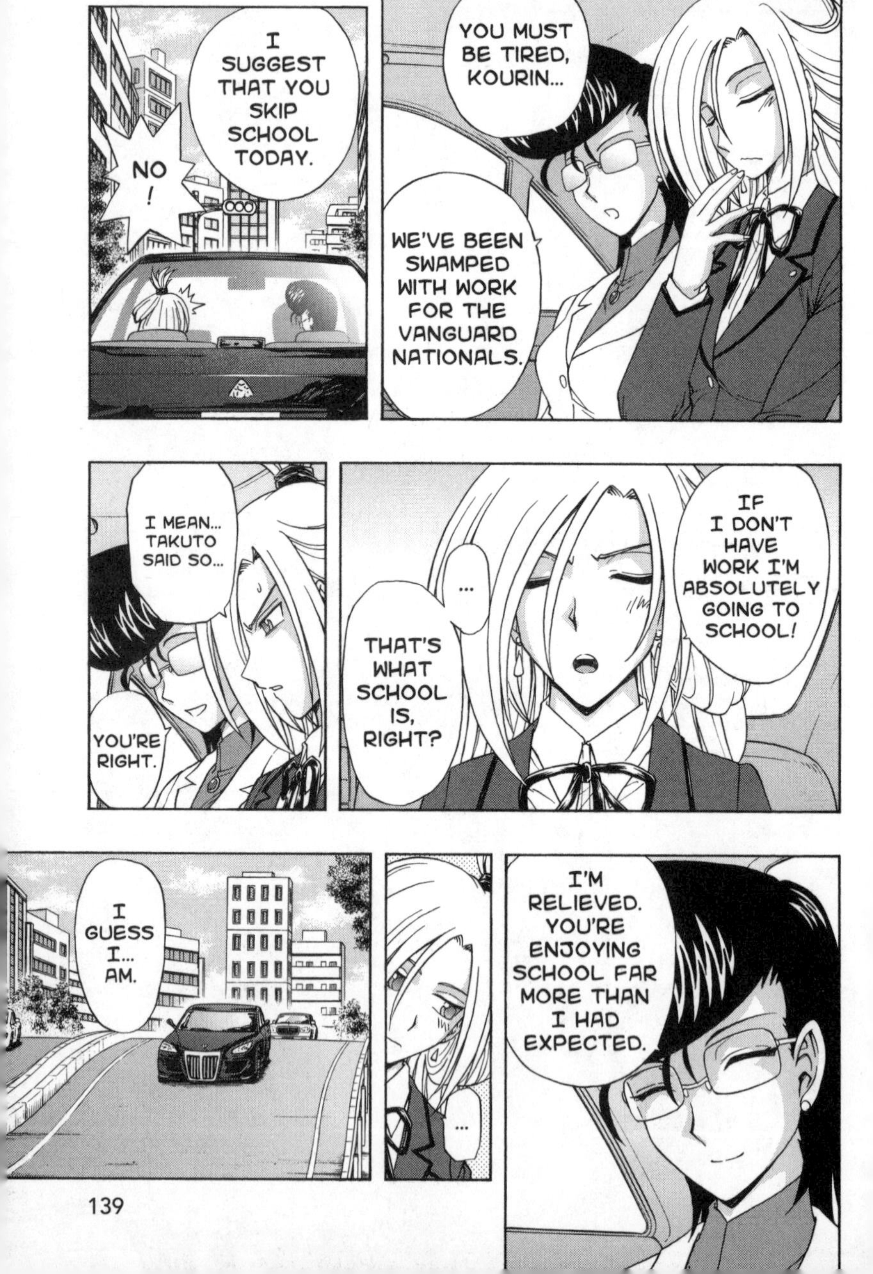

YOU MUST BE TIRED, KOURIN...
WE'VE BEEN SWAMPED WITH WORK FOR THE VANGUARD NATIONALS.
I SUGGEST THAT YOU SKIP SCHOOL TODAY.
NO!
IF I DON'T HAVE WORK I'M ABSOLUTELY GOING TO SCHOOL!
...
THAT'S WHAT SCHOOL IS, RIGHT?
I MEAN... TAKUTO SAID SO...
YOU'RE RIGHT.
I'M RELIEVED. YOU'RE ENJOYING SCHOOL FAR MORE THAN I HAD EXPECTED.
...
I GUESS I... AM.

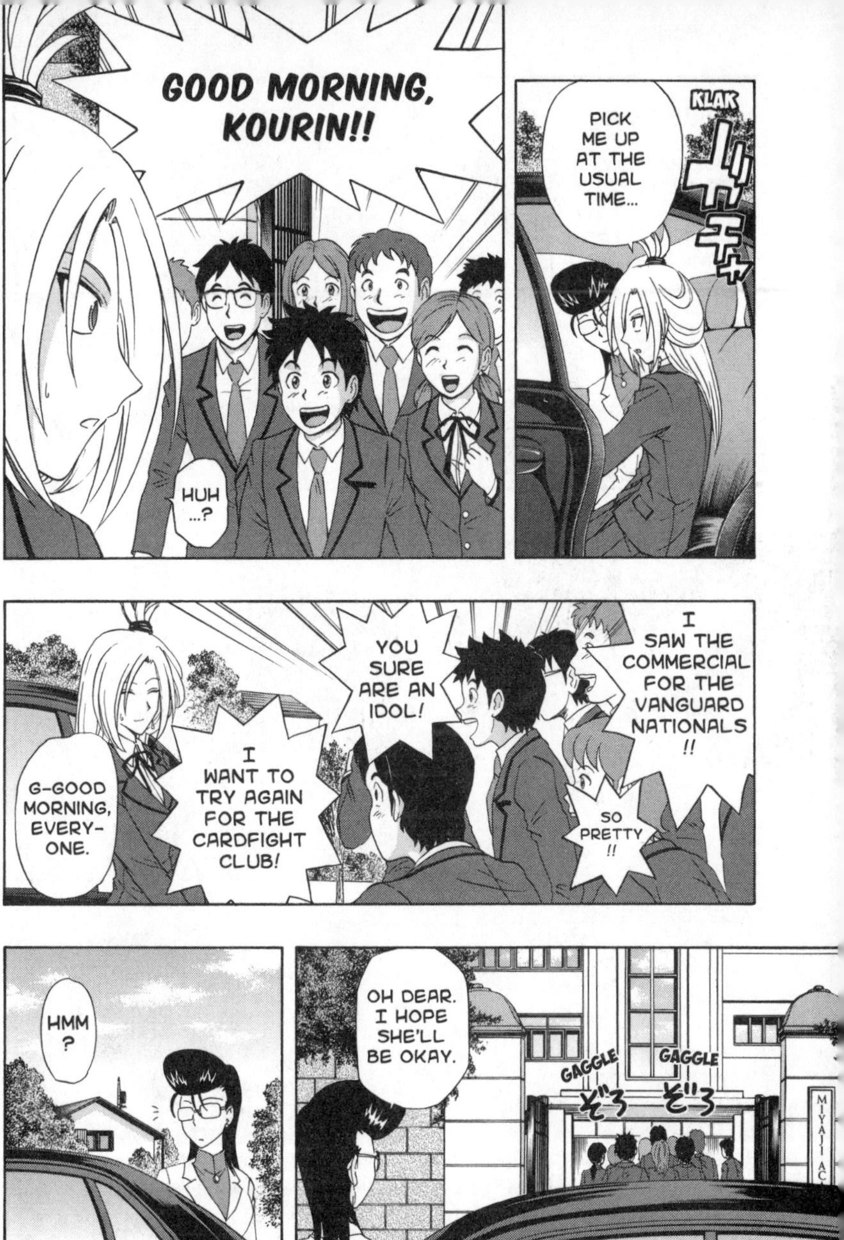
KLAK
PICK ME UP AT THE USUAL TIME...
GOOD MORNING, KOURIN!!
HUH ...?
I SAW THE COMMERCIAL FOR THE VANGUARD NATIONALS !!
SO PRETTY !!
YOU SURE ARE AN IDOL!
I WANT TO TRY AGAIN FOR THE CARDFIGHT CLUB!
G-GOOD MORNING, EVERY-ONE.
OH DEAR. I HOPE SHE'LL BE OKAY.
GAGGLE GAGGLE
ぞろ ぞろ
MIYAJI AC
HMM ?

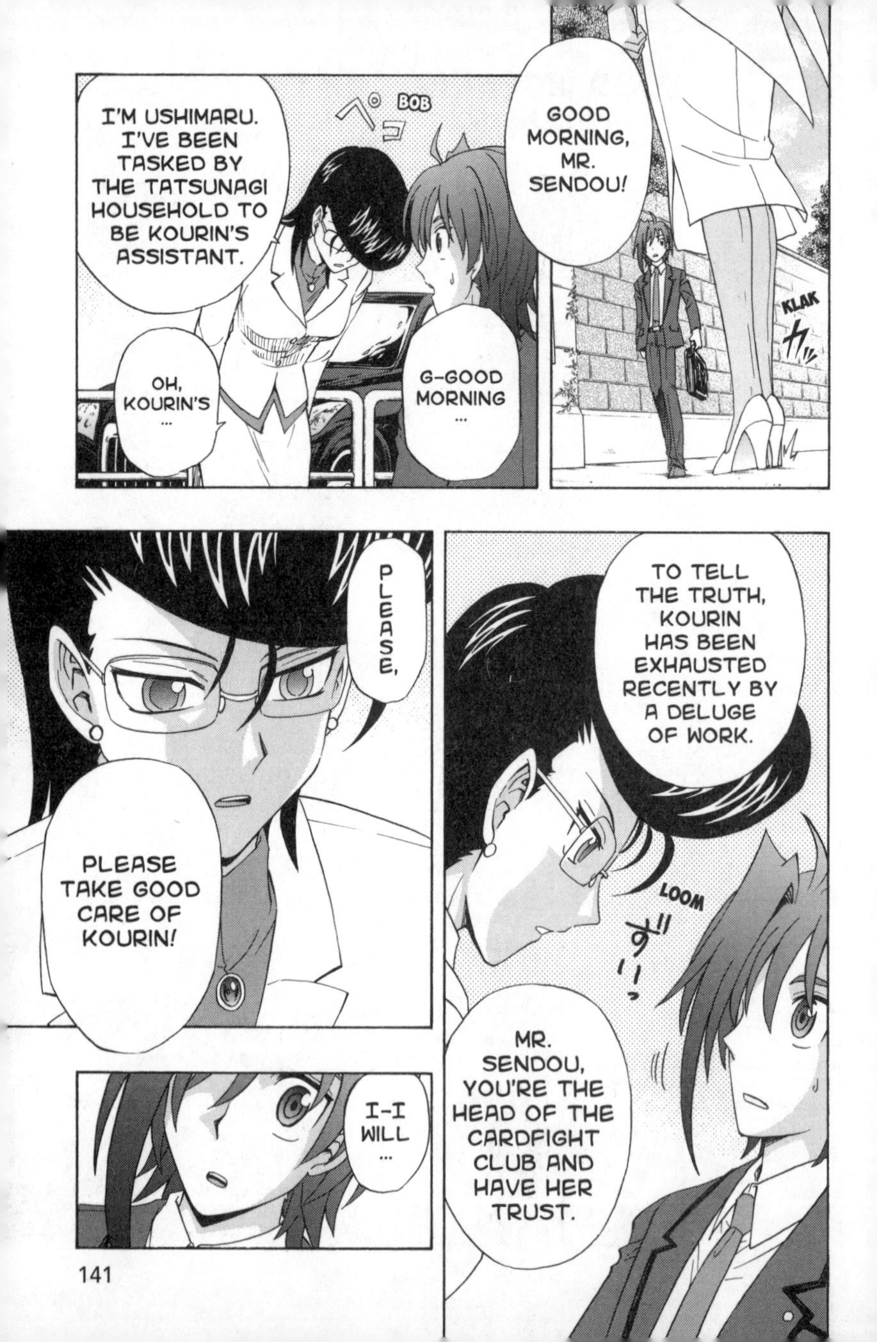
GOOD MORNING, MR. SENDOU!
KLAK
BOB
G-GOOD MORNING...
I'M USHIMARU. I'VE BEEN TASKED BY THE TATSUNAGI HOUSEHOLD TO BE KOURIN'S ASSISTANT.
OH, KOURIN'S...
TO TELL THE TRUTH, KOURIN HAS BEEN EXHAUSTED RECENTLY BY A DELUGE OF WORK.
LOOM
MR. SENDOU, YOU'RE THE HEAD OF THE CARDFIGHT CLUB AND HAVE HER TRUST.
PLEASE,
PLEASE TAKE GOOD CARE OF KOURIN!
I-I WILL...

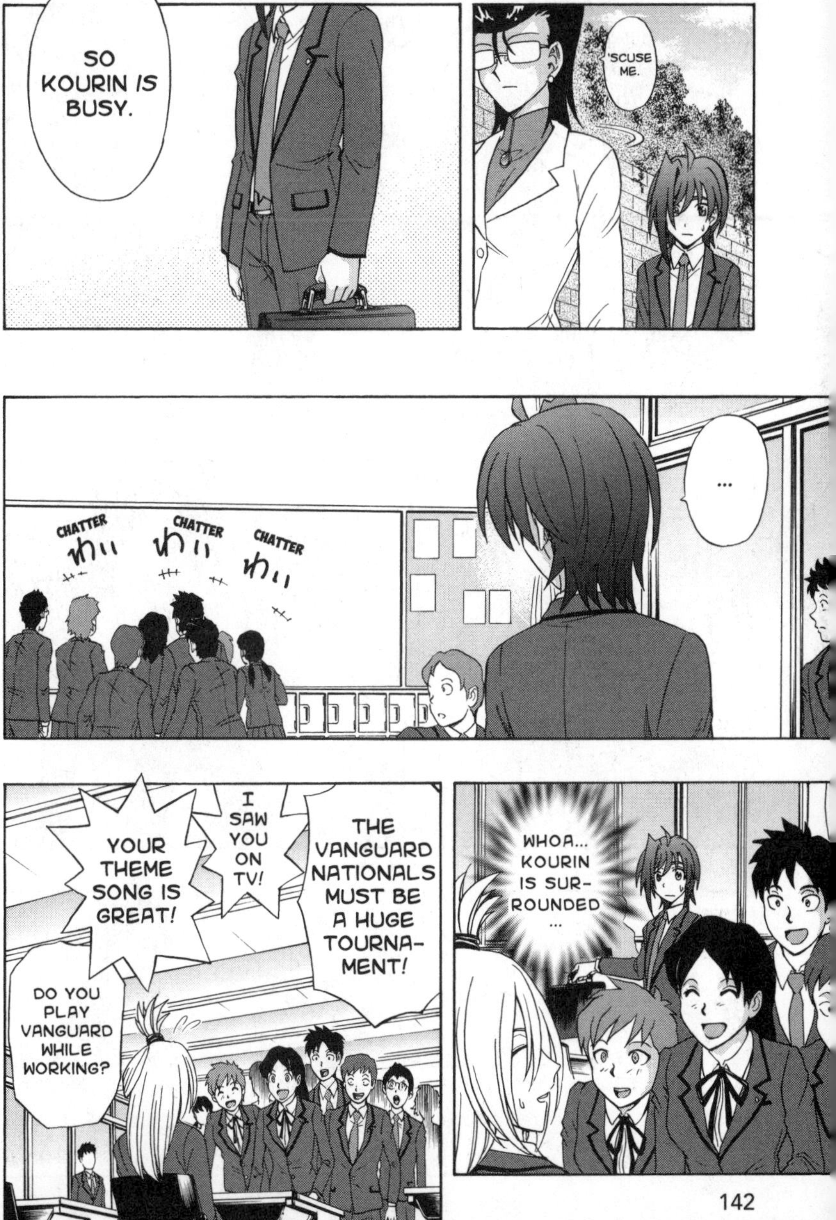
'SCUSE ME.
SO KOURIN IS BUSY.
...
CHATTER
わい
CHATTER
わい
CHATTER
わい
WHOA... KOURIN IS SURROUNDED...
THE VANGUARD NATIONALS MUST BE A HUGE TOURNAMENT!
I SAW YOU ON TV!
YOUR THEME SONG IS GREAT!
DO YOU PLAY VANGUARD WHILE WORKING?

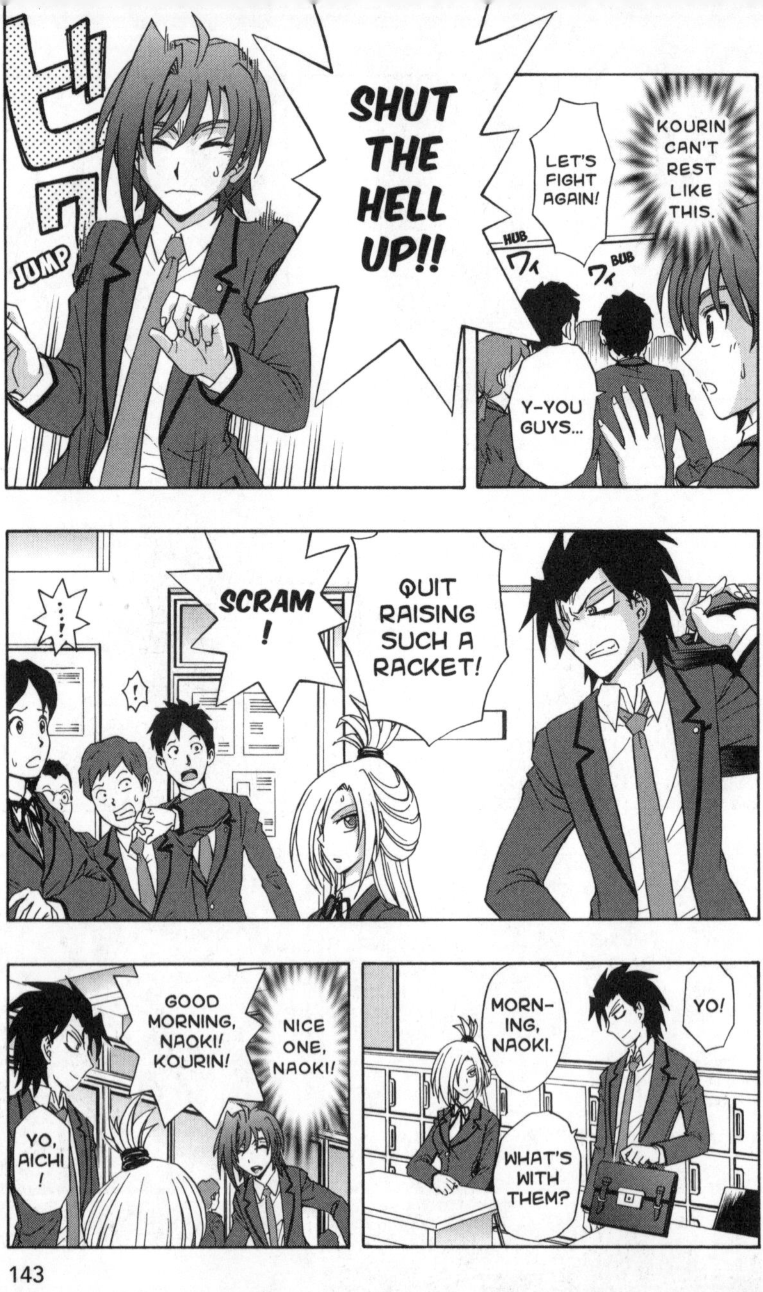

KOURIN CAN'T REST LIKE THIS.
LET'S FIGHT AGAIN!
HUB
BUB
Y-YOU GUYS...
SHUT THE HELL UP!!
JUMP
QUIT RAISING SUCH A RACKET!
SCRAM!
!
...!
YO!
MORNING, NAOKI.
WHAT'S WITH THEM?
NICE ONE, NAOKI!
GOOD MORNING, NAOKI! KOURIN!
YO, AICHI!

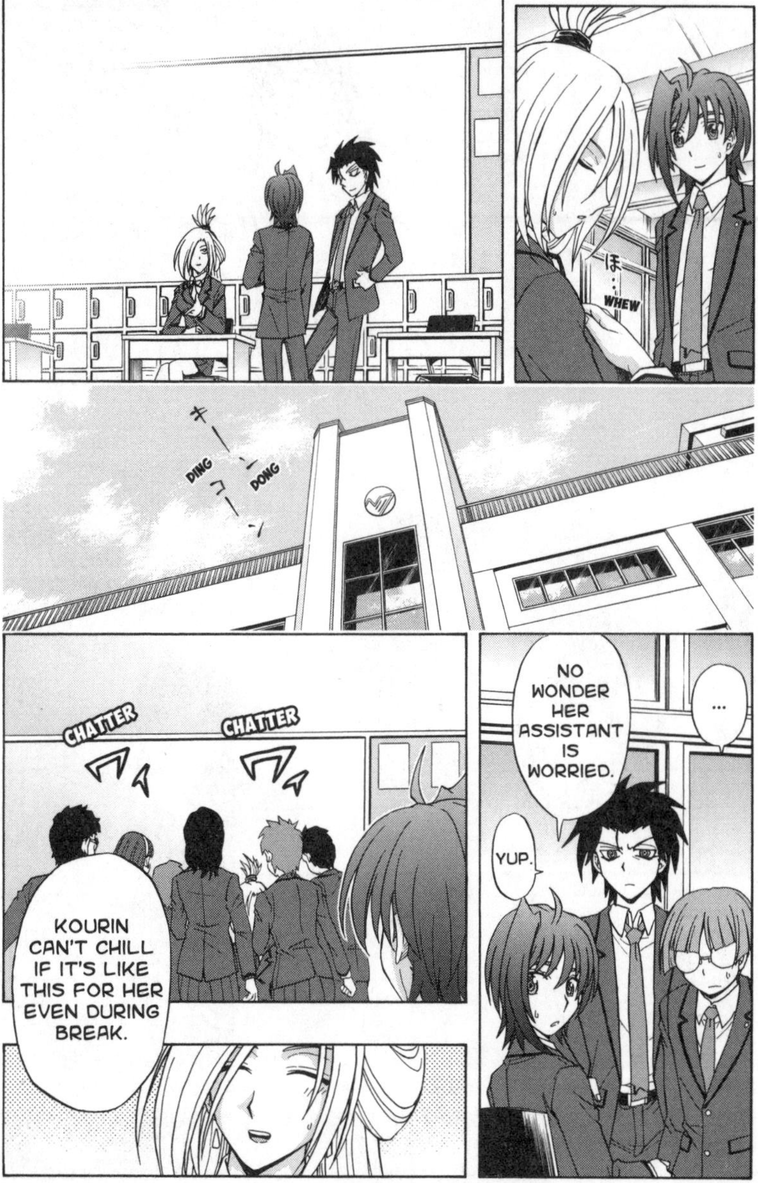
ほ…
WHEW
キーンコーン
DING DONG
...
NO WONDER HER ASSISTANT IS WORRIED.
YUP.
ワイ
CHATTER
ワイ
CHATTER
KOURIN CAN'T CHILL IF IT'S LIKE THIS FOR HER EVEN DURING BREAK.

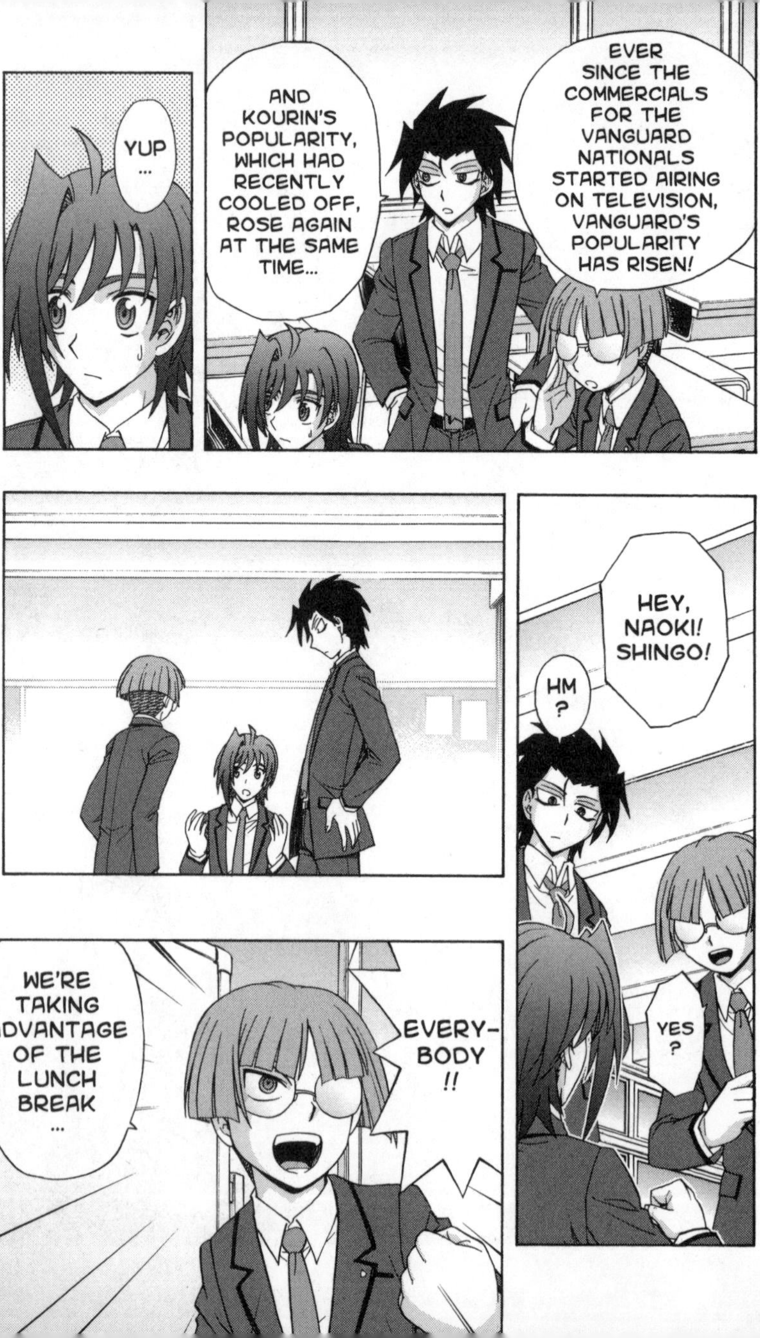
EVER SINCE THE COMMERCIALS FOR THE VANGUARD NATIONALS STARTED AIRING ON TELEVISION, VANGUARD'S POPULARITY HAS RISEN!
AND KOURIN'S POPULARITY, WHICH HAD RECENTLY COOLED OFF, ROSE AGAIN AT THE SAME TIME...
YUP ...
HEY, NAOKI! SHINGO!
HM ?
YES ?
EVERY-BODY !!
WE'RE TAKING ADVANTAGE OF THE LUNCH BREAK ...

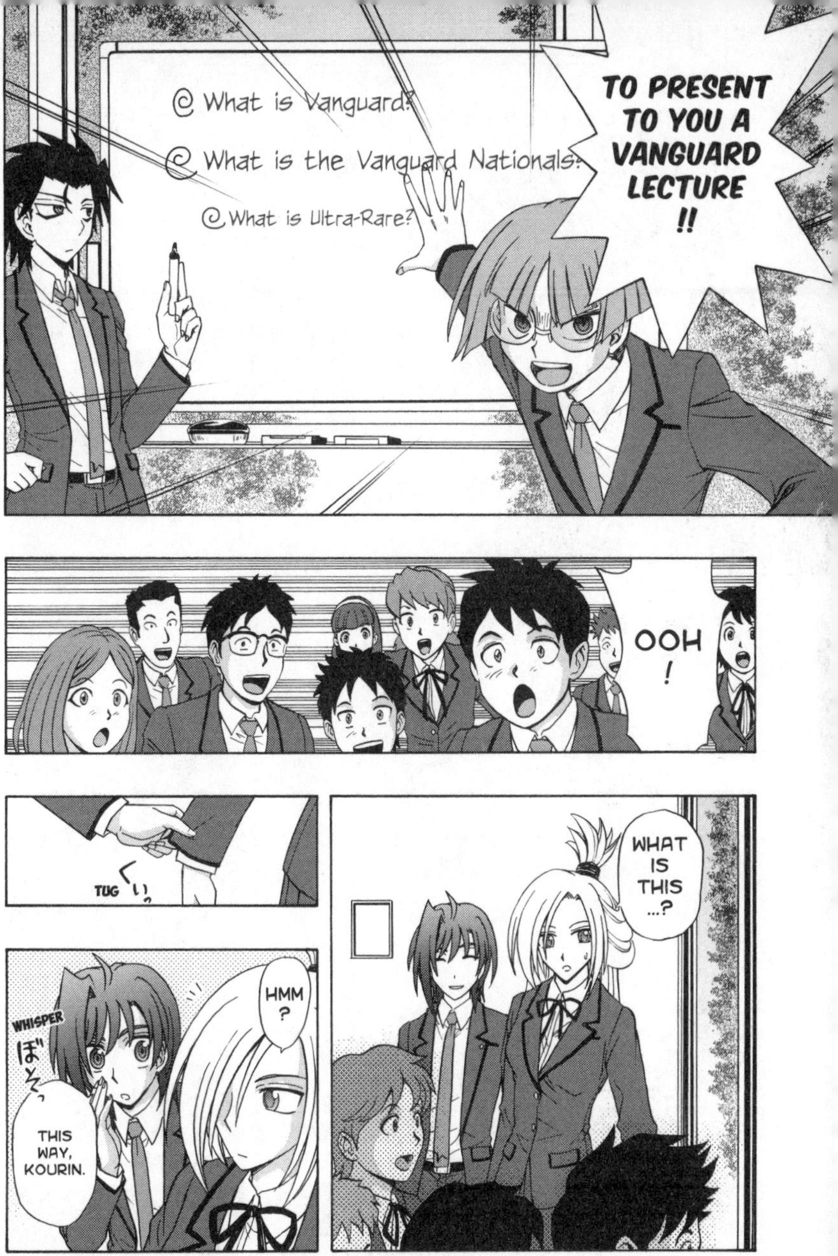
TO PRESENT TO YOU A VANGUARD LECTURE !!
What is Vanguard?
What is the Vanguard Nationals?
What is Ultra-Rare?
OOH !
WHAT IS THIS ...?
TUG くいっ
HMM ?
WHISPER ぼそっ
THIS WAY, KOURIN.

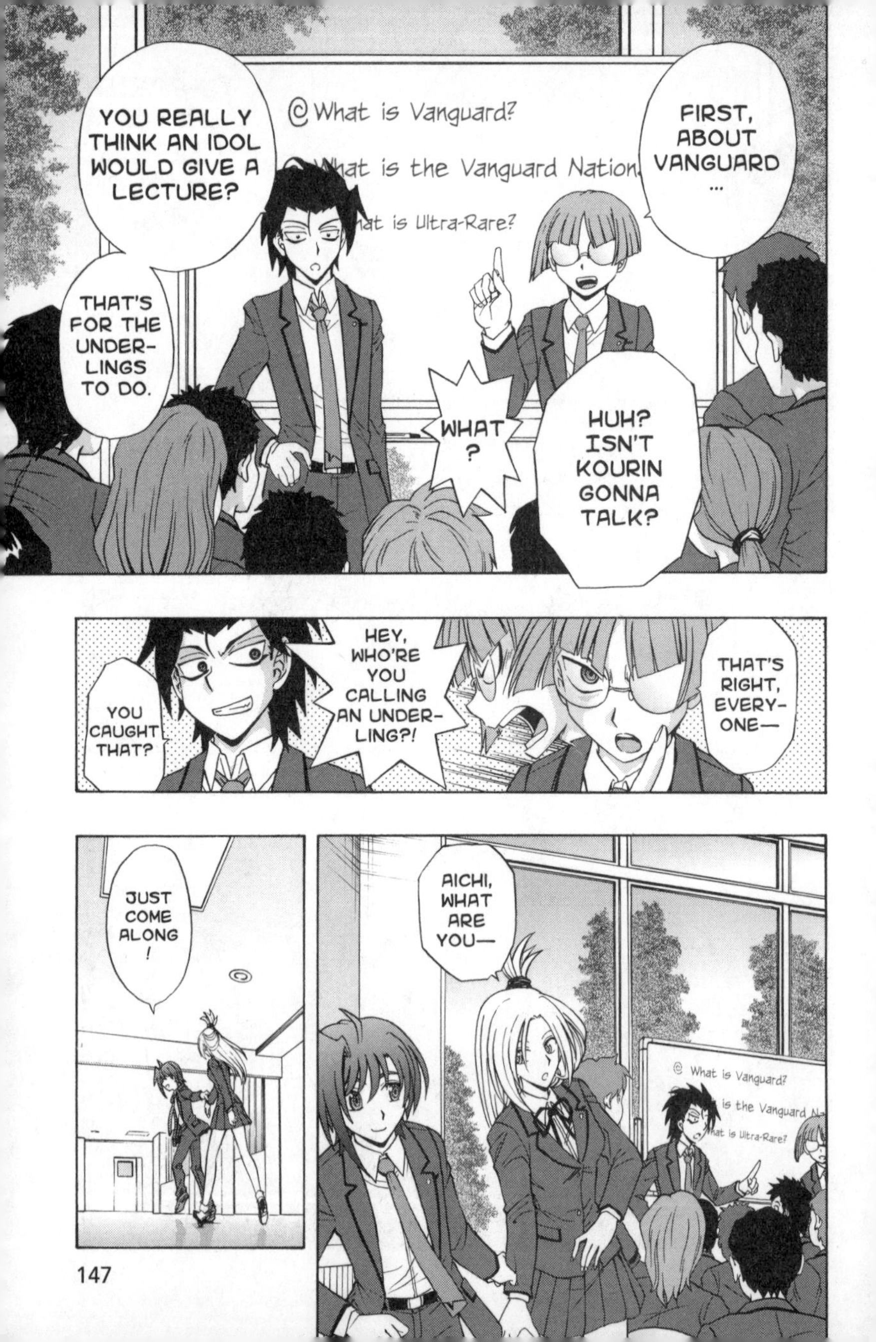
FIRST, ABOUT VANGUARD ...
What is Vanguard?
What is the Vanguard Nation
hat is Ultra-Rare?
YOU REALLY THINK AN IDOL WOULD GIVE A LECTURE?
THAT'S FOR THE UNDER-LINGS TO DO.
HUH? ISN'T KOURIN GONNA TALK?
WHAT ?
THAT'S RIGHT, EVERY-ONE—
HEY, WHO'RE YOU CALLING AN UNDER-LING?!
YOU CAUGHT THAT?
AICHI, WHAT ARE YOU—
What is Vanguard?
is the Vanguard Na
hat is Ultra-Rare?
JUST COME ALONG !

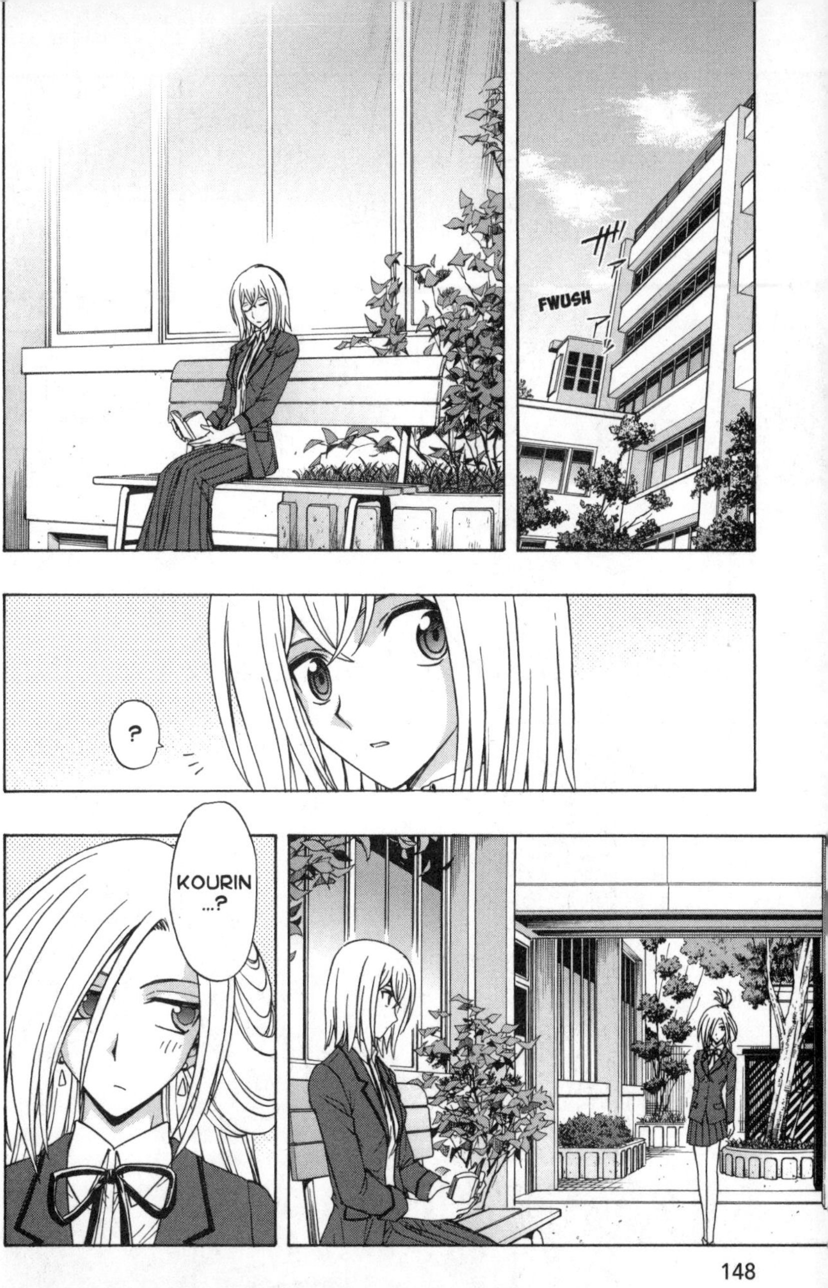
FWUSH
?
KOURIN ...?

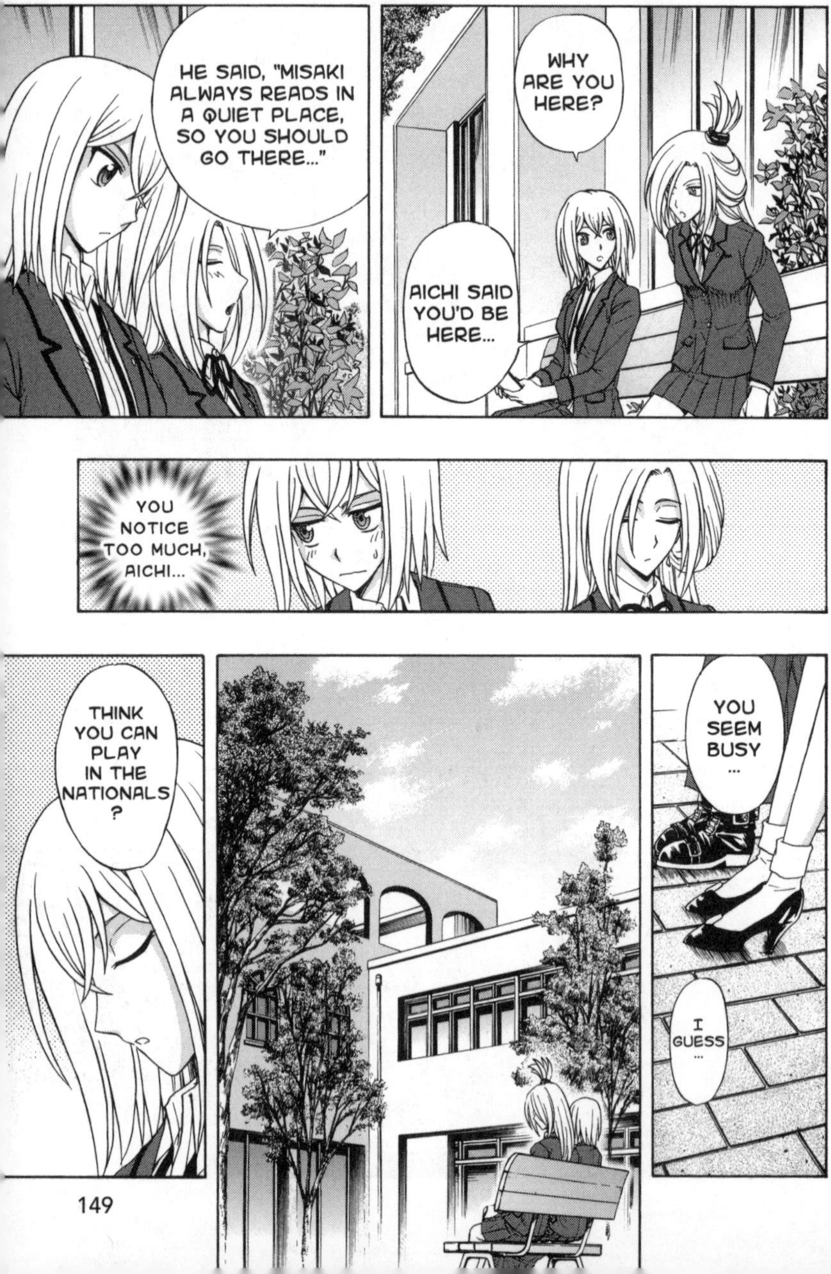
WHY ARE YOU HERE?
AICHI SAID YOU'D BE HERE...
HE SAID, "MISAKI ALWAYS READS IN A QUIET PLACE, SO YOU SHOULD GO THERE..."
YOU NOTICE TOO MUCH, AICHI...
YOU SEEM BUSY...
I GUESS...
THINK YOU CAN PLAY IN THE NATIONALS?

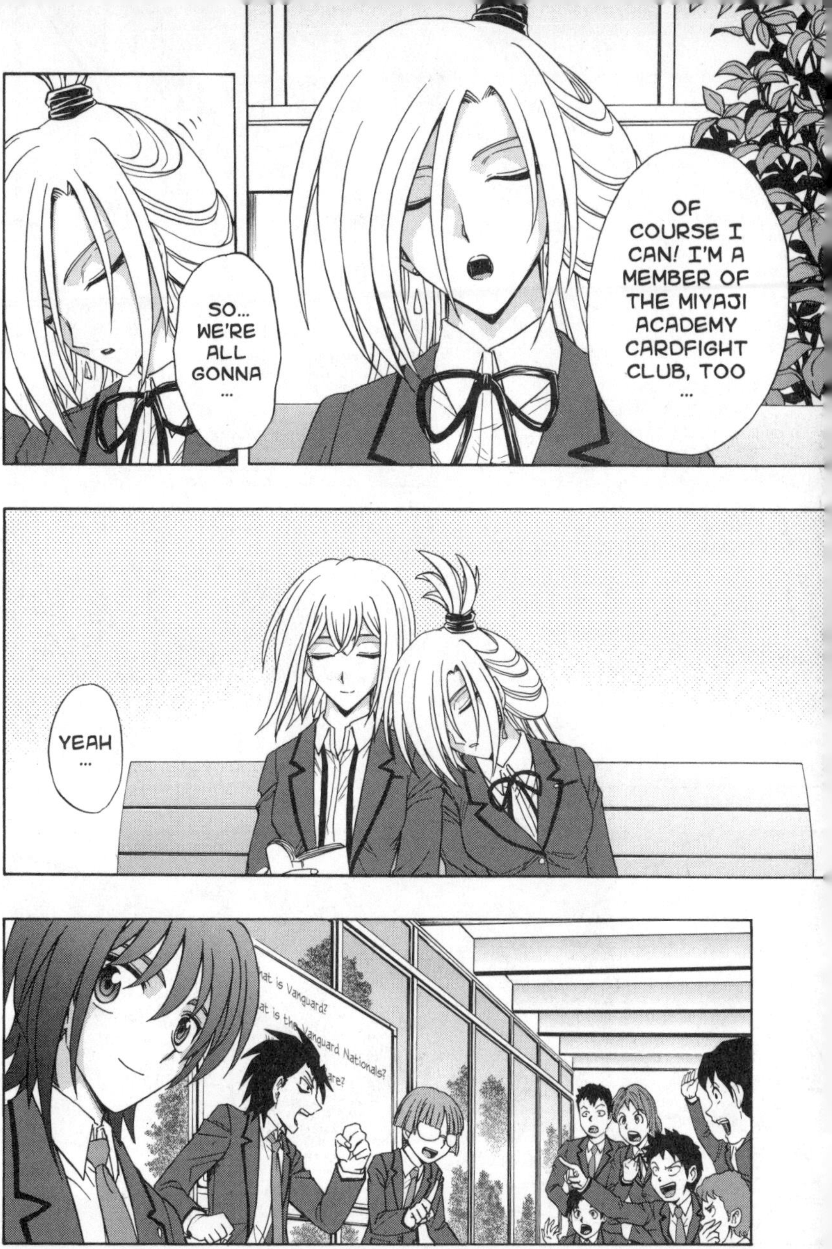
OF COURSE I CAN! I'M A MEMBER OF THE MIYAJI ACADEMY CARDFIGHT CLUB, TOO ...
SO... WE'RE ALL GONNA ...
YEAH ...

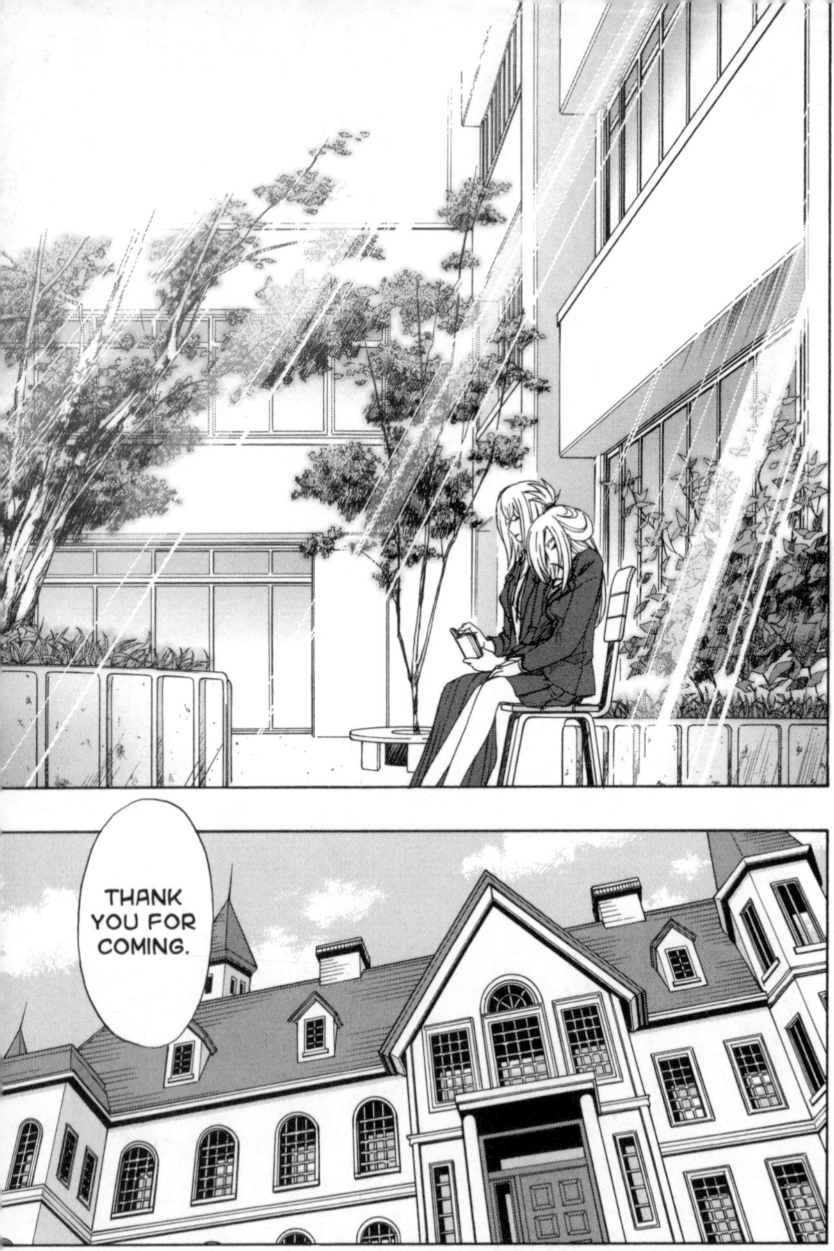
THANK YOU FOR COMING.

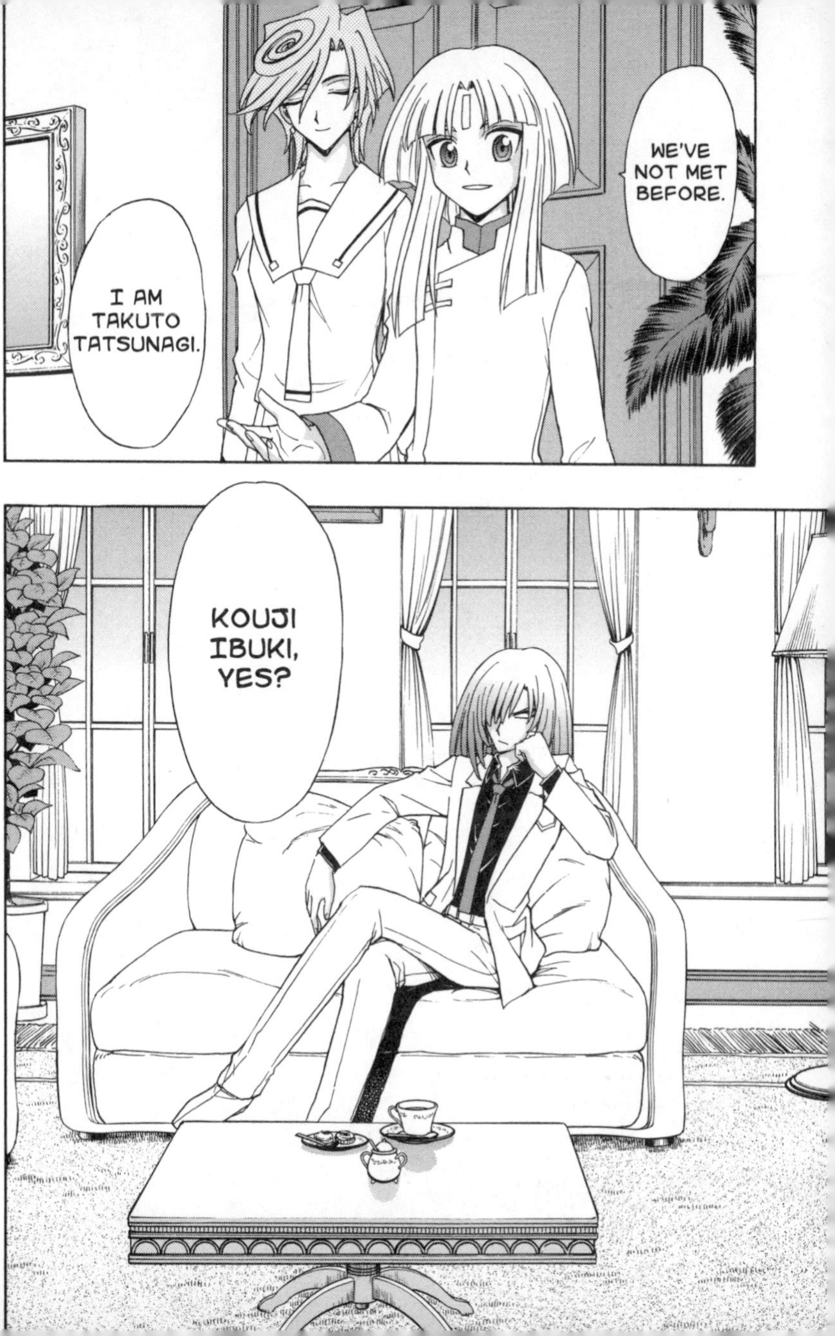
WE'VE NOT MET BEFORE.
I AM TAKUTO TATSUNAGI.
KOUJI IBUKI, YES?

CARDFIGHT!! Vanguard

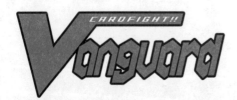

**BONUS!** CARDFIGHT!! Vanguard

# NEVER-BEFORE-SEEN IMAGE BOARDS

**Incandescent Lion, Blond Ezel**

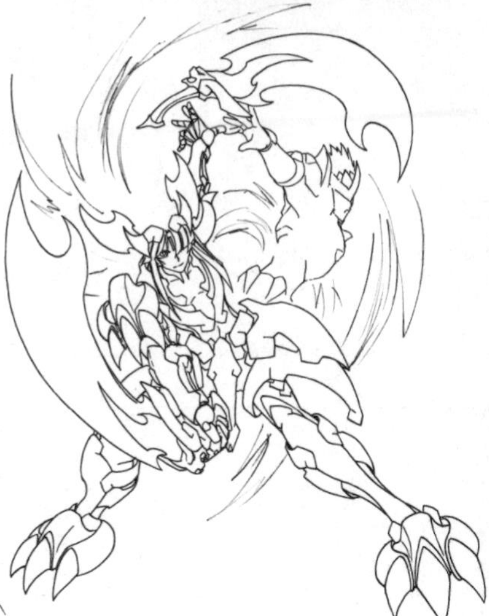

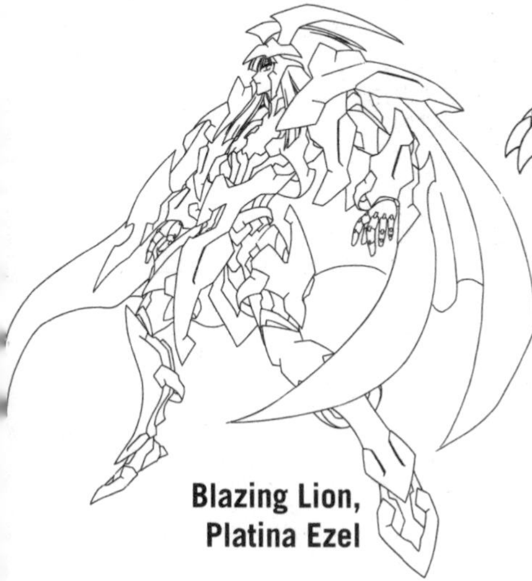

**Blazing Lion, Platina Ezel**

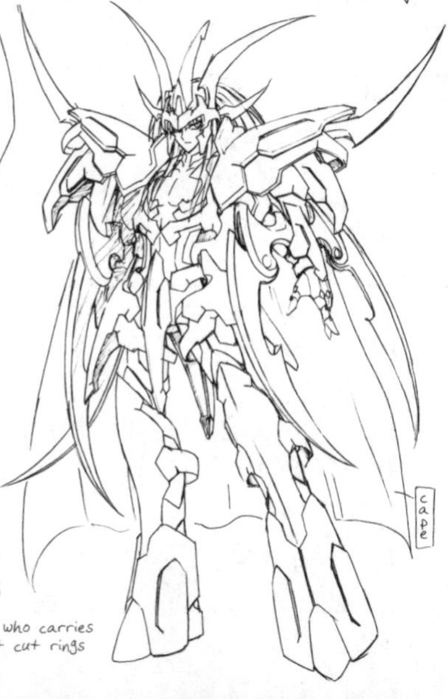
cape

**Salvation Lion, Grand Ezel Scissors**

Note: An Ezel who carries scissors that cut rings

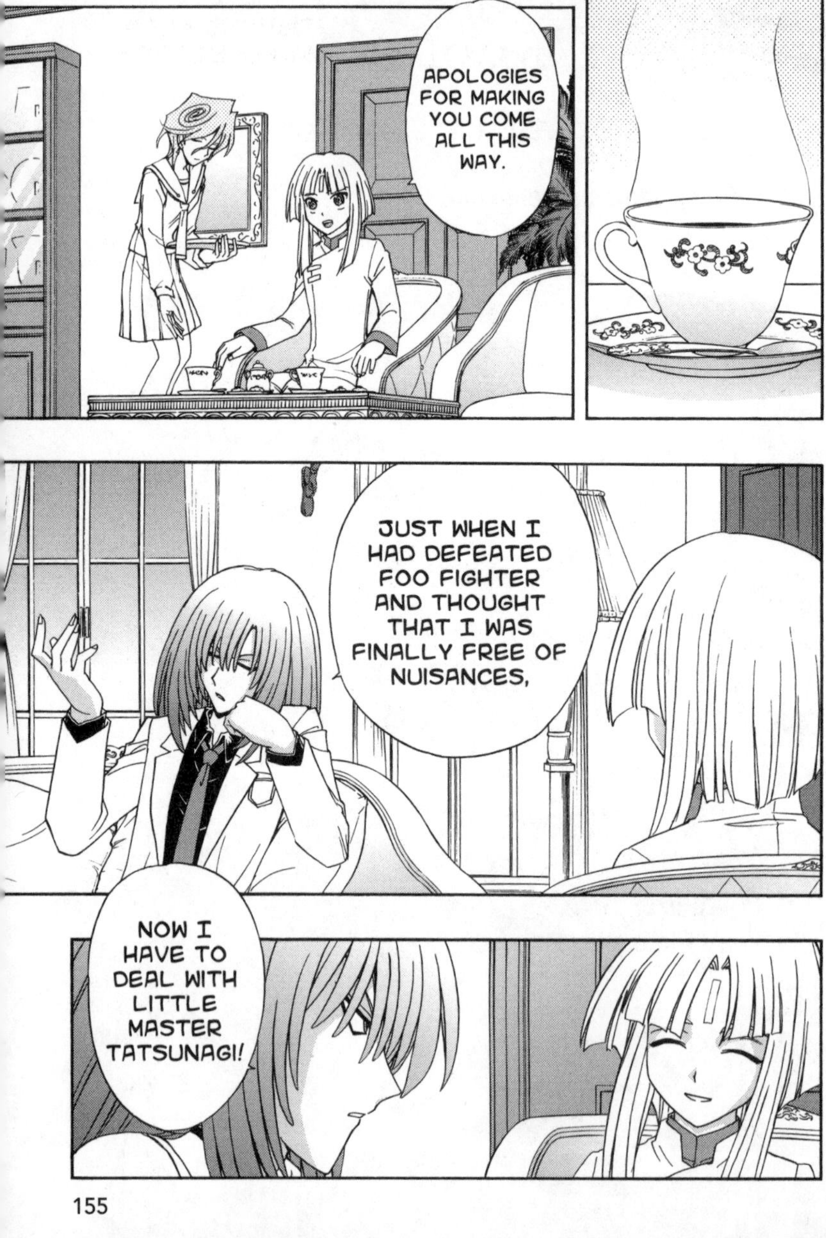
APOLOGIES FOR MAKING YOU COME ALL THIS WAY.
JUST WHEN I HAD DEFEATED FOO FIGHTER AND THOUGHT THAT I WAS FINALLY FREE OF NUISANCES,
NOW I HAVE TO DEAL WITH LITTLE MASTER TATSUNAGI!

# #037 THE SECRET OF "DELETOR"!

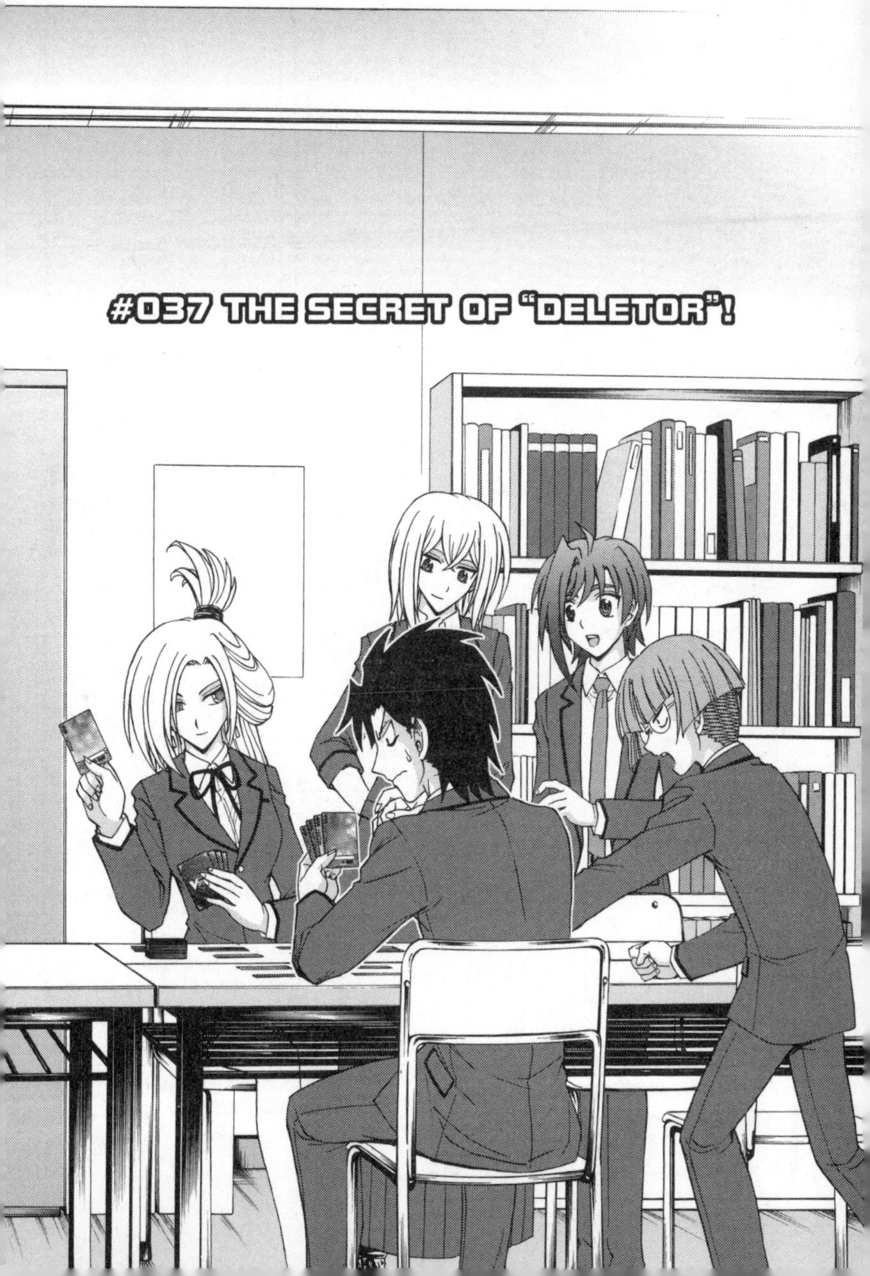

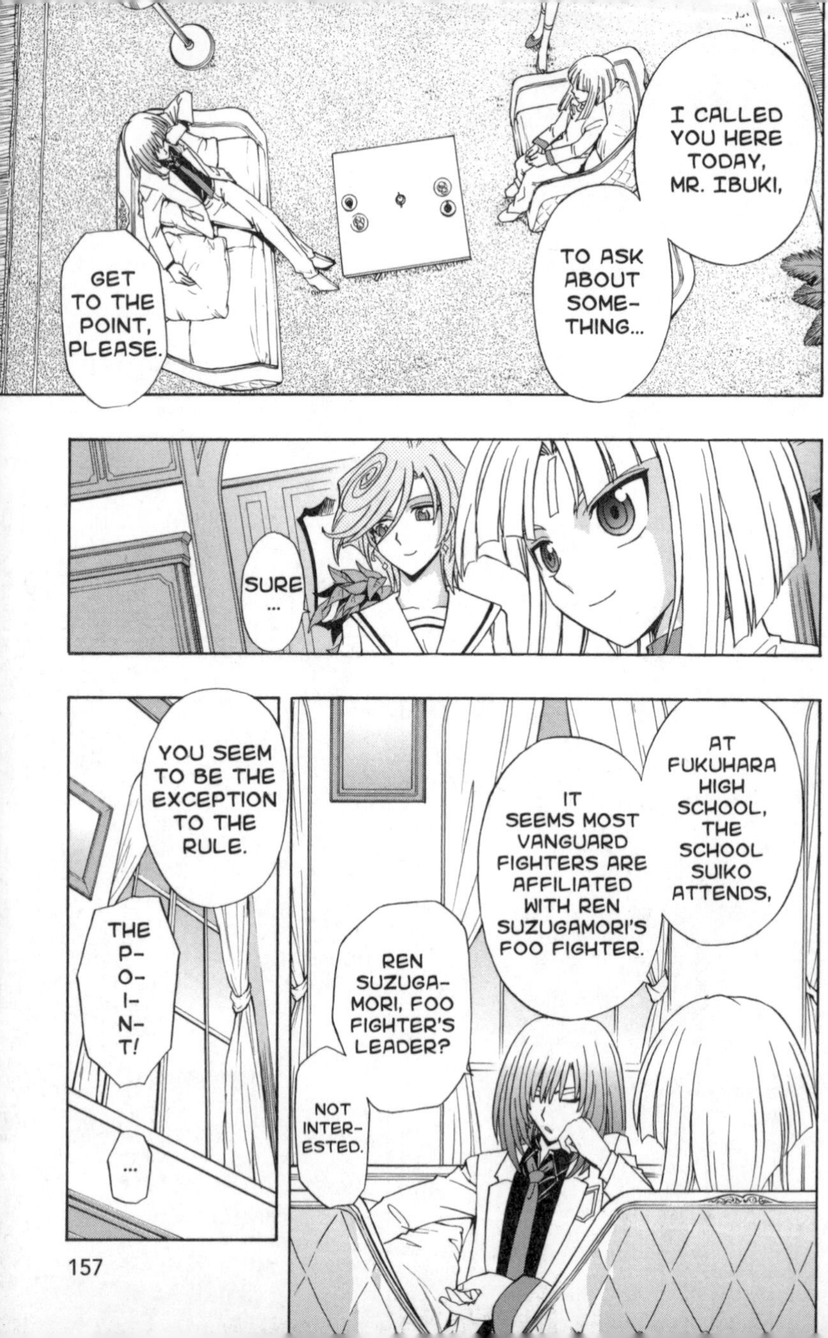
I CALLED YOU HERE TODAY, MR. IBUKI,
TO ASK ABOUT SOME-THING...
GET TO THE POINT, PLEASE.
SURE ...
AT FUKUHARA HIGH SCHOOL, THE SCHOOL SUIKO ATTENDS,
IT SEEMS MOST VANGUARD FIGHTERS ARE AFFILIATED WITH REN SUZUGAMORI'S FOO FIGHTER.
REN SUZUGA-MORI, FOO FIGHTER'S LEADER?
NOT INTER-ESTED.
YOU SEEM TO BE THE EXCEPTION TO THE RULE.
THE P-O-I-N-T!
...

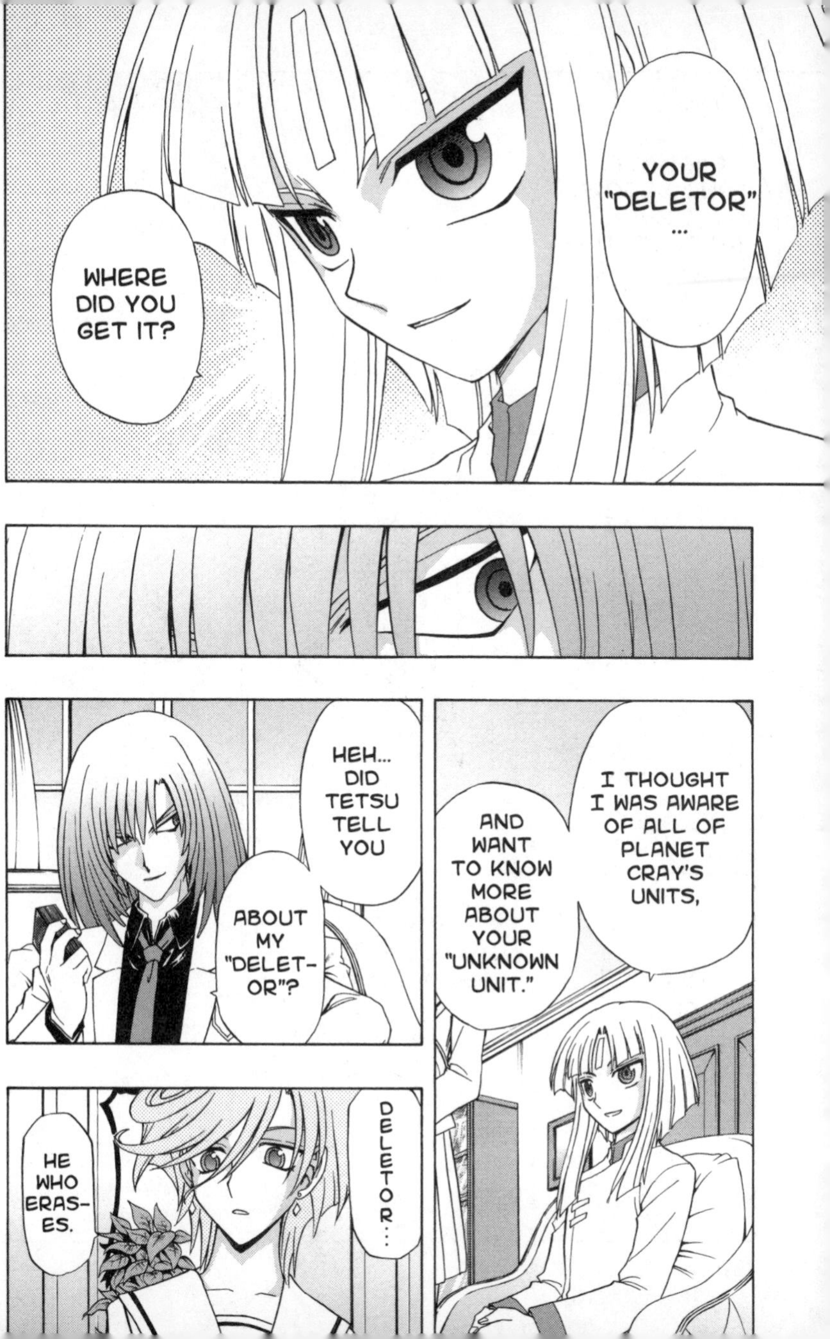
YOUR "DELETOR" ...
WHERE DID YOU GET IT?
I THOUGHT I WAS AWARE OF ALL OF PLANET CRAY'S UNITS,
AND WANT TO KNOW MORE ABOUT YOUR "UNKNOWN UNIT."
HEH... DID TETSU TELL YOU
ABOUT MY "DELET-OR"?
DELETOR...
HE WHO ERAS-ES.

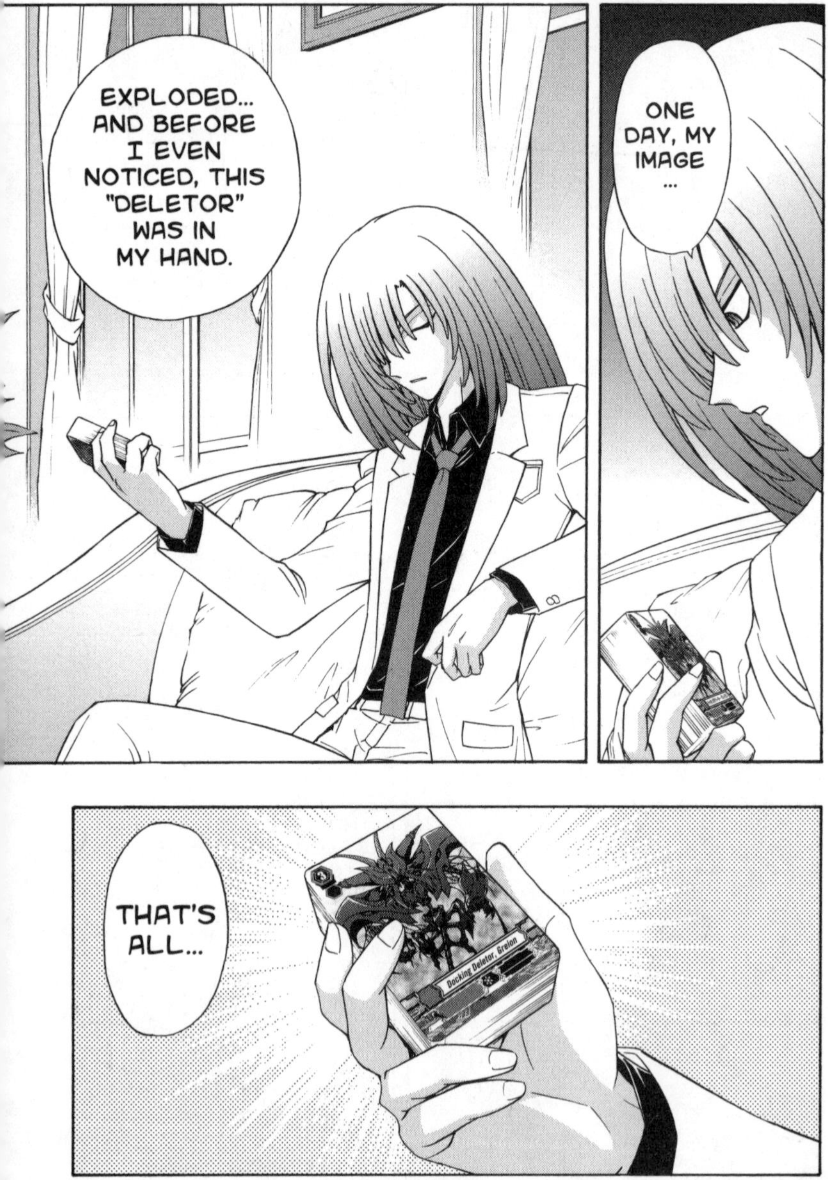
ONE DAY, MY IMAGE ...
EXPLODED... AND BEFORE I EVEN NOTICED, THIS "DELETOR" WAS IN MY HAND.
THAT'S ALL...
Docking Deletor, Greion

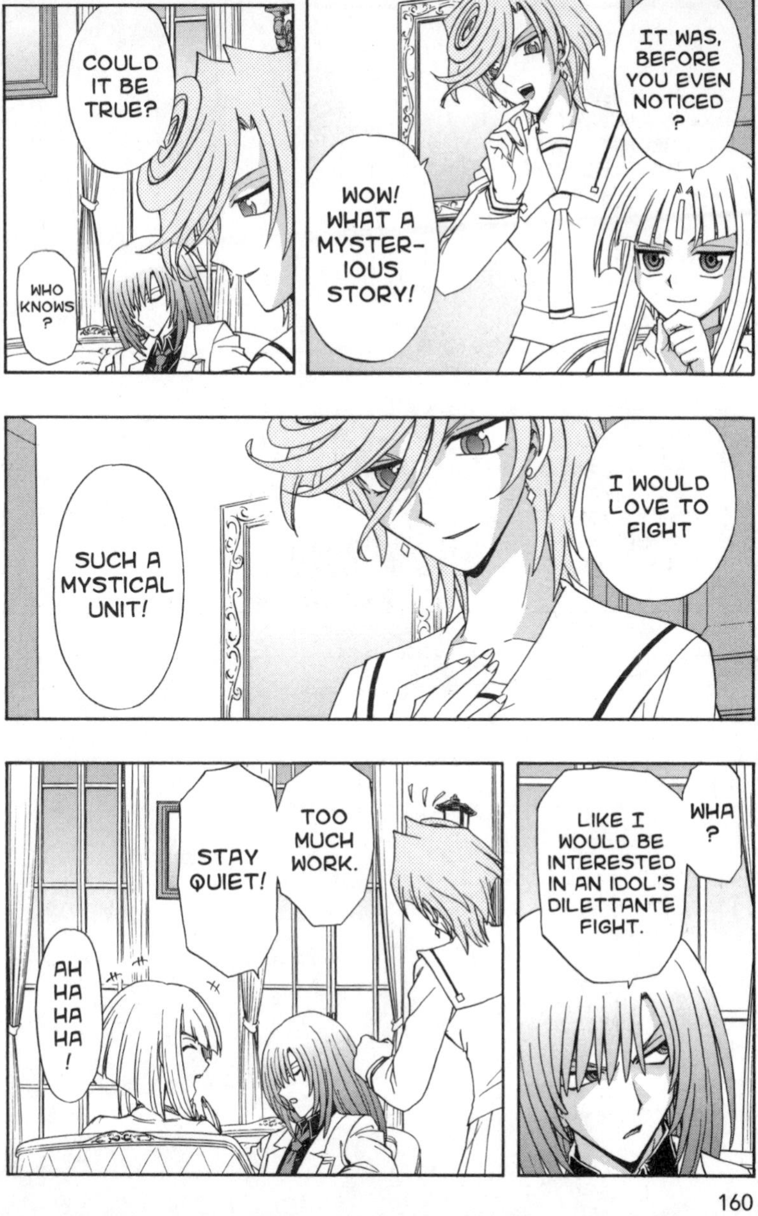
IT WAS, BEFORE YOU EVEN NOTICED ?
WOW! WHAT A MYSTER-IOUS STORY!
COULD IT BE TRUE?
WHO KNOWS ?
I WOULD LOVE TO FIGHT
SUCH A MYSTICAL UNIT!
WHA ?
LIKE I WOULD BE INTERESTED IN AN IDOL'S DILETTANTE FIGHT.
TOO MUCH WORK.
STAY QUIET!
AH HA HA HA !

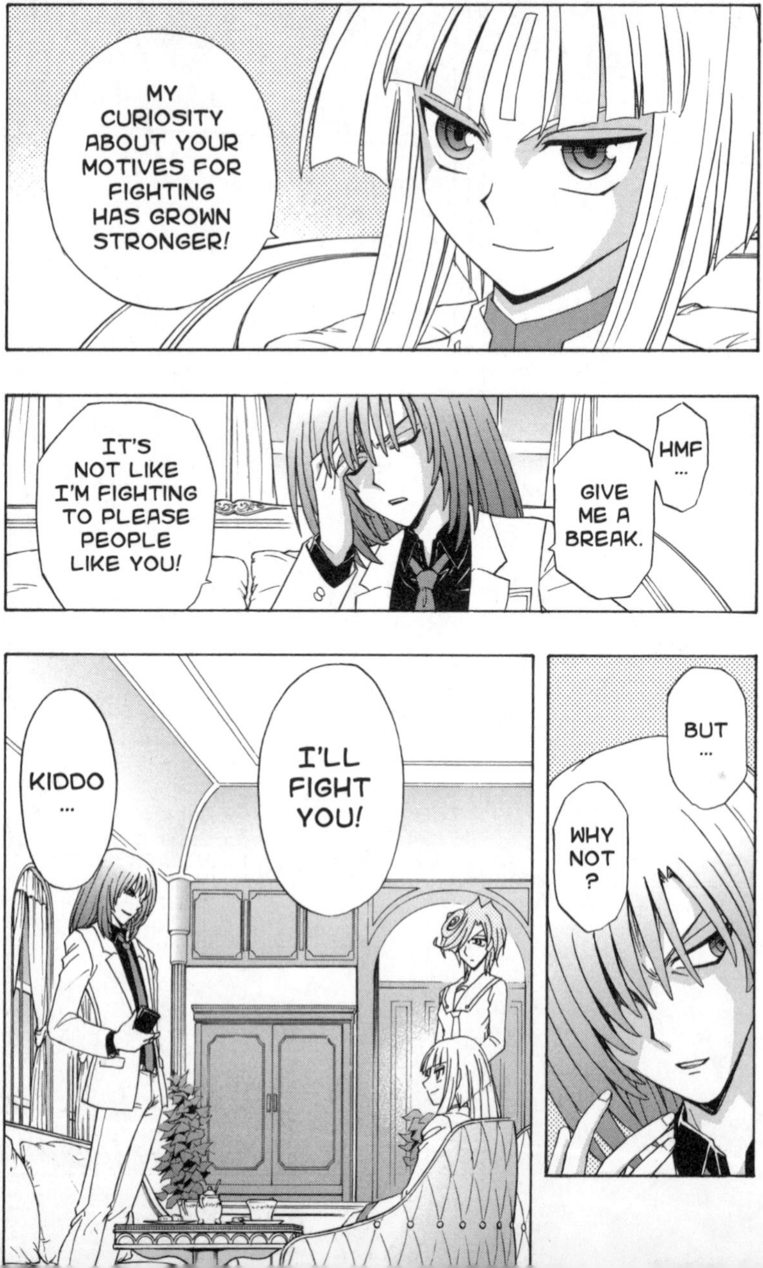
MY CURIOSITY ABOUT YOUR MOTIVES FOR FIGHTING HAS GROWN STRONGER!
HMF ...
GIVE ME A BREAK.
IT'S NOT LIKE I'M FIGHTING TO PLEASE PEOPLE LIKE YOU!
BUT ...
WHY NOT ?
I'LL FIGHT YOU!
KIDDO ...

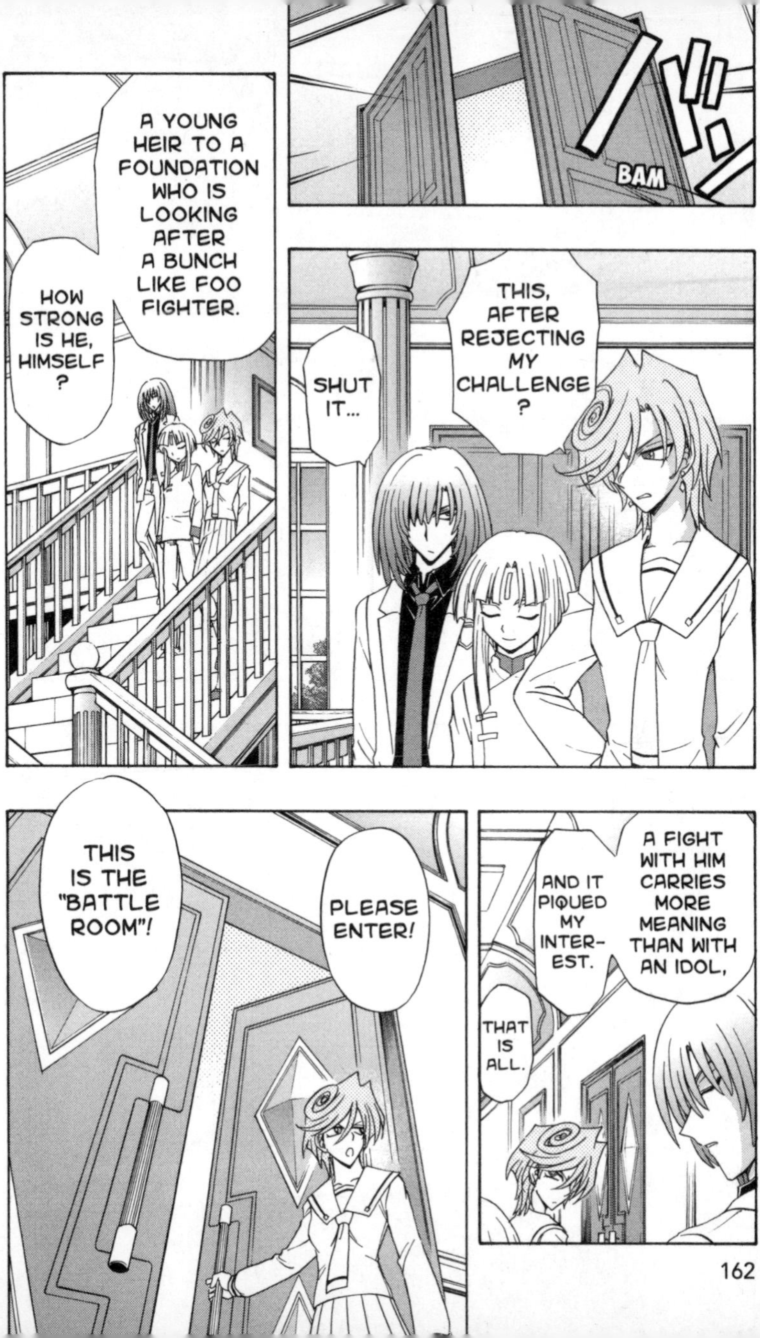
BAM
THIS, AFTER REJECTING MY CHALLENGE?
SHUT IT...
A YOUNG HEIR TO A FOUNDATION WHO IS LOOKING AFTER A BUNCH LIKE FOO FIGHTER.
HOW STRONG IS HE, HIMSELF?
A FIGHT WITH HIM CARRIES MORE MEANING THAN WITH AN IDOL,
AND IT PIQUED MY INTER-EST.
THAT IS ALL.
THIS IS THE "BATTLE ROOM"!
PLEASE ENTER!

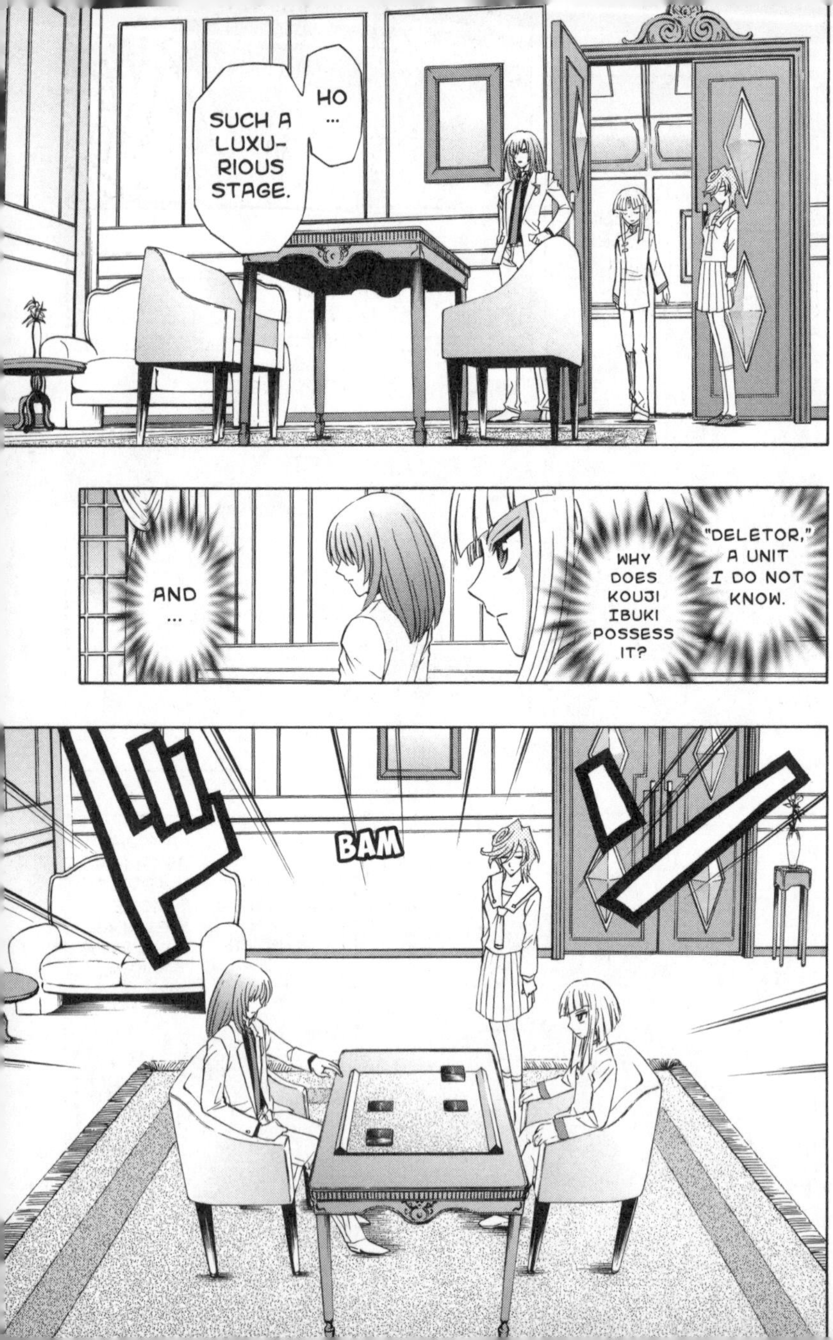
HO ... SUCH A LUXU-RIOUS STAGE.
"DELETOR," A UNIT I DO NOT KNOW.
WHY DOES KOUJI IBUKI POSSESS IT?
AND ...
BAM

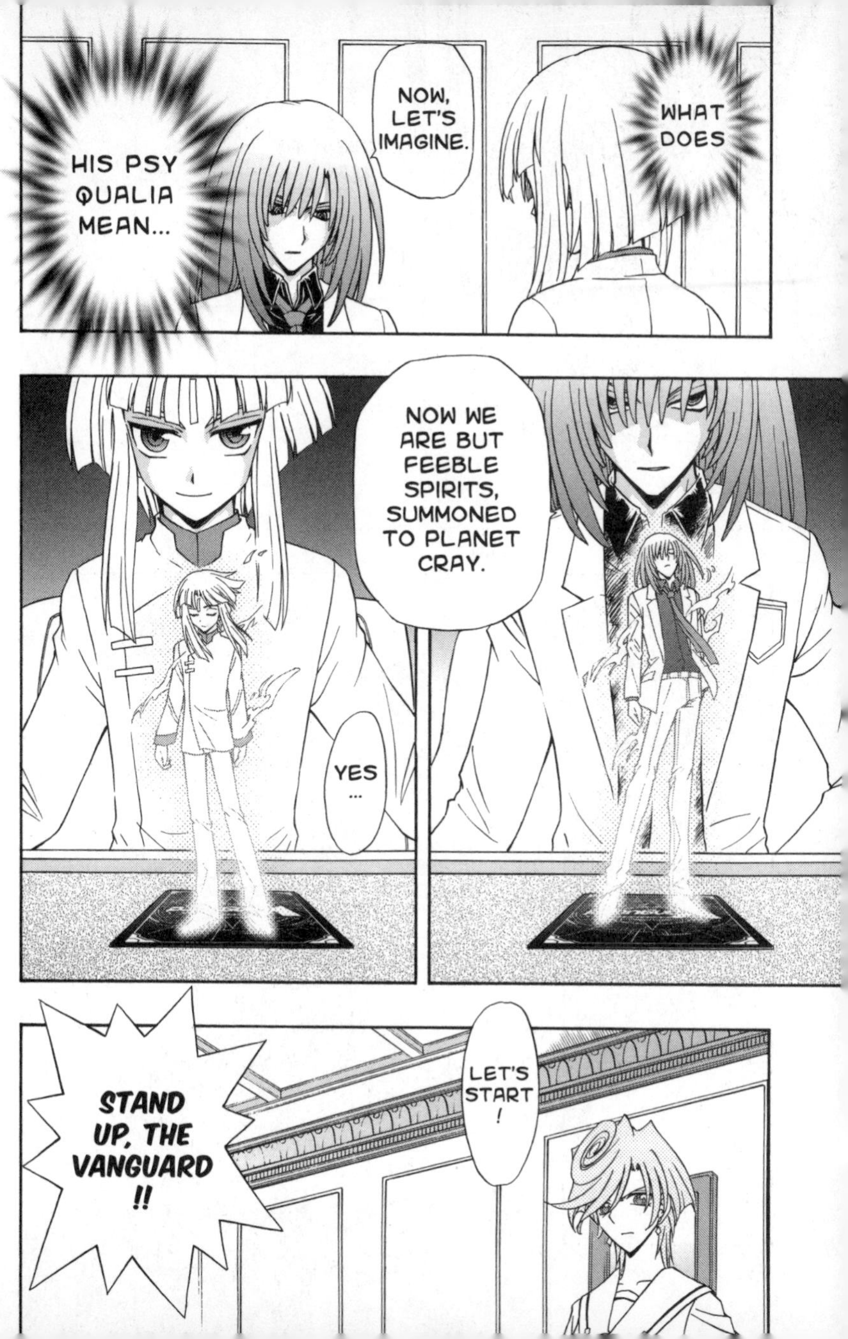

WHAT DOES
NOW, LET'S IMAGINE.
HIS PSY QUALIA MEAN...
NOW WE ARE BUT FEEBLE SPIRITS, SUMMONED TO PLANET CRAY.
YES ...
LET'S START !
STAND UP, THE VANGUARD !!

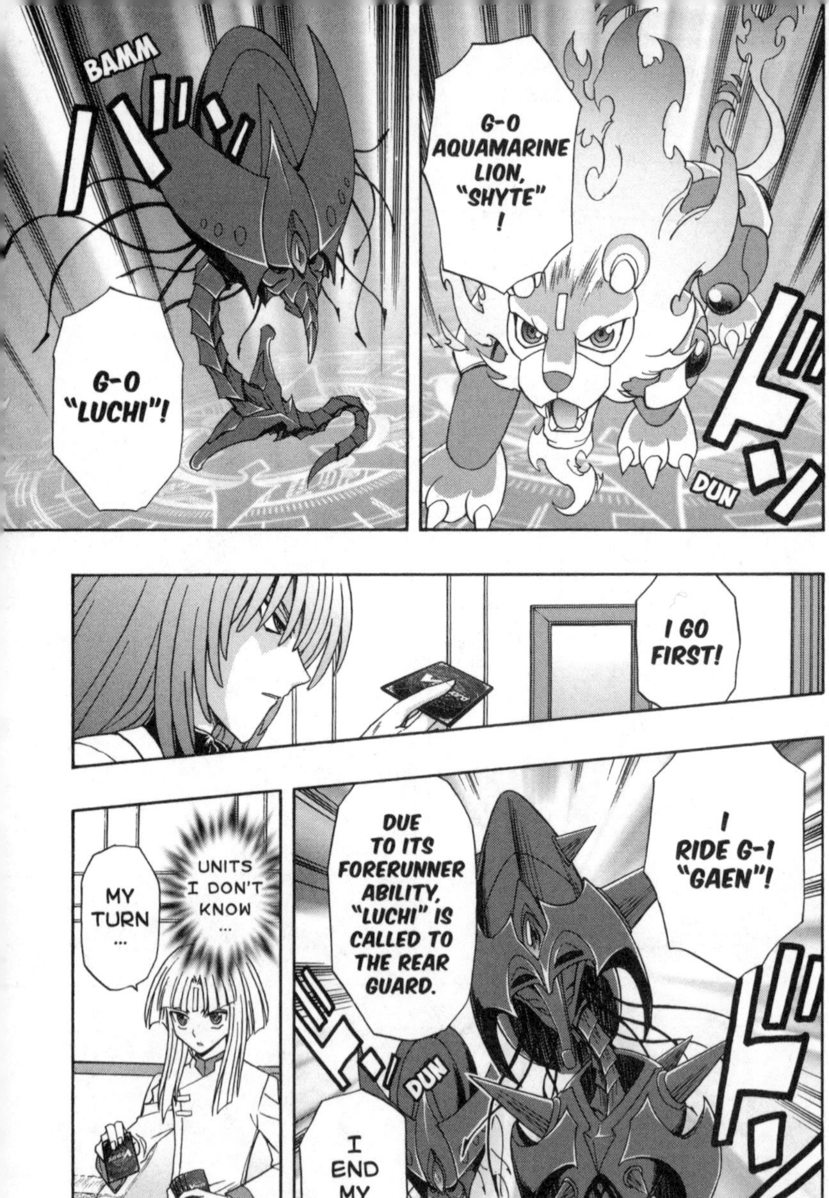
G-0 AQUAMARINE LION, "SHYTE"!
DUN
BAMM
G-0 "LUCHI"!
I GO FIRST!
I RIDE G-1 "GAEN"!
DUE TO ITS FORERUNNER ABILITY, "LUCHI" IS CALLED TO THE REAR GUARD.
DUN
DUN
I END MY TURN.
UNITS I DON'T KNOW ...
MY TURN ...

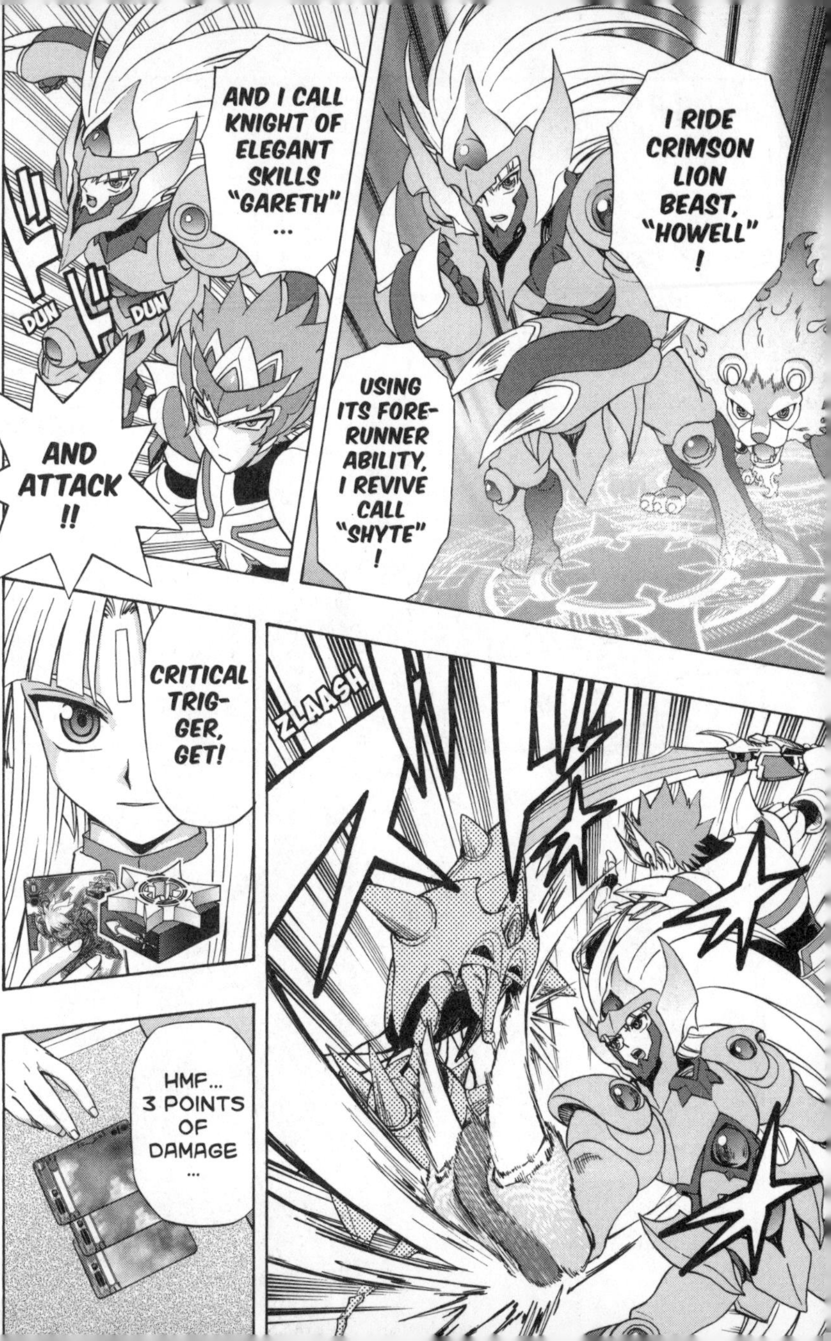
I RIDE CRIMSON LION BEAST, "HOWELL"!
USING ITS FORE-RUNNER ABILITY, I REVIVE CALL "SHYTE"!
AND I CALL KNIGHT OF ELEGANT SKILLS "GARETH"...
DUN
DUN
AND ATTACK!!
ZLAASH
CRITICAL TRIG-GER, GET!
HMF... 3 POINTS OF DAMAGE...

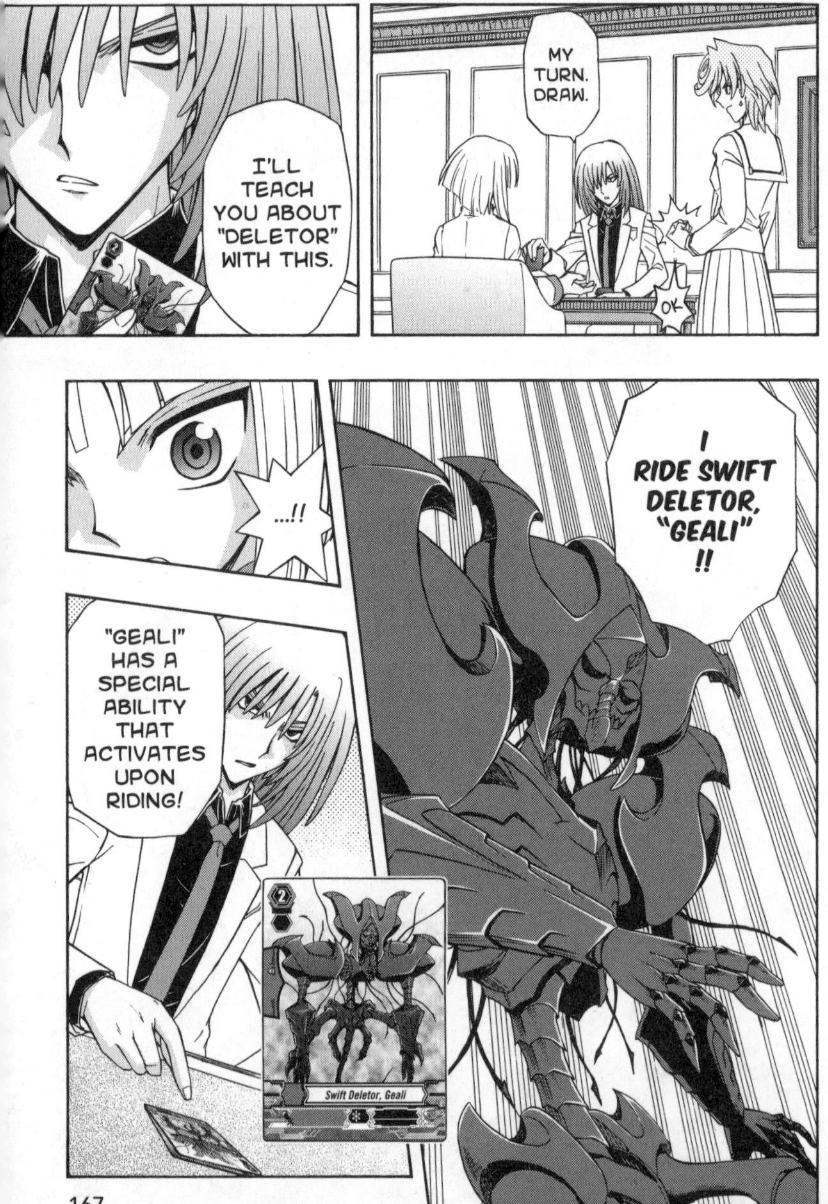
MY TURN. DRAW.
OK
I'LL TEACH YOU ABOUT "DELETOR" WITH THIS.
I RIDE SWIFT DELETOR, "GEALI" !!
...!!
"GEALI" HAS A SPECIAL ABILITY THAT ACTIVATES UPON RIDING!
Swift Deletor, Geali

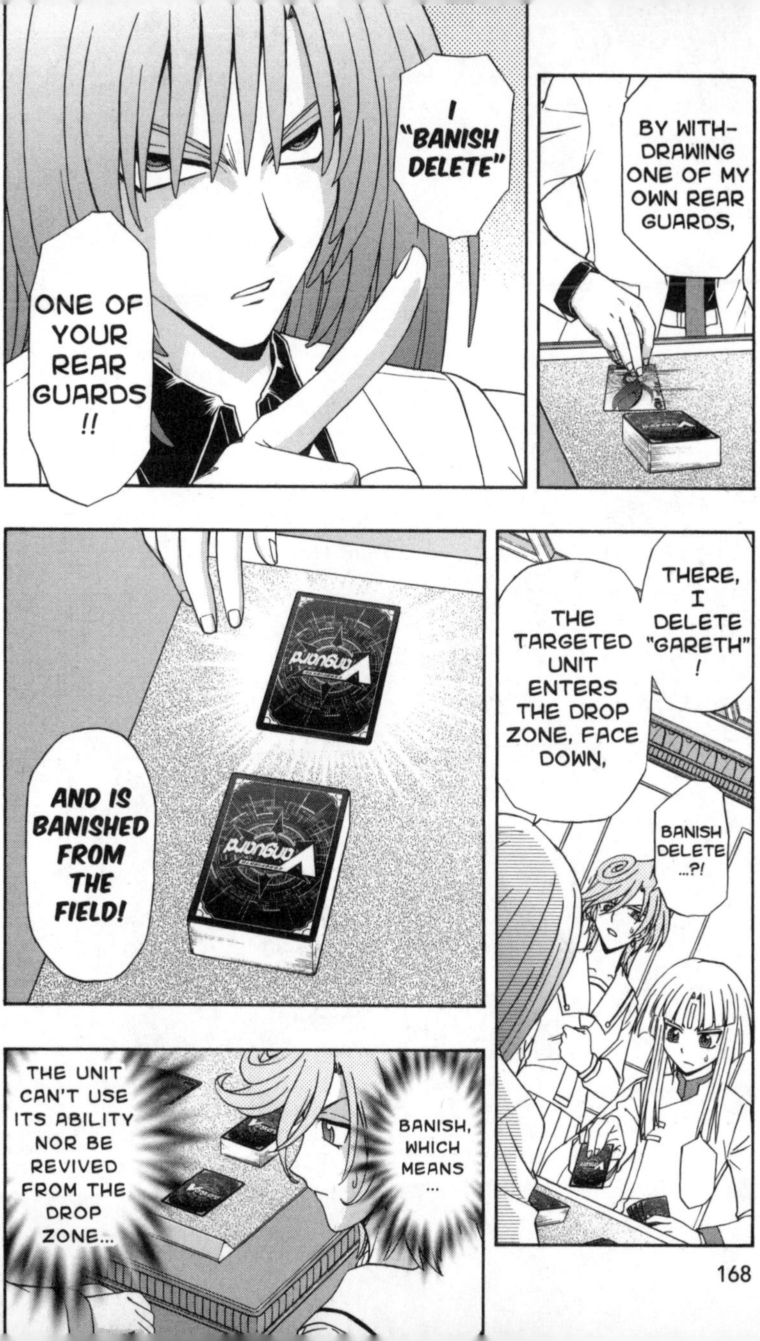
BY WITH-DRAWING ONE OF MY OWN REAR GUARDS,
I "BANISH DELETE"
ONE OF YOUR REAR GUARDS !!
THERE, I DELETE "GARETH" !
THE TARGETED UNIT ENTERS THE DROP ZONE, FACE DOWN,
BANISH DELETE ...?!
AND IS BANISHED FROM THE FIELD!
BANISH, WHICH MEANS ...
THE UNIT CAN'T USE ITS ABILITY NOR BE REVIVED FROM THE DROP ZONE...

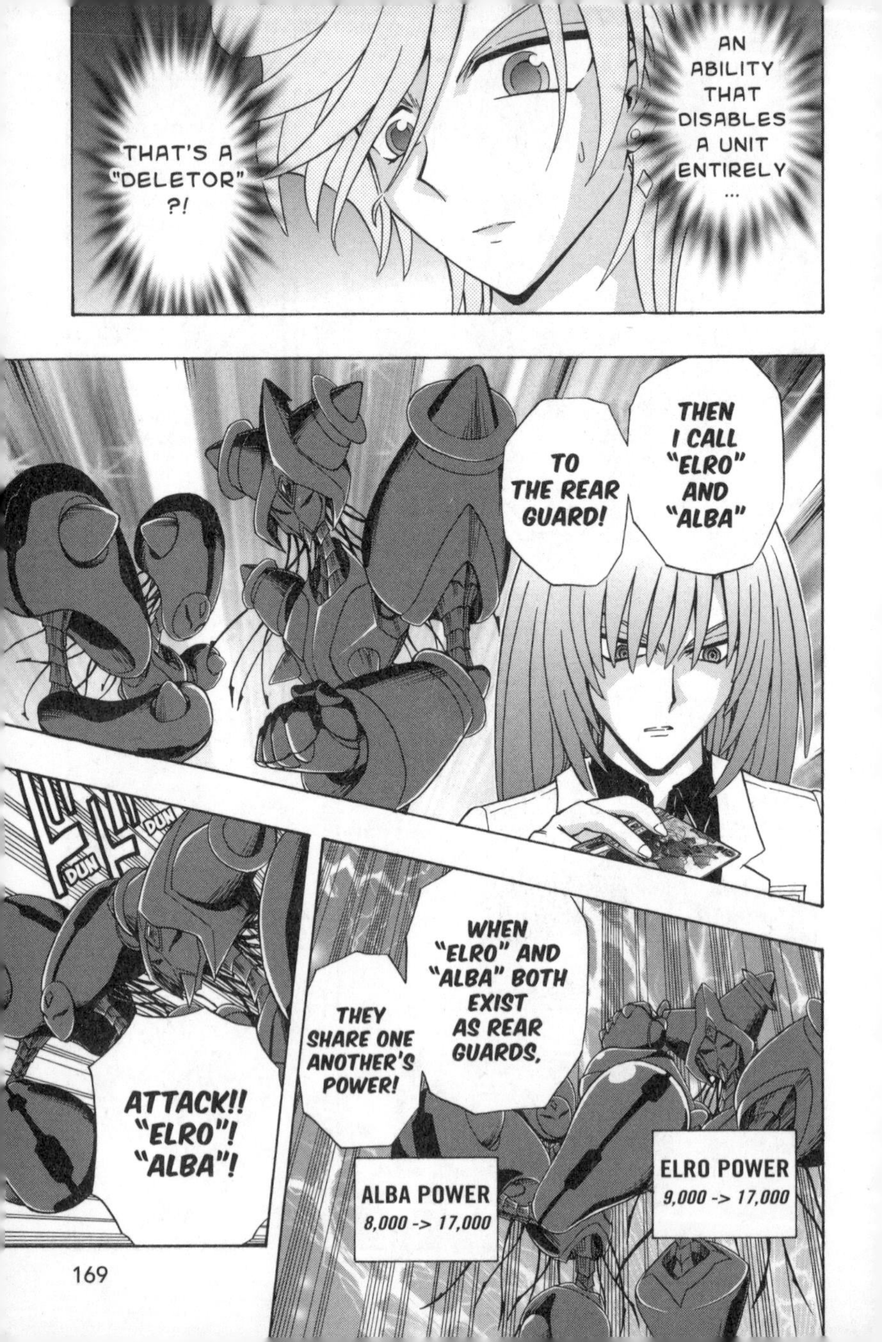
AN ABILITY THAT DISABLES A UNIT ENTIRELY ...
THAT'S A "DELETOR" ?!
THEN I CALL "ELRO" AND "ALBA"
TO THE REAR GUARD!
WHEN "ELRO" AND "ALBA" BOTH EXIST AS REAR GUARDS,
THEY SHARE ONE ANOTHER'S POWER!
ELRO POWER 9,000 -> 17,000
ALBA POWER 8,000 -> 17,000
DUN DUN
ATTACK!! "ELRO"! "ALBA"!

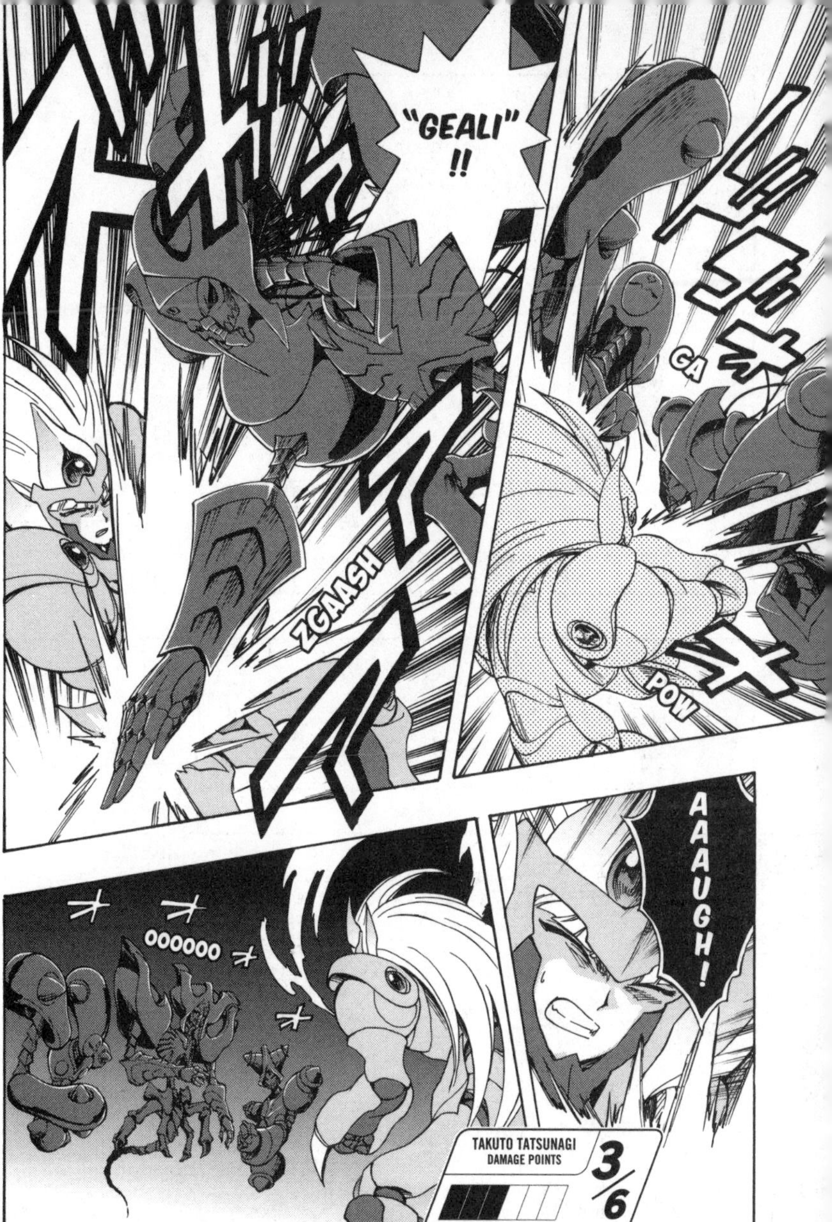
GA
POW
"GEALI" !!
ZGAASH
AAAUGH!
TAKUTO TATSUNAGI
DAMAGE POINTS
3/6
OOOOOO

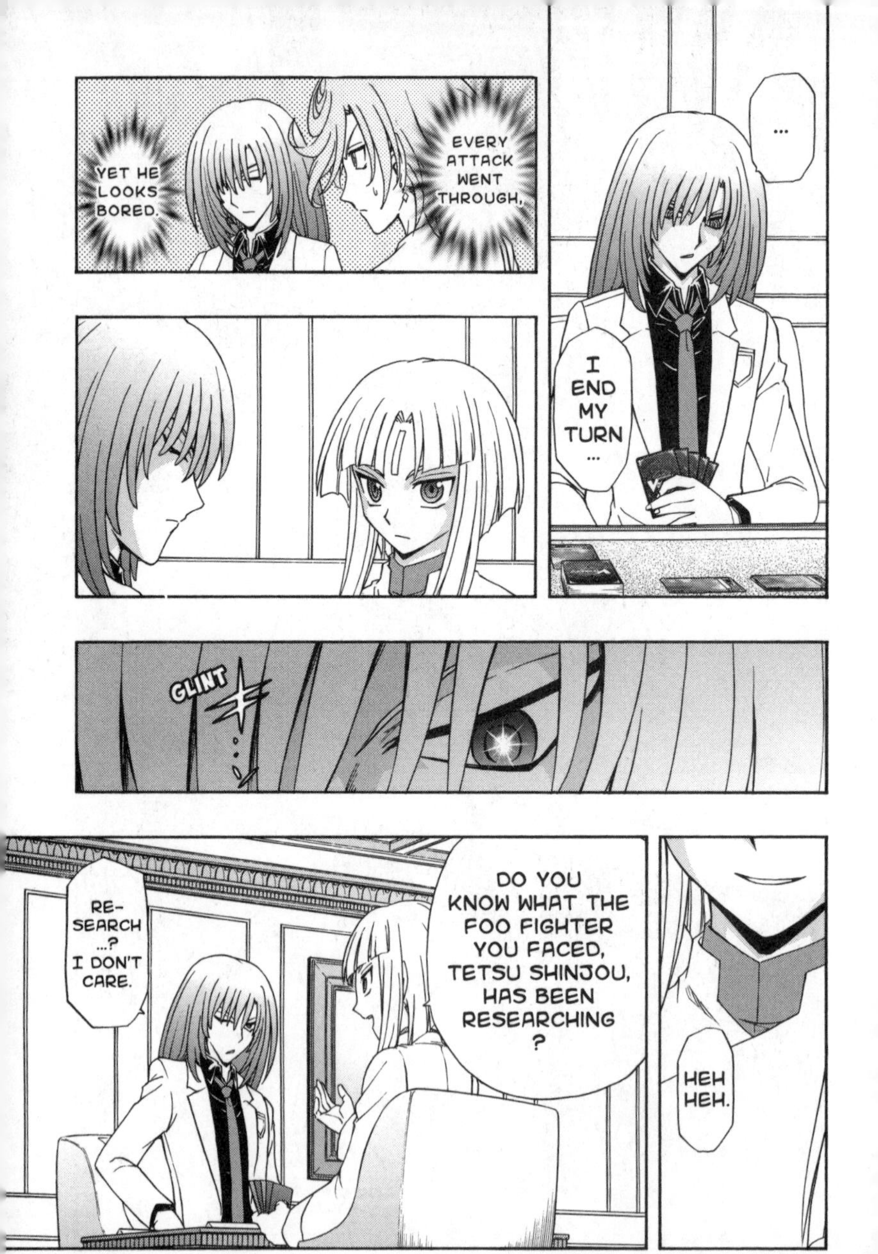
...
I END MY TURN ...
EVERY ATTACK WENT THROUGH,
YET HE LOOKS BORED.
GLINT
HEH HEH.
DO YOU KNOW WHAT THE FOO FIGHTER YOU FACED, TETSU SHINJOU, HAS BEEN RESEARCHING ?
RE-SEARCH ...? I DON'T CARE.

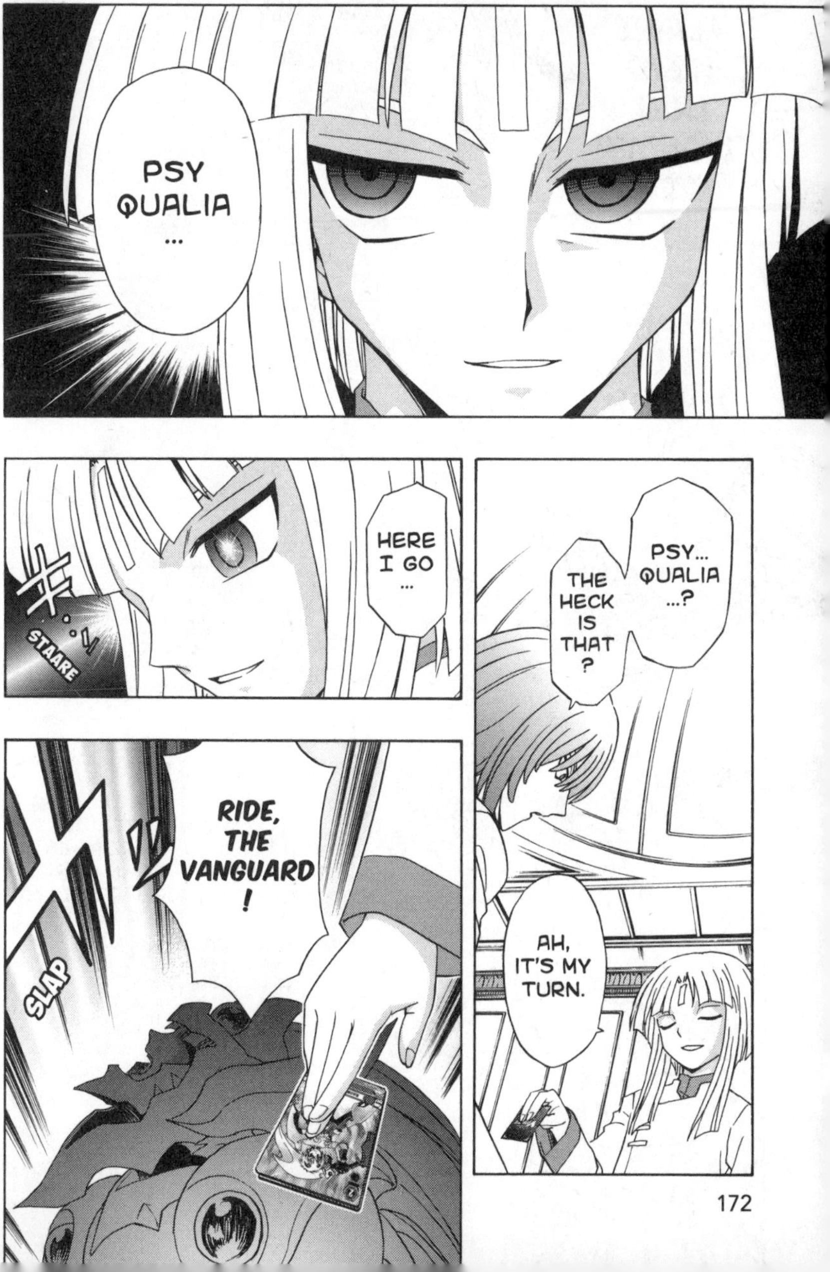
PSY QUALIA ...
PSY... QUALIA ...?
THE HECK IS THAT ?
AH, IT'S MY TURN.
HERE I GO ...
STAARE
RIDE, THE VANGUARD !
SLAP

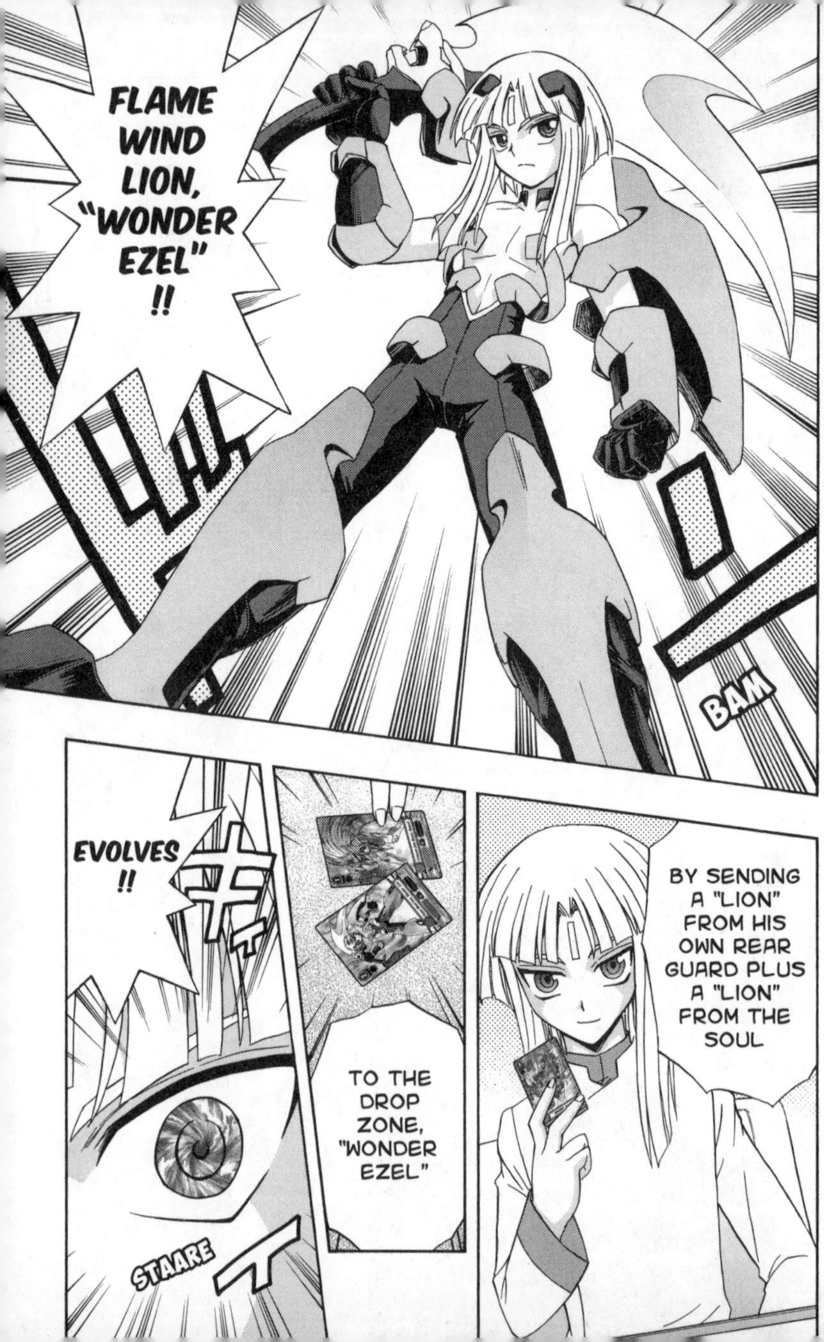
FLAME WIND LION, "WONDER EZEL" !!
BAM
BY SENDING A "LION" FROM HIS OWN REAR GUARD PLUS A "LION" FROM THE SOUL
TO THE DROP ZONE, "WONDER EZEL"
EVOLVES !!
STAARE

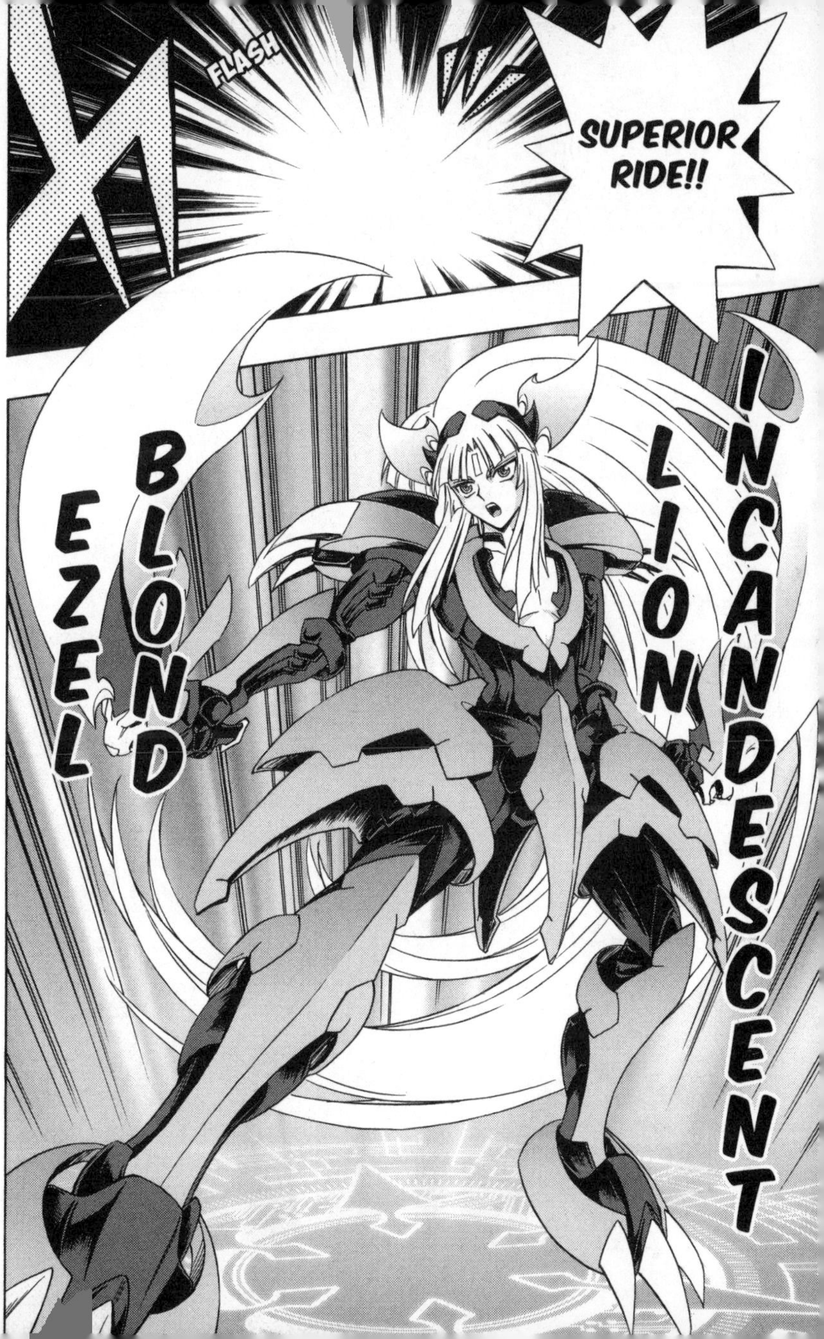
SUPERIOR RIDE!!
FLASH
INCANDESCENT LION BLOND EZEL

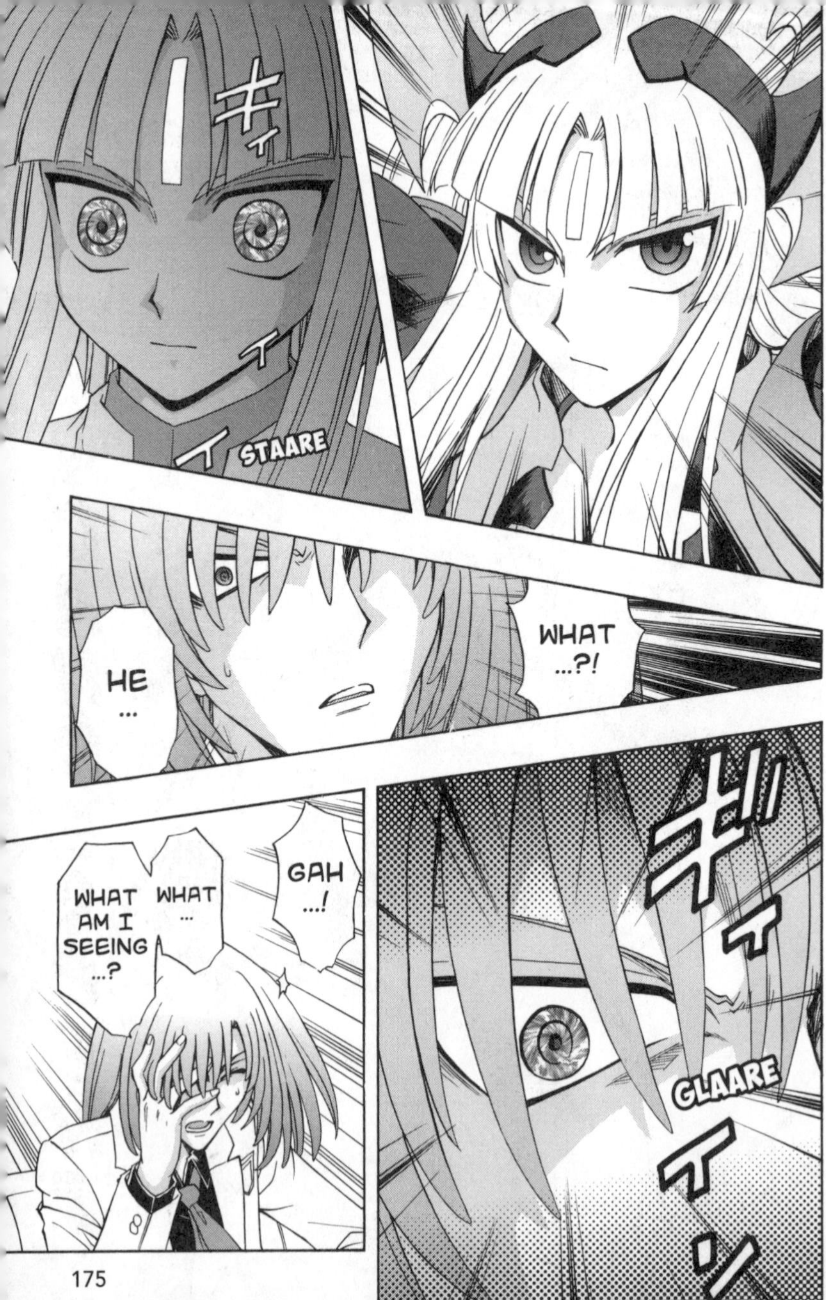
STAARE
WHAT ...?!
HE ...
GLAARE
GAH ...!
WHAT ...
WHAT AM I SEEING ...?

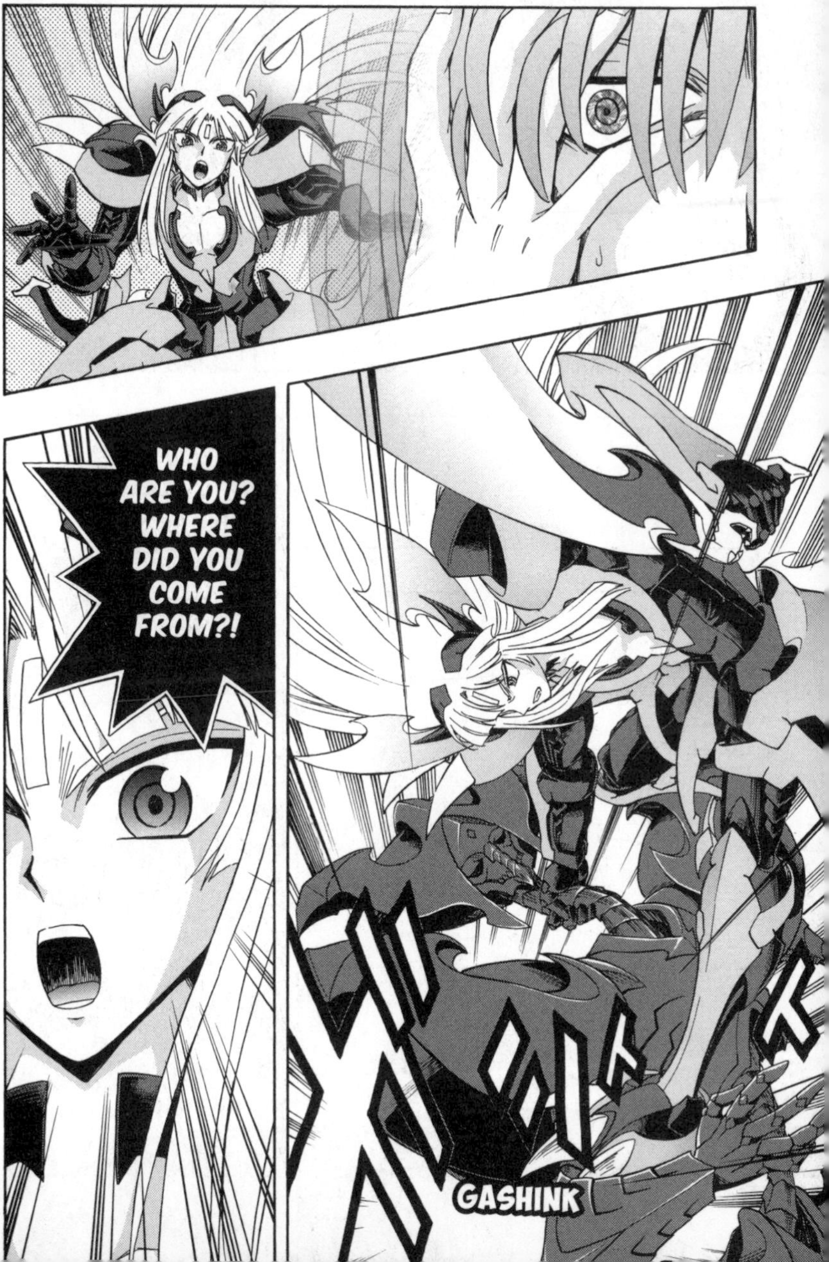
GASHINK
WHO ARE YOU? WHERE DID YOU COME FROM?!

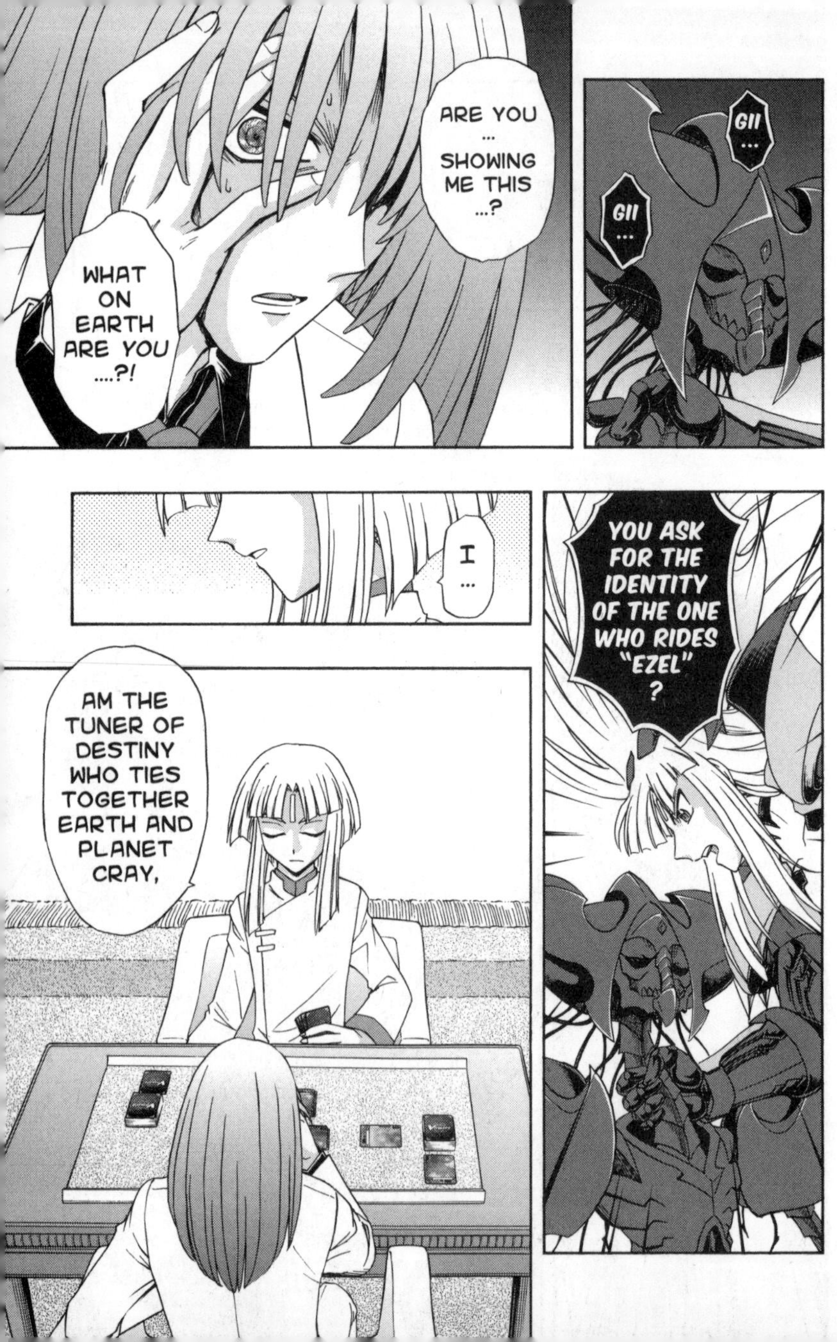
GII ...
GII ...
ARE YOU ... SHOWING ME THIS ...?
WHAT ON EARTH ARE YOU ....?!
YOU ASK FOR THE IDENTITY OF THE ONE WHO RIDES "EZEL" ?
I ...
AM THE TUNER OF DESTINY WHO TIES TOGETHER EARTH AND PLANET CRAY,

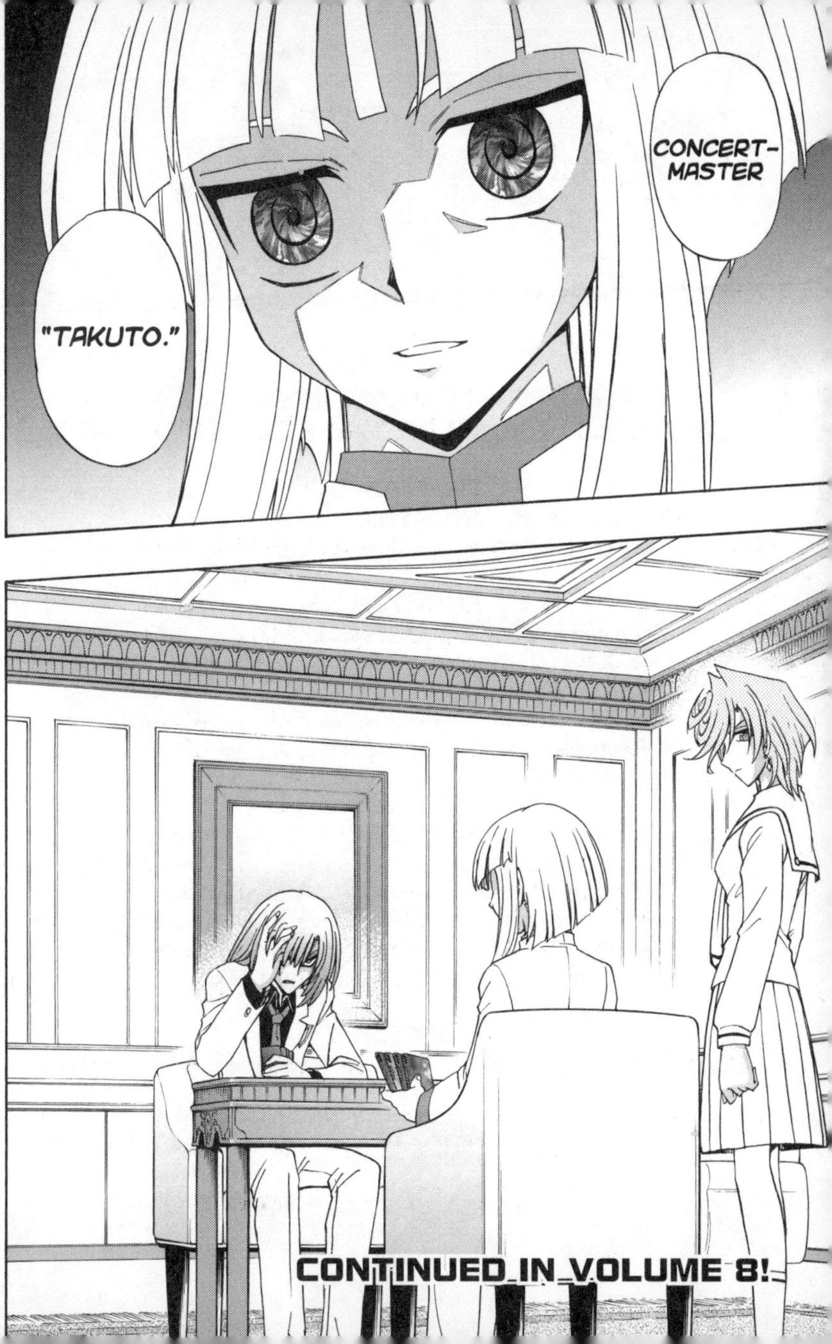
CONCERT-MASTER
"TAKUTO."
CONTINUED IN VOLUME 8!

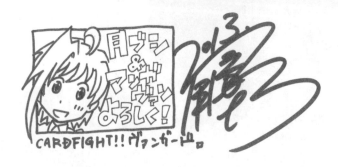

# CARDFIGHT!! VANGUARD VOL. 7
## ORIGINAL DESIGNS OF THE FEATURED UNITS

### CHAPTER 32
Starlight Melody Tamer, "Farah" / 碧風羽 (Foo Midori)
Alfred Early: Design: 伊藤彰 Akira Itou  Illustration: 三好載克 (Norikatsu Miyoshi)

### CHAPTER 33
Thousand Ray Pegasus / 由利真珠郎 (Shinjurou Yuri)
Essence Celestial, "Becca" / 喜久屋めがね (Megane Kikuya)
Wild Shot Celestial, "Raguel" / てるみぃ (tell me)
Marking Celestial, "Arabhaki" / パトリシア (Patricia)
Booting Celestial, "Sandalphon" / えびら (Ebila)
Eradicator, "Thunder Boom Dragon" / スズキゴロウ (Gorou Suzuki)
Dragonic Deathscythe / Eel
Yellow Gem Carbuncle / 齋藤タケオ (Takeo Saitou)
Lightning of Hope, "Helena" / 木下勇樹 (Yuuki Kinoshita)
Dragonic Kaiser, "Vermillion" / 竜徹 (Ryutetsu)
Demonic Dragon Nymph, "Seiobo" / 石田バル (Val Ishida)
Solidify Celestial, "Zerachiel" / ともひと (Tomohito)
Hot Shot Celestial, "Samyaza" / SALT

### CHAPTER 34
Blaster Dark: Design: 伊藤彰 Akira Itou  Illustration: 竜徹 (Ryutetsu)

### CHAPTER 37
Knight of Elegant Skills, "Gareth" / 竜徹 (Ryutetsu)

All Other Units / Akira Itou

# CARDFIGHT! VANGUARD
## VOLUME 7

Translation: Yota Okutani
Production: Grace Lu
            Anthony Quintessenza

Copyright © Akira ITOU 2013
          © bushiroad All Rights Reserved.
First published in Japan in 2013 by KADOKAWA CORPORATION, Tokyo.
English translation rights arranged with KADOKAWA CORPORATION, Tokyo
through TUTTLE-MORI AGENCY, INC., Tokyo.
English language version produced by Vertical, Inc.

Translation provided by Vertical, Inc., 2017
Published by Vertical, Inc., New York

Originally published in Japanese as *Kaadofaito!! Vangaado 7* by KADOKAWA
CORPORATION
*Kaadofaito!! Vangaado* first serialized in *Young Ace*, 2011-

This is a work of fiction.

ISBN: 978-1-941220-14-6

Manufactured in Canada

First Edition

Vertical, Inc.
451 Park Avenue South
7th Floor
New York, NY 10016
www.vertical-inc.com